Famous
Wisconsin
Artists and
Architects

ISBN 1-932542-12-4

Badger Books Inc.
P.O. Box 192
Oregon, WI 53575
Toll-free phone: (800) 928-2372
Fax: (608) 835-3638
Email: books@badgerbooks.com
Web site: www.badgerbooks.com

This book is dedicated to my mom Joy C. Hasslinger who pursued art training at the University of Wisconsin-Madison.

Joy C. Hasslinger, United States Navy ca. 1943
Charcoal drawing
Courtesy of the Grimm family

And to my great great grandfather, August Grimm, a nineteenth century artist in Frauenwald, Germany. He began as a porcelain painter, as was common for German artists. He then moved to oil painting. It is not known if his paintings survived beyond World War II Germany.

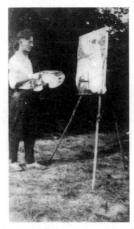

August Grimm ca. 1800's
Photo courtesy of the Grimm family

Contents

A Letter

It is my hope that you will enjoy this book for what it is. Which brings me to the question, what exactly is it? *Famous Wisconsin Artists and Architects* is a book for the general reader, art enthusiast, student, interested soul, exploring tourist, connoisseur of Wisconsin books — or smart orangutan. The book's purpose is to generate and spread awareness of Wisconsin's rich heritage in the visual arts. Wisconsin has literally thousands of artists and many skilled architects. In a work of this length, it is impossible to include them all. This presents the awful chore of weeding, indeed a challenge and a nightmare. I have included acclaimed artists as well as samplings of lesser-known artists. I've also compiled a further listing of others in the profession of visual arts, some recognizable and notable, and some who are not as well known.

Famous Wisconsin Artists and Architects is not a directory. If I wanted to write a directory, I'd find a job at the phone company. The book is not a scholarly work, and it is not meant to be. There are resources and research avenues for those interested in academic chronological detail. Am I experienced in the creative spheres of art and architecture? No, I come from a partially detached perspective. I dabble here and there as a hobbyist, sell a few works, and give things to my friends. My work is scattered. What I am is a tourist wandering through this visual forest, but I know what interests me, and I know the creative process.

An important factor in writing a book like this is that I love talking to people who know more than I do, or who have knowledge about uncharted territory. I've sought advice, opinions, and help from inhabitants of the field. Now I can be the middle person and pass the paint palette to you. Don't run with scissors, or fugitive colors, but run with the knowledge and visit the places where art and architecture make Earth an incredible place to live. Some artists will take you further into the universe if you dare. Nevertheless, use the book as a stepping-stone and an introduction to art in Wisconsin.

Famous Wisconsin Artists and Architects contains a mixture of brief essays and facts about artists and architects. I have included images when possible. A few sections that are more extensively written profile artists whose work is unquestionably recognized nationally and internationally. Others promised me they'd meet those criteria in this lifetime or another. The artists I've met have a common mission to their creativity. They explain it in varying ways, but I think it boils down to capturing a moment in time. If they become *famous* along the way, they'll consider it a bonus, but it's not their reason for doing what they do. Fame is usually relative anyhow except for a limited number of outliers. An artist can be a perfectionist at what he or she does, and turn out exquisite work, but prominence may remain as elusive as a dandelion seed carried by the breeze. Wisconsin, in that respect, is still part of the Wild West, but certainly it does have a strong art history and many artists expanded beyond the borders of Wisconsin.

Many people were enthusiastic about this project and helped me to stay afloat in such a vast sea of activity. Sometimes it was overwhelming and all I wanted to do was clean the house, train dust bunnies to disappear, eat popcorn, and watch funny movies. Nonetheless, the folks who graciously helped me are keepers of the knowledge — they have museums, galleries, exhibits, things to teach, and a sense of humor. This raft of adventure will take you sailing. What you do with what you find depends on what you're looking for, really.

Because you've read this letter, I'll disclose my three favorite artists. I like so much of what I see — some traditional, some contemporary, some avant-garde — that it's very hard to choose. Of the artists that I've written about in *Famous Wisconsin Artists and Architects,* my three favorites are Henry Vianden mainly because I love trees, Carl von Marr for his portraits, and Edmund Lewandowski for his lines, angles, and geometry.

My request is that after you've read this book, give a box of crayons or a glob of clay to a curious child, and teach that child how to *see.* Those two steps alone can start an avalanche. However, as my mother would say, "Don't draw on the wall!"

— **Hannah Heidi Levy**
October 2004

Artists and Architects

They started with a
bright idea

Photographers at Strobo Research Lab ca. 1948
Wisconsin Historical Society Image 2089

George Catlin

(1796-1872)

"George Catlin was the Audubon of American Indian Painting"

— **Porter Butts, *Art in Wisconsin***

A distinct parallel exits between <u>Audubon</u> painting birds and George Catlin recording the accurate portrait and life of the Native American. Both artists had a drive and a purpose in their work, to which history is indebted. We are fortunate these pioneers took on the nearly impossible task in an era when it was difficult to record anything pictorially. "I have designed to visit every tribe of Indians on the continent for the purpose of procuring portraits of distinguished Indians of both sexes in each tribe, painted in their native costume, accompanied with pictures of their villages, domestic habits, games, mysteries, religious ceremonies, etc., with anecdotes, traditions, and history of their retrospective nations" (Art in Wisconsin by Porter Butts). The artist set himself a grueling schedule to accomplish the work, reportedly because he was fearful for the Native Americans' future, their way of life, and their very existence. George spent summers sketching, and winters transforming his sketches into oil paintings. He published a record of his accomplishments in his North American Indian Portfolio with the purpose of educating a wide audience. During this ten-year project, the artist produced 507 canvases.

**"Wild Horses at Play" from the drawings
and notes of George Catlin, 1844
Wisconsin Historical Society Image 23621**

George was born in Wilkes Barre, Pennsylvania, in 1796. His grandfather was in the Wyoming massacre of 1778. His mother was captured at the surrender of Forty Fort, and later released. These were early memories of the famous artist that influenced his interest in the Native American. He studied law for a time, but doodled over most of his law books instead of taking the usual notes. Wisely, his parents let him pursue his artistic ambitions and sent him to Philadelphia in 1823 to study art at the Pennsylvania Academy of Fine Arts, but it's thought that he remained largely an untrained artist. He earned money from 1824 to 1829 painting miniature portraits in watercolor on ivory in Philadelphia. He also earned a reputation and soon found himself in Washington, D.C. receiving numerous commissions, including one from Dolly Madison. By 1830, he was financially set to begin the Wild West adventure.

In Wisconsin, Catlin traveled around Praire du Chien to paint Wabasha's band, and then by bark canoe he paddled to Dubuque. In 1836, he made it to Green Bay and traveled the

Fox and Wisconsin rivers, and then on to the pipestone quarry region of Minnesota. The rock formations of the region are named "Catlinite" after the artist. The artist and his paintings, including portraits that he did from time to time to support himself, became world famous. He was especially recognized in France and England for his book *North American Indians*. All of his work was self-financed.

Wisconsin recognizes George Catlin as the first artist of "international reputation" to enter its territory. He had a brother, Richard, who lived in Ripon, and his nephew Theodore, a noted artist, lived in Green Bay. George Catlin left much of his work in Wisconsin, including his self-portrait sketches. One of his Wisconsin paintings is of the Ojibwas at the Soo catching whitefish with scoop nets and racing canoes. "Spearing Fish by Torchlight" is a noted painting. Like Audubon, Catlin did not mess with nature. He painted as he saw without embellishment in any part of the painting.

James Otto Lewis

(1799-1858)

The Philadelphia-born James Otto Lewis was hired to preserve the Native American in art form. The Indian Department of the United States government and Secretary of War, J.A. Barbour hired him from 1823 to 1834 to produce the portraits. His first twenty portraits and one overall view of the fort, tribes, and soldiers were done at the treaty of Prairie du Chien in 1825 and simply labeled, "Painted on the Spot by J.O. Lewis." Nine tribes that included the Chippewa, Winnebago, Sioux, Sauk, and Potawatamie met for the treaty, which was organized by Governor Lewis Cass of Michigan, William Clark of Missouri, and commissioners. This important treaty opened up the Wisconsin territory to safe settlement. James Otto Lewis continued his portrait assignment in Fond du Lac, Green Bay, and Fort Wayne and Missennewa, Indiana, and ended with a portrait of Black Hawk in Detroit in 1833.

The work was published in 1835 in Philadelphia as "The Aboriginal Portfolio," which was issued in ten parts. This represented one of the earliest large projects in American lithography and was one of the first works to deal with subjects beyond the East Coast. The artist followed General Lewis Cass after the War of 1812 to Detroit where James was employed as a copperplate engraver, draftsman, and portrait painter.

The lithographs of Lewis today are in the $3000-$5000 range. Examples of the lithographs can be found at the West Bend Art Museum in West Bend, Wisconsin. All of the original paintings were destroyed in a fire at the Smithsonian Institution in 1865. The James Otto Lewis portraits are considered the most accurate and earliest depictions of the Native Americans and their society. Lewis' sketches were usually not done in the same regions that artist George Catlin, who also pictorially recorded the Native American, had visited.

The work portrayed in the lithographs is devoid of light and shadow and is flat. However, the artist was well aware of these limitations caused by intense wilderness events. James nearly lost his life on a few of these occasions. Upon the announcement of his Portfolio, the publisher stated that Lewis "sincerely trusts that the judicious and critical will regard it with a favorable and critical eye…[due to] the great and constantly recurring disadvantages to which an artist is subject, while traveling through a wilderness and in penciling by the way…" The artist was hired for a quick "historically and anthropologically correct record." Tough assignment; no opportunity for leisurely dabbling.

Kee-O-Kuck by James Otto Lewis
Collection of the West Bend Art Museum

Henry Vianden

(1814-1899)

"When you paint a tree, you have a king sitting for you." The words of the great father of Wisconsin art, Henry Vianden, also know as "The Bear," are colorfully musical notes that ring as true today as they did during his career. At the age of 35, Heinrich (Henry) Vianden, who was a professional artist arrived in Milwaukee as a German immigrant. The Milwaukee of 1849 was home to 20,000 people, one-third of them German immigrants. Henry's work had already been exhibited in European cities after his classical training in Munich. He became Milwaukee's leading professional artist, and had a lasting impact and influence on a generation of artists in Milwaukee. He encouraged his best students to seek training in Europe. The artist held classes on the grounds of his nine-acre property where he had built a Swiss chalet-style cottage. Apparently, a willow tree on the property was painted so many times by his students that it became known as the most painted tree in Wisconsin.

The most notable of Vianden's students was Carl von Marr (1858-1936), who was encouraged by Henry Vianden to study art in Europe. Consequently, von Marr studied in Munich and eventually became director of the Royal Academy of Art. A collection of 350 of the von Marr works can be seen at the West Bend Art Museum in West Bend, Wisconsin. Other esteemed students included Robert Koehler (1850-1917), Frank Enders (1880-1921), Robert Schade (1861-1912), and Susan Stuart Frackelton (1851-1932).

The prolific painter Henry Vianden was known as the "oak tree artist." He used a large amount of detail and generally used the green and brown palette of the photographic realism Düsseldorf style. According to biographer Peter C. Merrill, from an essay published in *Yearbook of German-American Studies*, vol. 22, University of Kansas 1987, the following story, as told by photographer Edward Steichen, is often repeated:

At one of Henry Vianden's exhibitions, a young lady approached him and said, "Mr. Vianden you paint such wonderful trees. What is your secret?"

Henry replied, "Secret? Vat is a tree? A tree is one hundred t'ousand leaves. You paint one hundred t'ousand leaves and dare you have a tree."

During the summer months, the artist traveled by horse and wagon to areas around the Wisconsin Dells and along the Fox and Kickapoo rivers. The trips lasted for weeks and several of his students would accompany him.

Henry Vianden was highly influenced by the strict realism of the Düsseldorf style, and I surmise this may have been a reflection of his early upbringing in addition to his art training. It is reported that, like his father, he began, as a decorative painter of fine porcelain. At the age of 14, Henry was apprentice to a goldsmith—all very exacting and detailed work. He remains an artist known for his landscapes and of course, trees. Other subject areas include figure, genre (human activity), landscape, and snow scenes.

The artist Louis Mayer said of Vianden in a *Milwaukee Sentinel* article, April 5, 1903, "He came like a seed to a foreign shore…if they [settlers] could not enjoy the possession of a painting, they would at least offer their children the opportunity to profit by the study of drawing, and so they sent them to Vianden."

One of Henry's paintings in particular has been of recent interest due to a hidden anomaly. The painting of a twisted old oak tree set amidst the backdrop of a storm is at the West Bend Art Museum. An observant child noticed a face behind the oak tree in the painting. Surprised, baffled, and thrilled, the museum staff had the painting x-rayed. Amazingly, a likeness of the artist was imbedded on the canvas, but mysteriously brushed over and rather concealed. Speculation as to the significance of the hidden portrait says that maybe the artist was painting his own sense of pain and loss. I have a hunch the artist-teacher-porcelain painter-goldsmith may have painted it as a test for a sharp-eyed student to discover along the road, which is exactly what happened.

Unitited (Traveler in a Stormy Landscape) by Henry Vianden
Collection of the West Bend Art Museum

"In the Dells" 1880 by Henry Vianden
Collection of the West Bend Art Mueum

Samuel Marsden Brookes

(1816-1892)

Samuel arrived in the United States in 1833 when his botanist father decided to take the family, including servants, pets, and rootstock, and emigrate from England. The family then traveled from New York and settled in a log cabin near Chicago in 1833. Formal art training for Samuel Marsden Brookes was scarce in this neck of the woods. Despite his father's disapproval, the young Brookes continued to observe the techniques of nomadic artists who traveled the frontier to paint portraits for a living. Around 1840, Samuel painted a miniature self-portrait on cardboard pasted to wood. This was one of his first paintings. In 1841, determined to pursue art, he paid an artist in Chicago for instruction in painting. Ambition stuck with the 25-year-old, and he began giving art lessons to others. Brookes strengthened his talents by painting miniature portraits for a variety of clients. He was on the fast track.

On the move, Samuel found his way to Milwaukee in 1842. From 1842 to 1845, he pursued a living as a traveling portrait painter, with a stint in London in 1846 where he studied art by copying works of the old masters. The Wisconsin works of Samuel Brookes include portraits of prominent citizens and Native Americans such as Chief Iometah of the Menomonee, a veteran of the War of 1812. Samuel Marsden Brookes was instrumental in forming an art union in Milwaukee for the sale of paintings. He and his business partner, Thomas Stevenson, another professional artist in Milwaukee, were commissioned by the Wisconsin His-

"Battle Axe Battleground"
Painting by Samuel Marsden Brookes and Thomas Stevenson
Wisconsin Historical Society Image 2531

torical Society to begin the establishment of a painting collection. Today the collection of more than 400 pieces includes four of the works by the team of Samuel Brookes and Thomas Stevenson. The four works include oil portraits of Morgan L. Martin of Green Bay, the noteworthy portrait of James H. Lockwood with the famed green glasses, Chief Iometah, and a landscape of the Pecatonica Battleground, a Black Hawk War site.

Beginning in 1858, Samuel started creating still-life paintings that included compositions of exotic fruit. Around this time, the artist moved to San Francisco with his wife and six children. Many of his canvases were destroyed in the 1906 fire. Samuel Marsden Brookes is celebrated for his depictions of fish and capturing the light of the scales—from cardboard on wood to exquisite oil paintings worth many times their weight in fish.

Bernard Isaac Durward

(1817-1902)

Bernard Durward is best known for portrait painting, still life, and religious art. He also admired the writers and poets of the day, such as Byron, Wordsworth, Tennyson, Keats, and Shelly. Putting art into words and art into image were probably equally important to the young Bernard. From a rare book in the family archives, *The Story of Durward's Glen* by Mary Grace Terry, comes a history of Bernard Isaac Durward. According to this source, he was born in Montrose, Scotland, the youngest of five children. Tragically, his father drowned when Bernard was three months old. At the age of 8 (1825), Bernard's mother sent him to the Grampian Hills to work as a shepherd. Later, he lived at the orphanage in Montrose, and it was here that he began what was to become his life's path. *Art in Wisconsin* by Porter Butts picks up the history at this point and contends that Bernard was apprenticed to the shoemaker James Thorne. The boy was allowed to use watercolor and his own home-made crayons to copy the illustrations found in Thorne's books. The very young artist also experimented with landscapes, and indeed brought a sketch of Sterling Castle at Perth with him to Milwaukee.

Durward's portraits grew in popularity in England, and he was known to have painted the portraits of a member of Parliament, Mr. Shirley, and his family. In 1845 Bernard Durward and his wife, who was a poet and artist, arrived in Milwaukee. Not having much money, only a shilling according to Mrs. Durward, Bernard painted a portrait of Tymothy Dore after following him down North Water Street and bartering to paint his portrait in exchange for a barrel of flour. Soon Bernard entered the business of portrait painting and set up a studio downtown. After painting a portrait of Solomon Juneau, his business boomed, and his clients included Mr. and Mrs. Byron Kilbourn, the Furlongs, Dahlmanns, Schleys, Hathaways, Alexander Mitchell, Bishop Henni (first bishop of Milwaukee), and others. In 1852, the artist accepted a "professorship of rhetoric" at the new St. Francis Seminary. His essays appeared in the *Milwaukee Sentinel* under the pen names "Porte Crayon" and "Delta."

A love of nature, pastoral scenes, woods, and wildlife drew Bernard Durward and his family to an area seven miles east of Baraboo, Wisconsin. Today, the area known as Durward's Glen, is around the Baraboo bluffs, is a retreat of the Order of St. Camillus, and is laced with nature trails. The Durwards bought this thirty-two acre glen in 1862 for $150. Bernard's writing was

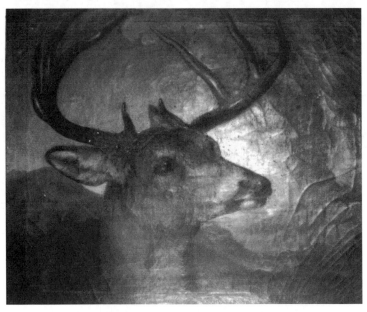

"Deer" by Bernard Durward
Photo courtesy of the Durward family

Bernard Durward
Photo courtesy of the Durward family

Isabella Dickie, 1856
Sister-in-law of Bernard Durward
Courtesy of the Durward family

influenced by religion, especially after the death of two of his children, Emma and Bernard Junior. Fifty of his poems were published in the *Milwaukee Sentinel* between 1852 and the start of the Civil War. His sympathies were with the South. "Milwaukee Bay" was considered one of the finest poems by a Wisconsin writer of the times. He was author and publisher of *Wild Flowers of Wisconsin, Colombo,* and The *Two Women,* among other books. The family home and the Glen were left to the Order of St. Camillus. Family portraits, other Durward paintings, and original writings are preserved at the Glen. Religion heavily influenced the poetry Bernard wrote. Equally as important to him was a love of nature. This is expressed by his words and paintings of the landscape and wildlife.

Bernard Durward had no formal schooling and no formal art training. Examples of his works are located at the Wisconsin State Historical Museum. According to Porter Butts' *Art in Wisconsin,* the painter is considered to "present evidence that an unusual talent, a step advanced from the likeness-makers had come to the Wisconsin frontier and developed there." His paintings "show him to be a better colorist and draughtsman than Brookes."

Mark Robert Harrison

(1819-1894)

The painter came from Yorkshire, England to Oneida County, New York, at the age of 3. At the age of 14, Mark Harrison began studying art with Bowerman in Toronto, Kimble in Rochester, and with Henry Inman of New York. He ended up with five years of training in the British tradition. The painter went to England in 1838 to continue studies at the Royal Academy. In England, he painted "The Charge of Cromwell at Marston Moor." This painting was sold, and more importantly, established a reputation for him in Europe. Harrison moved to Hamilton, Ontario, where he worked on individual paintings and large theatrical dioramas. In 1843, he painted "The Death of Abel," an 11' x 9' canvas that was shown in Europe and Canada. By last reports, the canvas is owned by the Canadian government. Tragedy struck in 1844 when all his sketches and finished works were burned, which left him to paint from memory and printed illustrations. For a time, he traveled with Julius Booth as an actor, and then in 1849 he moved to Oshkosh; and in 1892 he moved to Fond du Lac, Wisconsin, where he worked as a painter until the end of his life.

The artist hung his paintings in local offices and stores until someone offered to buy them. Wisconsin, and America for that matter, didn't provide much in the way of a market for the artist's paintings. Subject matter and themes were a problem. The larger allegorical paintings and Biblical paintings were shipped to New York and sent to England and France. Mark Harrison spent large

Untitled (Devil's Lake) by Mark Robert Harrison
Collection of the West Bend Art Museum

amounts of time on historical research, Indian history and lore.
He made numerous sketches of wildflowers and plants to catch
as much detail as possible. The noted historic Biblical paintings,
which were sold on the European market and to museums, include
"The Deluge," "Jephthah's Rash Vow," "The Angel Delivering
Peter from Prison," and "Peter Listening to the Cock Crowing."
Harrison received letters of appreciation from the poet Longfellow
for the artist's painted scenes from the poem "Minnehaha." But
his masterpiece is "Cleopatra's Triumph," a painting containing
300 figures and a profusion of Egyptian architectural motifs. This
canvas was completed in 1879 after years of researching.

The artist, reportedly reclusive from time to time, painted
many portraits of early pioneers and other men. He painted a
huge canvas of the historic defeat of Black Hawk. His typical
approach to painting of Native Americans was to study them from
literary accounts without using live models, thus the paintings are
idealized. Harrison painted "The Sioux Chiefs Under Sitting Bull
in Council at Little Big Horn River, Montana 1876" three years
after the event. In his book *Art in Wisconsin,* Porter Butts describes
the painting as producing "a curious disharmony between subject
and style that, happily, set no course for local artists, who simply
could not see what Harrison had imagined." The painting, along
with several others, is at the Wisconsin Historical Museum in
Madison, Wisconsin.

Alexander Marquis

(1829-1884)

The painter came from Glasgow, Scotland, and arrived in Milwaukee in 1850 where he proclaimed that he was a portrait painter and a drawing teacher. Not much is known about the artist other than that he possibly studied at the Scotch Academy in Edinburgh and was a gentleman's son. What is recorded is that in thirty years he painted more than three hundred portraits of Milwaukeeans and out of town clients. He received very little for his paintings and lived a life of poverty. Earlier work showed a refined style, but later paintings depicted a photographic style. In his book *Art in Wisconsin,* Porter Butts stated that Marquis was "not an especially gifted painter."

Alexander Marquis painted the portrait of Col. John W. Jefferson. The subject was thought to have been the grandson of President Thomas Jefferson and his slave Sally Hemings. A later report, based on DNA, suggests that John Jefferson is more likely the grandson of Randolph Jefferson, Thomas' younger brother. Col. John Jefferson was the leader of the Wisconsin 8th Infantry in the Civil War. The infantry unit was also known as the "Eagle Brigade." Its mascot, a trained eagle named Old Abe, flew over the battlefields.

In the portrait "Col. John W. Jefferson," oil on canvas painted in 1876 (one source says 1884), the artist neglected to paint over the right sleeve of the figure, thus letting some of the brown background come through. This resulted in a different blue than is used in the rest of the military uniform. Marquis is also criticized for "not painting the beard straight." However, the criticism does not take into account the texture of African American hair. Another criticism of the painter was that he "succumbed to the demand of photographic exactitude." Collectors prized his earlier work with its grace and style after the painted photography craze dwindled. He reportedly headed west in 1882 and died in Denver, Colorado, in 1884, although one source lists his death in 1917. The portrait, "Col John W. Jefferson," is at the West Bend Art Museum in West Bend, Wisconsin.

"Col. John W. Jefferson" by Alexander Marquis
Collection of the West Bend Art Museum

Frederick Stanton Perkins

(1832-1899)

The artist Frederick Stanton Perkins devoted much of his time in Wisconsin to collecting stone and copper antiquities of Wisconsin. This all started because of one summer in 1857 that he spent in Wyoming Valley, Pennsylvania, scene of the famous Indian massacre. Frederick found about thirty hatchets and stone implements that sparked a profound interest in the archaeology of native people. The curiosity and fascination transformed into a mission that he carried back with him to Wisconsin. He trekked through the roads, paths, and trails of Wisconsin, county-to-county, using detailed maps, stopping door to door, and leaving his business card, which stated he would purchase all copper, bronze, iron, stone, or "other evidences of man's primitive life in Wisconsin." Eventually, the artist-turned-archaeologist mortgaged his property to continue pursuing his collection. By 1885, Frederick, definitely a little on the obsessive side, or just a man with a plan, had established a monopoly in the ancient relic business. He had acquired 1,300 copper implements and 34,000 of stone, all found in Wisconsin. Frederick also collected a huge number from other states and foreign countries. The clients who became interested in obtaining pieces included the State Historical Society, Milwaukee Museum, Smithsonian Institution, College of the City of New York, the American Museum of Natural History, and private collectors of antiquities.

Of course, the artist did not begin his career avidly collecting the objects that enthralled him. Frederick Stanton Perkins was born in Oneida County, New York, in 1832, and arrived in Burlington, Wisconsin at the age of 4. He traveled to New York at the age of 21 and studied in the studio of Jasper Cropsey, consequently becoming the first and only Wisconsin artist to seek training rooted in the Hudson River landscape school. By 1862, he occupied his Milwaukee studio as a prominent portrait painter, with clients such as William Metcalf, E.P. Allis, and

Untitled (Floral Still Life) by Frederick Stanton Perkins
Collection of the West Bend Art Museum

Charles F. Ilsley.

Studying in Europe, spending three months in Florence, ten months in Paris, and another year in France, Germany, and England was on the Frederick Perkins itinerery in the years 1875-1877. After returning from Europe, the artist set out to paint and preserve in exact size and color every implement, relic, and charm in his collection. Two hundred detailed portraits of stone and 1,100 copper pieces were recorded with his brush. The meticulous artist annotated each specimen with the records he had kept. The life project required years of painting, and could have been done with photography, but size, color, and depth would have suffered, and obviously it would not have suited the painting spirit.

Lydia Ely (Hewitt)

(1833-1914)

Lydia Ely is not only known for her artwork, but also for her humanitarianism. Lydia announced on a return trip from Chicago to Milwaukee that she would "have a soldiers' home in Milwaukee" and would "not stop until it is an established fact." She organized a fund raising fair in 1863, which included an exhibition of nationally noted paintings and sculptures, and raised $100,000 that in turn effectively persuaded Congress to establish a permanent soldiers' home in Milwaukee as a state institution for returning Civil War veterans. Lydia and her "committee," obtained a charter for a permanent "soldiers' home as a state institution in 1865. Today, the establishment is one of the largest Veteran's Administration centers in the United States.

With that task out of the way, Lydia Ely, joined by fellow Chicago artists, traveled by horseback and wagon to Colorado in 1870 for two months. She made a point of traveling to remote sections of Colorado to sketch and paint the colorful and dramatic wilderness. Lydia spent the winter in Florida before traveling

Untitled by Linda Ely
Collection of the West Bend Art Museum

to England, France, and Italy to study the galleries. When she returned to Milwaukee, she started her own studio and school in what was known as the Iron Block in Milwaukee. The building still stands at the corner of Wisconsin Avenue and Water Street. For six years, she directed colossal exhibition shows in Milwaukee, including directing the Fine Arts Division of the Milwaukee Industrial Exposition in 1881.

The show in 1881 was a major event that represented French, Italian, English, and American works from New York, Chicago, and Milwaukee. The show included 452 oils and watercolors, and 869 drawings or other works created by numerous well-known artists. The sales were phenomenal. Lydia Ely turned her attention to yet another major project—the procurement of "Soldier's Monument," a statute by John Conway, sculptor. She solicited contributions for the monument, and even sold an autograph collection of hers with 3,000 names in it to Frederick Pabst for $5,000.

Lydia Ely is best known for her watercolor landscapes of the Colorado wilderness. She is important in Wisconsin and Milwaukee history as an art activist and for supposedly having established the first art exhibit in Wisconsin. Her energy really became her art.

Henry Hamilton Bennett

(1843-1908)

Photographer Henry Hamilton Bennett bought a photography studio in Kilbourn, Wisconsin, after his return from the Civil War. Today Kilbourn is known as Wisconsin Dells. Despite permanent damage to his right hand from a war wound, the photographer-artist managed to build his own photographic equipment — and his reputation. Invention through improvisation could have been his motto. Henry built a camera with an instantaneous shutter that allowed him to stop action. He also built a solar printing house on iron rollers that could be rotated 280 degrees to enable the printing racks to face the sun all day. These two inventions now reside in Washington, D.C., at the Smithsonian Institution. Henry's family operated the Bennett Studio from 1865-1908, and the descendents of the Bennett family still run the studio in Wisconsin Dells.

Henry started out as a portrait photographer, but soon felt the

"Down River from State Street Bridge"
Milwukee Wisconsin
H.H. Bennett Photograph
Wisconsin Historical Society Image 5377

"Kilbourn Railroad Station," Wisconsin Dells
H.H. Bennett Photography
Wisconsin Historical Society Image 7835

"Witches' Gultch View," Wisconsin Dells
H.H. Bennett Photograph
Wisconsin Historical Society Image 7298

Section #1728 of "The Battle of Gettysburg" Panorama Painting
by French artist Paul Dominique Phillipoteaux
H.H. Bennett photograph
Wisconsin Historical Society Image 25721

allure of the dynamic Dells landscape. His photos brought the
Wisconsin Dells, a modestly kept secret in the 1860s, into the
limelight. Photography in that era was a rather bulky endeavor,
but nonetheless Henry lugged his cameras, glass plates, tripod, and
"portable (if there is such a concept) darkroom" into the beautiful
wilderness with its magnificent canyons and grand Wisconsin
River. The photographer cleverly achieved a three-dimensional
effect in his photos by taking two photos of a subject from slightly
different angles to obtain a stereoscopic view of the landscape. By
1870, tourists started exploring this place that the Bennett photos
depicted. Not only did tourists find the dramatic landscape an
engulfing sight, they also found the Bennett photographs to be
a treasure. A most famous photograph is one where he caught
an image of a rope in mid air as it was thrown by a logger to the
shore. The technique he used to freeze this moment in time
was so advanced that he was accused of "trick photography."
The equipment to achieve this shot consisted of a cigar box and
a few rubber bands. Photographer Bennett was said to have
whitewashed the interiors of caves to make the interiors visible
on early glass plate negatives. I suppose that could be considered
"photographic technique."

Henry's talents were in great demand. He was commissioned
to photograph the landscape along the tracks of the Chicago,
Milwaukee, & St. Paul Railway. Thousands of his photos have
been displayed. In 1976, the Bennett Studio was placed on the
National Register of Historic Places. As Dennis McCann of the
Milwaukee Journal Sentinel wrote in 1998, "Think of him as the
father of the Wisconsin postcard, but so much more as well."

Panorama Painting

A Milwaukee Industry

The canvases measured as large as five stories high and 400 feet in circumference. This amazing accomplishment was pulled off by a number of artists who worked in the large panorama studios in Milwaukee around 1885. Two studios existed at the time, with the larger one owned by William Wehner of Chicago. He hired professionally trained European artists from German-speaking countries, although a few were recruited locally. So that the artists might feel at home, Wehner set up his business in Milwaukee, also known as "Little Munich" at the time. The popularity of panorama painting began in Paris around 1800. The price of a canvas was not less than $25,000, which was a huge amount in 1885 considering the cost of a house was a few hundred dollars. But the cost of producing such a canvas was very high because of the outlay in maintaining an ample studio, especially in severe winters.

Who bought the canvases and why? The paintings were a pre-motion picture means of bringing significant historical or religious events to life for a paying public. Essentially, the paintings were a part of the entertainment industry, but were also noteworthy in themselves as examples of fine art. Images in the foreground of the painting were life-size. Some of the canvases were viewed in the round while others were rolled in motion picture style in front of a seated audience.

The only Milwaukee canvas known to exist is "The Battle of Atlanta," which is on exhibit in Atlanta, Georgia. Nearly 19,000

square feet of Belgian linen was used as the support. The other
canvases mysteriously are unaccounted for today. However,
speculation has it that they were cut up, repainted a bit, framed,
and sold as smaller paintings, or used in theatrical sets, according
to expert representatives of the West Bend Art Museum.

The artists themselves were not framed and sold separately,
however they added to the 19th and 20th centuries cultural art
heritage of Wisconsin by influencing visual art and serving as
mentors, teachers, and peers who brought professional expertise
to a young land. Painters who worked with the William Wehner
American Panorama Company or successors included: Franz Biberstein, Theodor Breidwiser, Theodore Davis, Thomas Gardner,
Friedrich Wilhelm Heine, Louis Kindt, August Lohr, Richard
Lorenz, Herman Michalowski, George Peter, Franz Rohrbeck,
Bernhard Schneider, Wilhelm Schröeter, Johannes Schulz, Thad-
deus von Zukotynski, Amy Boos, Otto Dinger, Otto von Ernst,
Karl Frosch, Feodor von Luerzer, Albert Richter, Robert Schade,
Gustav Wendling, Paul Wilhelmi, and Conrad Heyd.

Information for this essay is from the book German-American
Artists in Early Milwaukee *by Peter C. Merrill, and from the West
Bend Art Museum's article "Milwaukee's Panorama Painting Industry" available at the museum. Many of the artists noted have works
included in the museum's collection.*

Bernhard Schneider

(1843-1907)

Bernhard was born in Luneburg, Germany, in 1843, and he
did not arrive in Milwaukee until 1885. He was hired to work
for the American Panorama Company and worked with Richard
Lorenz and Franz Biberstein in painting the huge canvases titled
"Logan's Great Battle" and "The Battle of Atlanta." The artist was
trained in Düsseldorf, and was considered by his contemporaries

Unititled (Cedarburg) by Bernhard Schneider
Collection of West Bend Art Museum

to be the "most able landscape artist of his time," according to
Art in Wisconsin by Porter Butts. After the panoramas, the artist
moved to Cedarburg, Wisconsin, where he painted scenes of the
Milwaukee River. The artist remained a bachelor and lived as
a roomer with the Barth family in Cedarburg. He paid for his
accommodations with large canvases, often scenes from Ozaukee
County.

His style is realism in genre (human activity), landscape,
historical scenes, and regionalism. Bernhard's work was exhibited at the Art Institute of Chicago as well as in numerous other
exhibitions. The painting "Artist by the Lake" was auctioned in
December 2001, for $15,000. The artist had great technical skill
and this shows consistently in his oil paintings. According to the
sources at the West Bend Art Museum, "his exquisite landscapes
remain as some of the state's most obscure and underrated works
of art."

Franz Biberstein

(1850-1930)

Franz Biberstein was a painter who never left his native Solothurn, Switzerland, far behind. He came to Milwaukee at the age of 36 and brought with him the expertise characteristic of many German artists of the time who settled in Milwaukee. Franz's training was at the Royal Academy of Munich, although he was defiant of the strict standards that were an integral part of the German academic painters. Preferring to paint heavily from nature rather than paint the usual Greek and Roman history

"Mt. Sir Donald" by Franz Biberstein
Collection of the West Bend Art Museum

compositions, the artist sought instruction in Carlsruhe with the artists Pilotti and Dietz.

In Milwaukee he set up a studio in a building with eleven other German artists, among them were John Fery, George Peter, and Robert Schade. Biberstein is noted for his style in realism. He joined the Milwaukee Panorama Company in 1886. Prior to this, he had experience working in Germany with the German panorama company in Frankfurt-on-the-Main. Biberstein, also a fine portrait painter, worked in oil on canvas and painted many notable landscapes, but his preference was to paint high mountain peaks that reminded him of the Swiss Alps. The artist is noted for his paintings of the Canadian Rockies and Mt. Sir Donald in the Selkirk Mountains of British Columbia. He was considered a master of color who did not adhere to the subdued palette of the German School. The painting "World's Columbian Exposition, Chicago" sold for $34,500 in 1996. The artist retained his sketches of valleys, glaciers, peaks and mountain vistas as a part of his library and the tools from which he studied. Around 1908 Franz turned to raising ginseng after severe losses in a trust company failure. Not to let misfortune rule the day, and with his experimentation and knowledge of color photography, he invented a method of reproducing portraits on canvas and then painting them with transparent colors. Biberstein was a member of the Wisconsin Painters and Sculptors organization.

Frederick Wilhelm Heine

(1845-1921)

Artist Frederick Heine began as a copper and steel engraver's apprentice in 1859 in Leipzig, Germany. He then studied at the Leipzig Academy from 1866-1870, followed by the Weimar Academy from 1870-1872. During the years 1861-1866, the artist was a book illustrator and designer for the house of Otto Sparner

"Muir Inn" by Frederick William Heine
Collection of the West Bend Art Museum

in Leipzig until 1866 when he became a war correspondent and sketch artist with the Prussian army in Austria. From 1870-1871 he was a field artist in the Franco-Prussian War, and in the years 1872-1885, the artist painted in Dresden.

The artist ventured to Milwaukee from Germany at the request of William Wehner, business promoter for the panorama painters. Artist Frederick Heine and August Lohr directed twenty German academy-trained painters to work on the panorama projects. Continuing to be industrious, the artist had a studio at 59 Oneida Street where he conducted his art school, painted in watercolor, and did commercial work. The Heine School of Art opened in 1888 in Milwaukee. He had success in selling his watercolors; especially those of marine scenes near Fish Creek, Wisconsin, and the redwoods of California. By the time World War I was in full swing, support for German artists was in jeopardy, and arson destroyed his studio. The artist then turned to church mural painting. Frederick Heine painted murals for the Old Pabst Theater café, the Edelweiss restaurant, and the Jung café in Milwaukee.

In the work of panorama painting, Frederick provided the sketches for the battlefields represented, and then projected the drawings by lantern onto the approximately 19,000 square foot canvas used for each painting. The painter spent six months in San Francisco following the Spanish-American war. Here he worked with George Peter, who was a staff painter for the Milwaukee Museum, Franz Rohrbeck and Franz Biberstein on the panorama "The Battle of Manila." Frederick and George Peter then went to Jerusalem in 1903 to sketch a panorama of the city, and exhibited it at the 1904 World's Fair in St. Louis. Not forgetting scenic Wisconsin, the artist made trips to Door County. Another favorite spot was Muir Woods, California. Reportedly, the artist died in 1921 of food poisoning from a tainted can of peas.

Richard Lorenz

(1858-1915)

Richard Lorenz is primarily known as for his paintings of horses, genre scenes, and landscapes. He was one of William Wehner's artists recruited in Germany and brought to the United States to work for the American Panorama Company in Milwaukee. Richard was born near Weimer, Germany, on a large family farm. He was sent to Weimer at age 15 to study sculpture and drawing at the Royal Academy of Art. The renowned painter, Heinrich Albert Brendel (1827-1895), whose specialty was horses and other animals, was his teacher. Richard also studied with the landscape painter Theodor Hagen and the portrait artist Max Thedy. Richard had a desire to be a Biblical painter because he wanted to portray nomadic people in the wilderness. The American West provided him the ample opportunity in such a way that he is recognized as one of the most important painters of western genre following Frederic Remington.

After reportedly working on the panorama company's best-known production, "The Battle of Atlanta Cyclorama" (now in

Atlanta, Georgia) in 1886, Richard traveled west to San Francisco. The artist sketched scenes from Chinatown and the Monterey coastal areas. He later took his talents to San Antonio, Texas; Oregon; Colorado; and Arizona. Richard returned to Milwaukee in 1888 and took a position as director of the Milwaukee Art School. His most famous student was Frank Tenney Johnson.

The majority of the artist's work is devoted to scenes of the West, especially storm scenes of the Great Plains. Prior to World War I, he was considered the most important art teacher in Milwaukee. His students included famous artists Alexander Mueller, George Raab, and Gustave Moeller. The paintings of Richard Lorenz were frequently exhibited and highly collectible in Milwaukee. Other exhibits include the Art Institute of Chicago, the Chicago 1893 Columbian Exhibition, the Pennsylvania Academy, and the St. Louis Exhibition in 1904, the Munich Exhibition in 1891, and the Paris Salon in 1901. In 1898, he began painting at the Crow Reservation and was influenced by stories he had heard

"Horse Market Mid Winter" by Richard Lorenz
Collection of the West Bend Art Museum

about the Indian victory over Custer at Little Big Horn. Although he is only quietly recognized, Richard Lorenz had an enduring brilliance in his ability to paint horses, and human figures in the backdrop of the American West. The Milwaukee Art Museum held a retrospective of the artist's work in 1966. Of the 103 works, half of them were of the American West.

Robert Schade

(1861-1912)

Robert Schade was versatile in his subject matter. He was known for portraits and still life, but painted landscapes and murals. Robert Schade was born in Tarrytown, New York, to German immigrants. The family moved to Milwaukee when Robert was 2 years old. He began to study art at the age of 15 in a school operated by the Milwaukee Art Association. That was an eager first step for him. Soon he was taking private lessons from the great artist Henry Vianden, who, after two years, sent his prodigy off to Munich. In Germany, the young artist enrolled at the Royal Academy in 1878, returning to Milwaukee in 1881. He spent several years traveling back and forth between Milwaukee and Germany. During these times, he studied drawing from life under Julius Benezier, drawing from the antique under Alexander Strachuber, and painting under Alexander Wagner.

Robert pursued his art career in Milwaukee and opened a studio in the Arcade Block on Milwaukee Street, and later moved the studio to the ever-popular Iron Block, where many of his contemporaries were located. The artist taught at the Milwaukee Art School from 1884-1886 and in 1885 took up panorama painting for August Lohr and Friedrich Heine of the American Panorama Company. He worked on the panorama painting "Jerusalem on the Day of the Crucifixion."

The artist made another trip to Munich to again study with

Alex Wagner, an artist known for his historical scenes. However, Robert Schade's art does not typically reflect historical scenes. The artist eventually returned to Milwaukee and taught at the Wisconsin Art Institute, directed by Richard Lorenz. One of Robert Schade's students was George Raab. Robert Schade was a founding member of the Society of Milwaukee Artists in 1900. The organization exits today as the Wisconsin Painters and Sculptors.

**"Mayme"
by Robert Schade
Collection of the
West Bend Art Museum**

**Untitled (Still Life)
by Robert Schade
Collection of the
West Bend Art Museum**

Conrad Heyd (Untitled)
Collection of the West Bend Art Museum

Conrad Heyd

(1837-1912)

Conrad Heyd, born in <u>Bavaria</u>, immigrated to New York at the age of 23. A self-taught artist, he found work as a decorative artist in a carriage shop, and ultimately developed his talents as a realism portrait painter by soaking up knowledge and technique from New York artists. The young Conrad was swept into the Civil War where he served with the Union Army and by no accident, was assigned to paint portraits of the Union Generals. The artist moved to Milwaukee in 1868, then two years later to Prairie du Chien, then Oshkosh, and finally back to Milwaukee in 1881. He established a studio in the Iron Block. The esteemed artist painted portraits of Wisconsin governors and other distinguished clients. His paintings can be seen at the Milwaukee County Historical Society and the State Historical Society of Wisconsin in Madison.

The artists of the day touted Conrad Heyd as "the foremost artist of Wisconsin" according to an entry in the Porter Butts' book *Art in Wisconsin.* Artist Louis Mayer wrote, "There was no real portrait painter until Conrad Heyd came to this city [Milwaukee] in 1868." He was acclaimed for his technical skills and ability to obtain a photographic likeness. Conrad was a founding member of the Society of Milwaukee Artists. He also worked with the popular artist Francesco Spicuzza. Other art included landscapes, miniature, and panorama, although he is primarily known as a portrait painter. The artist's work on famous people won him fame beyond the borders of Wisconsin. His work can be found in several collections.

Vinnie Ream Hoxie

(1847-1914)

A girl born in Madison, Wisconsin, on September 25, 1847 was to become a world famous sculptor by the age of 18. Her name was Vinnie Ream. Many of her playmates were children from the Winnebago (Ho-Chunk) tribe. The Native Americans have been credited with teaching Vinnie how to draw and paint. Madison, at the time was a settlement of 632 people living on the isthmus between Lake Mendota and Lake Monona. In 1848, Wisconsin became a state, and Vinnie's father, Robert Ream, a surveyor and mapmaker, had become the local postmaster and was active in Democratic politics of the day. In 1838, Robert Ream had acquired a log house that became known as the Madison House, which became an inn and stagecoach stop. Guests were allowed to sleep on the floor at a price of two pence per foot. Governor Henry Dodge and Judge Doty were rivals when the Madison House became a center of Democratic politics. By 1850, Robert Ream, Vinnie's father, held the positions of deputy state treasurer and deputy secretary of state. Madison had a population of three thousand people in 1851.

Robert became disenchanted with Wisconsin politics when the Whigs came into power. The family moved to Washington, D.C., and continued their involvement in Democratic politics. But their stay in Washington was short-lived. Robert decided to accept an assignment in Kansas as a clerk to Surveyor General John Calhoun. The family eventually settled in Leavenworth, Kansas, and managed the Shawnee House hotel. It was here that the young Vinnie played with river bottom clay and sculpted likenesses of her friends, her brother Bob, and the family dog, along with just playing in the mud and making mud cakes.

By the age of 10, Vinnie was in school in Columbia, Missouri where she studied art with William Alexander. Around this time, she did a noted oil portrait of Martha Washington. At age 11, Vinnie began writing poetry, with many of the poems printed in newspapers throughout the West. One famous poem, titled "Hard Times,: possibly inspired by the Dickens novel *Hard Times*, talked about the underdog role of women, who were blamed for problems of men's gambling and expensive living.

Around the beginning of the Civil War, Robert Ream moved the family back to Washington D.C., where there was a need for mapmakers. Vinnie's brother, Bob, had joined the Confederate Army. Washington had a Capitol dome that was still under construction. The dirt streets of Washington D.C., turned into a sea of mud in snow and rain. Abraham Lincoln was the president. Vinnie worked in the grim hospitals that were filled with wounded and dying Civil War soldiers. She sang for them and wrote letters for the incapacitated soldiers. Her voice attracted crowds, and she was hired by the E Street Baptist Church at $150 per year to sing. It was about this time when an unimaginable number of men had been consumed by a brutal war that the U.S. government set into action the Deficiency Act of 1862, which authorized the employment of women in government. In an effort to boost her family's limited income, Vinnie sought a $500 per year job as a postal clerk. The maximum salary of $600 for women was set by Congress. Men in the same positions were allowed to earn $1,200 to $1,800 per year. On November 10, 1862, Vinnie signed an oath of allegiance and signed a document that stated she was above the age of 16.

Women worked under miserable conditions in the dead letter office, always placed out of public sight in the sweltering high balconies which overlooked the main floor. They were not allowed to open mail because "immoral things are sometimes found in them," and this supposedly would "corrupt the morals of women." During her free time, Vinnie would study the art of the nation's capital. She continued her school studies at home, eagerly reading the poetry of Edgar Allan Poe and Byron, and continued her own writing. Vinnie never learned to play cards, a popular amusement of the day, and disliked the thought of wasting time on trivial pastimes. She said, "It always seemed a poor sort of employment." Vinnie once told her mother, "I must do something really worthwhile with my life. I feel that I am to have some special work in the world. I do not know what it is, but I must be ready for it when it comes." Perhaps the statement originated in the uncertainty of the times. Vinnie could often see smoke rising from the valleys of Virginia, and hear the sounds of cannon fire as she walked down Pennsylvania Avenue.

A sculptor, Major Clark Mills, who had received a commission to sculpt the equestrian statue of George Washington, asked permission from Vinnie's parents to do a sculpture of the lovely Vinnie Ream. She found herself in amazement of Mills' studio with its eclectic mix of sculptures, fever medications, sketches, books, a hat full of eggs, and mechanical hardware. She watched him carefully as he modeled the clay. Vinnie insisted, "I can do that!" He tossed her a few handfuls of clay, and she went to work. Mills was astonished at the finished product that emerged a few hours later. Vinnie had sculpted the likeness of an Indian Chief's head and his headdress. He later remarked that he thought the piece represented more vitality and character than he had man-

TOP LEFT: Abraham
Lincoln Sculpture by
Vinnie Ream
Washington, D.C.
Wisconsin Historical
Society Image 8349
TOP RIGHT: Statue
"Sequoia" completed in
1915 by sculptor George
Julian Zonay after the
death of Vinnie Ream.
Wisconsin Historical
Society Image 8663
RIGHT: Vinnie Ream
Hoxie, sculptor
Wisconsin Historical
Society Image 3627

aged to produce in his entire career.

Vinnie became a student-helper to the sculptor. Soon after, Vinnie announced to her mother that it was her intention to be a sculptor. The Ream family was adamantly opposed to such an outrageous notion. Vinnie paid little attention to the upheaval. She had a mind and talent of her own, regardless of her status at that time in history. Women did not have the right to vote, girls were barely educated, and any type of career such as this was certainly unheard of and unladylike, and it was nearly criminal to speak of such an idea. To earn money in addition to her job as a postal clerk, she set up a booth called the "Post Office" where she wrote letters for donations. In between working, Vinnie studied sculpture with Clark Mills. She became acquainted with many of the politicians of the Washington scene when they would seek the atmosphere of the studio for relaxation.

The quality of Vinnie's work improved as her reputation grew. After relentless effort, she received permission from President Lincoln to sculpt a bust of him. At first, Lincoln was reluctant, and said he didn't see why a young woman would want to bother with such a common man. He had seen the artist before in the upstairs corridor near his private office and living quarters. People seeking job appointments would wait outside Lincoln's office to catch him for a moment when he'd step outside. It was reported that Vinnie would be in the corner with her sketchpad to catch a few lines of Lincoln's face as he dashed down the corridor. Apparently Lincoln noticed the frequency with which Miss Ream would be waiting in the hallway. When he questioned her, she told him that her name was Vinnie Ream and that she was a sculptor. "So you're the Western sculptor. We are old friends [referring to their Midwest connection in common]."

Vinnie was less than five feet tall and weighed about 90 pounds. The towering Lincoln invited her into his office to begin her sculpture work as he prepared his second inaugural address. She became a regular visitor to his office over the next few months, having set up a makeshift studio there. Vinnie later wrote, "He seemed an absolutely heartbroken man. Sometimes at these sittings, his face wore a look of anxiety and pain, which will come to one accustomed to grief. Never was there grief like Lincoln's. He was still suffering from the blow of his child's death while great affairs convulsed the nation." By March of 1865, Vinnie had nearly completed the bust. Lincoln seemed pleased with the likeness. On April 14, 1865, Abraham Lincoln was assassinated. Vinnie was inconsolable, and could barely look at her work of art.

After the Civil War, Vinnie continued to study French, German, and textbooks on anatomy, improper as it was for ladies to study the science. Her brother Bob returned to Washington with his bride, a Chicksaw woman named Anna. Not willing to let an opportunity go by, Vinnie had Anna pose, and the result was a nude full-length statue titled "Indian Girl." News and gossip spread that the bold female artist worked with nude models. When a reporter questioned her about this, the undaunted artist replied, "The Lord modeled a good many people in the nude." Vinnie was a prolific artist with a passion she felt no obligation to defend. To honor the goal of the Lincoln Administration to keep the Union intact and restore it, Vinnie created the sculpture "Union Restored," which is composed of four female figures that depict four directions of the compass. In April 1866, members of the Senate and House of Representatives signed a letter proposing that Vinnie Ream be commissioned to do a full statue of the late President Lincoln. The resolution H.R. 197 passed in July of 1866 on a vote of 57-7, and then went on to the Senate where it met opposition and debate. Finally, it was passed, and the 18-year-old female artist was commissioned for $10,000 to do a life-size model of Abraham Lincoln.

Word traveled fast. The *Milwaukee News* boasted with the headline, "Congress Captured by Wisconsin Girl." But there was also plenty of negative press to go around. Vinnie was attacked by an envious East Coast art aristocracy as well as a few outspoken members of Congress. Who was this unknown, beautiful young

artistic genius who had no training in Europe and did not conform
to anybody's ideas about art? How dare she have the talent to
take on such a project and have a coveted U.S. government commission. Who was this "uncouth, uneducated upstart from the
outlandish West?" Eventually these questions would be answered,
as the young woman bravely forged ahead to mark her place in
history. Ream's studio was actually in the Capitol, and she was
daring enough to obtain and carefully clean the blood-stained
clothes Lincoln was wearing the night he was shot, and use these
as a model for the Lincoln sculpture. Mary Todd Lincoln had
doubts about this unknown artist, and she was sure her husband
had not been acquainted with the young woman. The White
House staff was routinely careful not to let the intensely jealous
Mrs. Lincoln have knowledge of female callers, Vinnie Ream
being no exception.

After nearly two years of working on the plaster model of
the Lincoln sculpture, Vinnie requested the first $5000 of the
appropriation. Two senators, Charles Sumner of Massachusetts
and Jacob Howard of Michigan, tried to stonewall the payment.
The oblivious Sumner had not viewed the sculpture even after all
members of Congress and the president were specifically invited to
do so. The forces that judged the sculpture exquisite and a work
of art that touchingly captured the "expression of sadness mingled
with benevolence," easily won the battle. The appropriation was
approved on April 29, 1869.

Success always seems to travel with a few bumbling companions. Just as the money was approved, an article came out in the
St. Louis Democrat that again blasted Vinnie. The women's rights
leader Elizabeth Cady Stanton described Vinnie as a "mature
Botticelli cherub" after Mrs. Stanton failed to obtain Vinnie's
signature on a petition titled: "A Plan to Move on the Works of
Man the Monster." Several of the men listed in this vindictive
document had been of help to Vinnie in her young career. She
staunchly stood up to the criticizing woman and said, "Mrs. Stanton, I am not of your thinking in this matter. I'm not a woman's

rights advocate ma'am. No help has any woman given me here."
The mature Botticelli cherub stood her ground.

Another woman, an influential Washingtonian named Calhoun, complained to the *New York Daily Tribune,* and said that Vinnie was "coarse, spiteful, and injurious." The vindictive woman had never seen Vinnie's work, but she was quoted as saying she "just knew it was bad." The cat spats continued relentlessly. Vinnie was accused of "decorating her studio with flowers, wearing long hair, and attracting the men and thereby lobbying. No girl can keep haste and pure with three hundred wretched men [Congress] around her." To this remark, Representative Thaddeus Stevens quipped, "Well out of all the three hundred men, there has never been an effort to do as much harm to Miss Ream as one woman can make."

The *St. Louis Democrat* dethroned the critical women by printing a piece that strongly stated, "These literary women are the most reckless of Bohemians...Little Ream is the Venus Victrix—she has met the enemy and they are hers." Nonetheless, the cruelty and the furor of attempts to crush her were taking a personal toll on the young woman. She faltered briefly and considered a change in career. But a letter from her father, Robert Ream cheered and encouraged her. He was in New Orleans and discovered his little daughter was talked about not only in Washington, but also all over the country. He wrote:

Vinnie,
What have you ever done to cause your name to be hawked about and be mixed up in such a manner? You are made notorious against your will, your name and fame are bound to outlive you. Just think, when we are all dead and gone, someone will write a novel about you and another will write a play. Your studio in the Capitol will be a grand tableau in the play. Bingham and Butler will be in the play and there will be spoons and broken statues...and Thaddeus Stevens will be one of the heroes.
(signed) Robt. L. Ream

Vinnie left the criticism of disapproving women behind, took the heartening words from her father, and traveled with the plaster sculpture of Lincoln to Rome, Italy, and arranged to procure the finest white marble. It was a glorious trip. In Europe, she was jolted into profound popularity and inundated by invitations from famous people to numerous social events. She had risen above the envy and pettiness of her critics in America, and she was now stronger than ever before. On January 25, 1871, the marble statute of President Abraham Lincoln was unveiled in the Rotunda of the Capitol in Washington D.C. The Rotunda was crowded to capacity and waiting people outside pounded on the doors in an attempt to gain entry. The Marine band played. Emotions ran high, and tears flowed, as the statue was unveiled. Senator Morrill of Vermont, chairman of the Committee of Arrangements, stepped to the front and proclaimed, "Four years ago, a little girl from Wisconsin occupied a little place in the Post Office Department, at $600 per year. She had faith that she could do something better. Congress, with equal faith and liberality, gave her an order for the statue of the late President Lincoln. That statue and the artist are now before you, and bespeak your sympathy." The applause was deafening. Senator Trumbull of Illinois said, "That Is Mr. Lincoln!"

Vinnie's critics had not ceased to exist. She was again blasted by abrasively snippy foes in the *New York Daily Tribune*. They said it was an outrage that she had been commissioned $10,000. This careless negative criticism was a definitive case of "be careful of what you pray for." Vinnie's expenses to make statue actually came to about $10,000, so in an effort to pay the artist fairly for her work, Congress granted Vinnie an additional $10,000. In the end, yes, $10,000 was outrageous, and ultimately the figure of $20,000 was deemed more fitting. Caveat: Criticism is easy; art is difficult. — Philippe Nericault Destouches (*Le Glorieux 1732* Act II Sc.5).

The works of Vinnie Ream are found at the Capitol in

Washington D.C., the State Historical Society of Wisconsin, the Wisconsin State Capitol in Madison, the National Museum of American Art at the Smithsonian Institution, Arlington National Cemetery, State Historical Society of Iowa, Georgetown University in Washington D.C., Cornell University, Ford's Theater collection; National League of American Pen Women, Chicago Historical Society, Oklahoma Historical Society, New York Historical Society, State Historical Society of Missouri, Historical Society of Washington D.C., National Museum of Women in the Arts, and other locations. Her personal papers were given to the Library of Congress.

Much of Vinnie Ream's art is reportedly missing, lost, or undiscovered. She was evicted from her studio at the U.S. Capitol by Reconstruction radicals, and her works were said to be "broken to pieces." Many of the portrait busts were not rendered in a hard material such as marble or bronze. Most of the major recorded works are treasured in historical societies and in several institutions in Washington D.C. Vinnie's last work was a life-size statue of Chief Sequoya. Sculptor George Julian Zolnay finished the sculpture after Vinnie's death in 1914. Chief Sequoya stands in the Capitol building in Washington D.C.

"The first real work I ever did was the sketch of an Indian. I hardly expect that I will ever do another piece of work after this is finished.

As the work I did was the statue of an Indian, so will the last be."

— Vinnie, two days before her death

It has been said that Vinnie's insight "looked straight into the soul." She was an optimistic rebel, and, God forbid, a woman. Vinnie grew up ahead of her time in the bloody framework of the Civil War. She had no delusions of being invincible in such a time of turmoil. At a young age she wrote, "We are all passing by…." Vinnie endured tremendous personal hardships, but became an integral and undisputable part of American politics and art. Vinnie believed that natural ability and opportunity is useless unless it is pursued avidly. Trivial unproductive pastimes and arrogant rivals did not interest her. Through poverty, unrelenting criticism, maliciously negative publicity, and family tragedy, she gave art her best efforts. Vinnie shut out distractions, no matter how overwhelming and devastating. The artist was distinguished with having a gracious personality that was displayed without exception to everyone she met. To quote one account, "She takes you cordially by the hand." George Brandes, Danish critic, described her as "a soul without a trace of bitterness, an intellect whose work is not a labor." In art history, she is considered the most prominent American female sculptor of the nineteenth century.

Author's Note: *In researching this book, I found, the story of Vinnie Ream Hoxie to be one of the most fascinating biographies that I encountered. Had Vinnie lived later in the 20th Century, and not in the chaos and tragedy of the Civil War, I believe she would have gained a greater degree of favorable notoriety in a more liberal society. On the other hand, I have faith that her compassion and trusting youth captured the living Lincoln in such a spiritual and dramatic way that her genius was born at a time in history that was her destiny. This short essay was researched through an excellent and detailed biography of Vinnie Ream Hoxie titled* A Labor of Love *by Glen V. Sherwood (SunShine Press).*

Susan Stuart Goodrich Frackleton

(1851-1932)

Not enough can be said about female artists in Wisconsin. Individually and collectively they were, and are, a driving force in the art world. Susan Frackleton, born in Milwaukee in 1851, was one of the earliest significant influences. Her path had been paved earlier, however. Around 1842, Wisconsin began to encourage women to follow the arts "as a desirable part of education." This

Susan S. Frackleton Studio
Milwaukee, Wisconsin 1901
Wisconsin Historical Society Image 8857

edict coincided with the arrival of Mrs. Gray who was hired to take charge of the Madison Female Select School. Introductory courses included reading, spelling, and English "branches" that included "natural, mental, and moral philosophy." Instruction in French and Latin was "six dollars extra." For drawing and painting, the price was "four dollars extra," according to Porter Butts' *Art in Wisconsin.*

Susan Frackleton was a student of Henry Vianden along with student Carl von Marr, and studied landscape painting, later studying in New York. Susan delved intensely into the field of ceramics and china painting, where she has become known as one of America's most renowned ceramicists. She organized the Milwaukee Art Association with the motto and seal, "Keep the fire alive." The Wisconsin Art Institute, the first school organized for professional art instruction in Wisconsin, was formed in 1888 through the creative efforts of Susan Frackleton. The school later became known as the Milwaukee Art Institute.

Susan Frackleton is best known for her salt-glazed stoneware and china painting. The artist seemed to have a practical sense about her. In 1901, she invented and patented the portable gas kiln used to fire ceramics. She was written about in *A Woman of the Century* in 1893. Because of her efforts, it is reported that more than 500 women were able to follow her methods and become self-supporting. In 1886, she wrote the technical book *Tried by Fire* (D. Appleton & Co., New York). A Susan Frackleton piece now is a rare find, and a large work can be valued in the $20,000 to $30,000 range. Typical pieces range from $5000-$8000. Her book *Tried by Fire* is considered rare and sells for about $800. The Sinsinawa Dominican Sisters maintain a collection of pieces that are occasionally on loan to museums.

Susan Frackleton received numerous awards, including rec-ognition of her book by London's South Kensington Museum, the U.S. Potters' Association, and many other organizations and institutions. She is the founder of the Wisconsin School of Design and a leader among women entering the arts and crafts movement of the twentieth century.

Theodore Robinson

(1852-1896)

Even though Theodore Robinson had his strongest affiliation
with France as an American expatriate, he lived in Wisconsin
sporadically from the age of 3. At a very early age, Theodore had
an overwhelming desire to develop a career in art. A student at
age 17, he began his training at the Chicago Academy of Design,
but a significant problem with asthma prompted him to try living
in Denver, Colorado. A year later, he returned to Wisconsin. At
the age of 22, he moved to New York to further his schooling at
the National Academy of Design and the Art Students League,
where he was instrumental in development of the League. Then
it was off to Paris in 1876 with a return to New York in 1879. A
return to Wisconsin was inevitable when his finances failed. Not
to let luck get him down, the 29-year-old artist returned to New
York, took a teaching position, and was employed on decorative
projects. Theodore traveled New England and painted views of
Nantucket, but finally he was drawn back to France at the age of
32. He lived in Giverny for the next five years, associating with
a number of American art students, who were later to become
famous.

Probably most significant to Robinson during this period in
his life was his association with the master French Impressionist
Claude Monet. The two were close friends and often critiqued
each other's work while working in Monet's backyard. Consequently, Theodore Robinson, although an American impressionist, was probably the most traditionally French in style. His trips

back and forth to New York made him a purveyor of the Impressionist movement in America. His canvases were exhibited and
his popularity grew. In December 1892, Theodore again moved
back to New York and began using his impressionistic style to
paint colorful New England scenery. During this time, he supported himself by teaching art for Evelyn College in Princeton,
New Jersey, and for the Brooklyn Art School. Tragically, when
he was just 44, his life and his art were cut short by a fatal asthma
attack in New York City in 1896. Brief though it was, Robinson's
intense career in art had a major impact on American Impressionism. He believed strong skills in drawing and a realistic depiction
of nature were paramount.

The Theodore Robinson painting "Boats at a Landing" was
auctioned in May 2003 for $2,136,000.

Carl von Marr

(1858-1936)

*"I am no longer a dreamer; my instructors are very demanding
and exact discipline every minute. They say self-discipline is an artist's
most important tool."*
— **From a letter to his father, John Marr**

The University of Wisconsin awarded Carl von Marr an honorary doctorate in 1929. In 1924, he was awarded an honorary
membership to the American Association for Art and Literature.
The road to these achievements was a long one teeming with
tremendous achievements in art, and life-threatening drama in
Europe. Carl von Marr was an American expatriate who found
his career in Europe, but established his strong reputation both
in Europe and in the United States. He was born in Milwaukee
in 1858, and at the age of 15, he joined his father John Marr in
business as a wood-engraver artist in an engraving firm. The

"John Marr — Father" 1891 oil on canvas 50.5" x 50.5"
Collection of the West Bend Art Museum

young Carl became a student of the professional artist Henry Vianden, who had trained in Germany in the Düsseldorf style before immigrating to the United States. Vianden encouraged his best students to seek more training in Europe.

In 1875, at the age of 17, Carl traveled to Germany to study at the Weimar Academy of Fine Arts and the Berlin Academy of Fine Arts. The young artist then settled in Munich at the Royal Academy of Fine Arts. He returned to the United States after completing his art training and went to work for Harper's Publishing Company in Boston. Carl then returned to Milwaukee where he taught avocational art classes and worked in illustration for a living. Dissatisfaction and perhaps the impatience of youth prompted Carl to return to Germany at the age of 24 in 1882. He stated in an interview, "I believe I could better endure physical starvation, if it came to that, than starve mentally as I had been doing in America" ("Carl von Marr" by Thomas Lidtke for the *Wisconsin Academy Review,* March 1986).

The enormous painting, "The Flagellants" (oil 13'10" x 25'8") was begun in 1884. It was a five-year project from first sketches to completion. The painting portrays a band of repentant devotees, people who roamed through Europe in the 13th and 16th centuries. As they walked the roads, the wanderers whipped themselves

Carl von Marr in his studio
Collection of the West Bend Art Museum

in an effort to save sinners. The painting won numerous awards and was on exposition at the Chicago World's Fair in 1893 where it found worldwide acclaim and attracted attention from the German art critics. The monumental painting was purchased by the city of Milwaukee and today it remains on long-term loan to the West Bend Art Museum in West Bend, Wisconsin.

Not only had Carl von Marr made a transition in his life to continue his pursuit of art in Europe, but also the artist made a transition in his style of painting. "Summer Afternoon" was done in the German Impressionist style rather than the academic style. At the age of 35 in 1893, while in California working on the commissioned painting "Summer Afternoon" for Phoebe Apperson Hearst, the artist was offered a professorship at the Royal Academy in Munich, and later was offered similar positions at the academies in Berlin and Vienna. The great artist was now recognized internationally in Europe and North and South America. In 1909 he received the Order of the Red Eagle from Kaiser Wilhelm of Prussia, thus placing the prefix "von" before his name. King Victor Emanual of Italy honored him in 1912 with a barony through knighthood.

The European titles and political affiliations as adviser to the Bavarian government came with a price. The Bolsheviks placed von Marr on their "forty most wanted" list. He was wanted dead or alive and the incentive was that others on the list would be spared by his capture. What's an artist to do? He fled to Switzerland and hid in the forested mountains. Eventually a kind peasant hid the artist in his house and then in a pigeon loft in the barn before a search party arrived. The startled pigeons took off in flight at the same moment the approaching searchers fired a warning shot. The peasant blamed the late night pigeon flight on the gunfire. Nevertheless, the searchers demanded to inspect the loft. Carl flattened himself against the shadows on the far wall, and both he and the peasant escaped imprisonment or execution. Carl was later captured, but he talked his way out by convincing his captors he was of no importance.

"Summer Afternoon" 1892 oil on canvas 52.75" x 81.5"
Collection of the West Bend Art Museum

"Bertha Marr — Mother" 1891 oil on canvas 50.5" x 50.5"
Collection of the West Bend Art Museum

Elsa, Carl's wife, died shortly after Carl shed his fugitive status. They had only been married three years. She had been the widow of a fellow painter before Carl married her. Elsa's two daughters from her previous marriage served as Carl's subjects in many of his paintings. Carl von Marr continued his career as more awards and honors distinguished his art. He was appointed director of the academy in Munich in 1919 at the age of 61. He retired from the academy in 1923.

The artist had made his contribution to art. He now had a conviction to aid other artists, not for the sake of art necessarily, but for the fundamental desire to lend compassion to the struggle of others. The 1930s arrived with more trouble brewing in Europe—this time in the form of Nazism. Carl von Marr became involved in helping Jewish artists flee Germany. It was said that Adolph Hitler was particularly fond of the painter's work and even owned a portrait of the famous artist.

Remembering his own relentless persecution as a political enemy, Carl von Marr had no sympathy and no use for Hitler or his dictatorship.

Carl von Marr died in Munich on July 19, 1936 from cancer. His paintings are known, not only for their technical excellence, but also for their uncanny ability to capture the personality of the subject through expression of the pose and careful attention to positions of facial muscles as they deal with emotion. The West Bend Art Museum, West Bend, Wisconsin, houses 350 works by Carl von Marr. The collection includes his drawings, academic work, portraits, genre (human activity), impressionistic, and symbolic works. The collection portrays his stylistic phases.

Author's note: *Special thanks are extended to the West Bend Art Museum and director Tom Lidtke for information and assistance on the subject of Carl von Marr. Much of the information in this essay comes from the article "Carl von Marr" by Thomas Lidtke written for the Wisconsin Academy Review, March 1986.*

John Fery

(1859-1934)

The artist John Fery is best known for his paintings of the western United States, and in particular his paintings of Glacier National Park and parts of Wyoming such as the Tetons and Jackson Lake. If you've ever admired a large old painting of scenery used as an ad for one of the great railways, you may have run into a John Fery or a Franz Biberstein painting. "Railway stations and hotels served in a real sense as the first 'art galleries' in the West, at a time before traditional art institutions were even envisioned in the region," notes William Gerdts in *Art Across America*. One of Fery's patrons was James J. Hill, builder of the Great Northern Railway whose successor was the Burlington Northern. The Great Northern Railway was the only convenient access to Glacier National Park in those days, and it owned the only hotel there. That John Fery found his niche and his love in painting Western scenery connected to a railway was a "portable" destiny of sorts. He was able to travel to Seattle, Washington and Salt Lake City, Utah, and pursue his scenery painting. One of his favorite places was Jackson Lake, Wyoming, and it is said that he painted 35 pictures of the lake while renting a lodge owned by the cousin of the artist John Singer Sargent. Typical paintings also depict the Pacific Northwest, California, and Wisconsin. The railroad purchased 362 works, many of them panoramas as large as 10 x 12 feet.

Strasswalchen, Austria, is the recorded birthplace of John Fery. Some say he was born in Hungary. That is likely inaccurate, but he is partly of Hungarian descent. At the age of 27, John, his wife Mary Rose, and their first-born child, Fiametta, immigrated

"Elk in Yellowstone Park" by John C. Fery
Collection of the West Bend Art Museum

to the United States. Four years later, in 1890, John Fery made his first trip to the American West. He and his family lived in Milwaukee from 1903-1910, and again from 1923-1929. The family then moved to Orcas Island, Washington.

It appears that Fery was a self-taught artist, but was greatly influenced by academic art. Some claim he studied art at the Düsseldorf Academy. He was a prolific artist much in demand, and he painted quickly with broad strokes. Most of his paintings today are privately owned, many in the Milwaukee area. Numerous paintings and sketches were destroyed in a tragic fire at his home in Washington. Institutions that own his paintings include places in the Milwaukee area, Burlington Northern, Inc., and the Church of Latter-day Saints Museum in Utah. Architectural paintings include the Steinmeyer estate at Okauchee Lake, Wisconsin, and the Spadena house in Beverly Hills, California. John Fery produced many large paintings, some as big as 10 by 12 feet, but the smaller pieces are actively sought after today by collectors of Western art. "Cascades of Canyon Creek" sold in 1999 for $16,500.

Frank Enders

(1860-1921)

Frank Enders is known as one of Wisconsin's painters and etchers, but he is probably just as strongly associated with the name Henry Vianden, who was his teacher. Frank Enders was a Milwaukee native whose father owned a saloon in Milwaukee's German community in the 1860s. The industrious boy was employed as a sign painter from the age of 15 to 17 in the painting shop of Henry Baumgaertner. At the age of 19 he went to Munich, Germany to study at the Academy. That adventure lasted until he was 24. He returned to Milwaukee and opened a studio on Oneida Street and became involved in Milwaukee's active art scene as secretary of the Milwaukee Art Association,

Untitled by Frank Enders
Collection of the West Bend Art Museum

and was later named director of the art gallery in the Milwaukee Exposition Building. Later he became a founding member of the Society of Milwaukee Artists.

Like so many artists, Frank had a Western travel bug. He ended up in Denver, Colorado, and then traveled on to San Juan and Santa Fe, New Mexico. During his stay in the southwest, the artist took an interest in images that included scenery, and the Native Americans and their villages. After a brief stopover in Milwaukee again, he painted his way through St. Louis, Omaha, Chicago, and New York. Murals were in vogue and in demand at the time. Returning to Milwaukee, the artist set up a new studio at 7th Street and Grand Avenue, and later on 3rd Street.

The artistic gift of Frank Enders can be seen in his paintings of Wisconsin scenery, especially around waterways and their villages. His subjects also included allegory, figure, human activity genre, still life, and portrait. Frank Enders' freedom with the brush gave his oil paintings an impressionistic style much of the time, but he is most closely associated with the school of realism from Munich where he had much of his intense training. The painting "Disregarded Advice" sold for $6,500 in 2001. The work of Frank Enders has been exhibited at the Art Institute of Chicago, the National Academy, and the Pennsylvania Academy.

Adam Emory Albright

(1862-1957)

Adam Emory Albright became famous for his depiction of children at play in his landscape paintings of rural America. He started out, however, as a landscape artist. It wasn't long before he began to add children to the landscapes after he was influenced by the poetry of James Whitcomb Riley. Perhaps inspirational to his work was the birth of his twin sons, Ivan Le Lorraine Albright and Malvin Marr Albright (Zsissly). The boys became

"Afternoon Ride"
by Adam Emory Albright
Collection of the West Bend Art Museum

his models for the canvases that depicted growing boys in rural settings. They spent summers at the artist colony in Brown County, Indiana, where their father produced some of his finest paintings. Adam Emory Albright was born in Monroe, Wisconsin. He studied at the Academy of Fine Arts and was one of the first students at the Art Institute of Chicago from 1881-1883. He then went on to study with Thomas Eakins at the Pennsylvania Academy of Fine Arts from 1883-1886.

Another Wisconsin connection to Adam Emory Albright is his association with the artist Carl Marr (Carl von Marr), with whom he received training in Munich, Germany. Traveling on to Paris for more training, Albright became arguably the finest Paris-trained figure painter before the Columbian Exhibition. The artist moved on to colorful Impressionism after the Columbian Art Exhibition. He set up his own studio in Chicago in 1890.

The twin sons, born in 1897, went on to become established artists in their own rights. Ivan LeLorraine Albright (1897-1983) was well known and successful as a Chicago painter, although he began his career as an architect studying at Northwestern and at the University of Illinois. His brother Malvin Marr Albright (pseudonym Zsissly) (1897-1983) became a noted sculptor.

"Summer Outing," oil on canvas 36 inches by 72 inches, sold in March 1990 for $63,000. Albright's paintings are bright, sunny, and full of life and activity. His paintings have been widely exhibited, especially at the Art Institute of Chicago.

Mathilde Georgine (Mathilda Georgina) Schley

(1864-1941)

The famous artist-writer was the first-born of nine children in Horicon, Wisconsin, to a German-born mother who taught her young daughter Mathilde how to read and write German before Mathilde began attending first grade in Mayville and Juneau, Wisconsin. Later, the artist-to-be became a telegraph operator for a short time. Moving to Kansas where relatives lived, Mathilde became a drawing instructor and started to exhibit her work. The artist later returned to Wisconsin, lived on her parent's farm, but shortly moved to Watertown, Wisconsin, where she and her sister Lydia opened a dressmaking business, and then moved the business to Milwaukee where it became exceedingly successful. The entrepreneur sisters spent summers in Beaver Dam. Mathilde and sister Lydia spent profits from their business and built the Schley Apartments in Milwaukee, where they subsequently lived.

Mathilde concentrated her art studies in Milwaukee. She was taught by Otto von Ernst, Richard Lorenz, and Alexander Mueller, and was probably associated with the Milwaukee Art School and the Milwaukee Art Students League. Not feeling confined to the German academic style of painting, she branched out to an impressionistic and pointillist style, preferring to use a palette

"Boathouse at Beaver Dam, Wisconsin"
by Mathilde Georgine Schley
Collection of the West Bend Art Museum

"The Rose
Garden" by
Mathilde
Georgine Schley
Collection of
the West Bend
Art Musuem

knife instead of a brush—a woman of independent thinking. The paintings include still life, buildings in rural Wisconsin, floral, and portraits of relatives. A painting showing Lydia in a landscape setting in 1926 "Germany" is considered one of her best. Mathilde had an admiration for nature, and was intrigued by the full moon. But she also had a great interest in architectural structure, and painted the Octagon House in Watertown. This is her only painting that is known to be in a public collection. Today, the painting hangs in the Octagon House Museum. Her other paintings remain with family members.

The artist offered few of her paintings for sale, but she exhibited them widely, including exhibits in New York, Chicago, Milwaukee, and other cities in the United States. She was a member of the Wisconsin Painters and Sculptors and other professional associations, and was listed in professional directories including American Art Annual and Who's Who in American Art.

Mathilde was intensely interested in the history of German immigration to the United States. She researched and wrote numerous articles written in German that were published in German-American newspapers throughout the United States. The collected articles were compiled into two privately printed books, *Deutshamerika* (1935) and *Fritz, Pät, Jules und Hänk* (1940). The books are illustrated with reproductions of her paintings. Copies of the books were placed in several libraries that included the library at Harvard University.

According to author Peter C. Merrill, the artist was known for "being high strung and capable of brief emotional outbursts." Nonetheless, she had a wide circle of friends both in the world of art and in publication. In 1928, she traveled to Europe where she was the only woman invited to attend an international press exhibition in Cologne, Germany. Eugene B. Meier, Jr. of Palatine, Illinois, grandson of Celia, one of Mathilde's sisters, has undertaken the task of researching the life and work of the remarkable female artist. Copies of the artist's publications and some of Meier's manuscript are located at the Max Klade Institute for German-American Studies in Madison, Wisconsin.

George Raab

(1866-1943)

The versatile artist George Raab was born in Sheboygan, Wisconsin, the youngest of seven children. He made the move to Milwaukee to further his opportunities in art. The year was 1888, and his timing was right; the Layton Art Gallery opened, and the Milwaukee Art Association was founded. Although he received a major part of his training in Milwaukee at the Wisconsin Art Institute, the artist was heavily influenced by European art, and spent several years training in Europe beginning in 1891, with short trips back and forth to the United States.

During his time in Milwaukee in 1889, at age 33 he was a partner in the firm of Feiker and Raab, Photographers. In 1890, he was a partner in the firm of Bresler and Raab, Crayon Artists. Mr. Bresler, who was the same age as George Raab later became a well-known art dealer and importer. George Raab was a student of Richard Lorenz, the most important art teacher in Milwaukee during this period. Raab's teachers also included Robert Schade, whose German influence from the Munich Academy can be seen in some of the Raab still-life paintings. It's interesting to note that this particular group of classmates at the Wisconsin Art Institute comprised a core whose work and accomplishments later shaped the art history of Wisconsin and beyond its borders, especially in the areas of expressionism and abstract art. The classmates included Louis Mayer, Jessie Schley, George Mann Niedecken, Alexander Mueller, Gustave Moeller, and Carl Reimann.

According to Peter C. Merrill in his book *German-American*

TOP LEFT:
Lillian Gabriella Bresler
by George Raab
TOP RIGHT:
Untitled by George Raab
Both from the collection of
the West Bend Art Museum

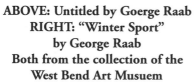

ABOVE: Untitled by Goerge Raab
RIGHT: "Winter Sport"
by George Raab
Both from the collection of the
West Bend Art Musuem

Artists in Early Milwaukee, George Raab's work is characterized by
loose brushwork that reflects the influence of late 19th Century
Munich style and some of the French Impressionists. Some of
his work, however, picks up the style of the French Impressionists. The artist used a variety of media working in oil, watercolor,
pastel, and crayon. He hand-colored his linoleum and wood block
prints, which took on geometric abstract of architectural subjects.
The artist also worked in low relief bronze portraits. George is
primarily known for his landscapes of Wisconsin and Illinois. The
early paintings were done in oil; however later in the 1930s he
moved more into watercolor and block prints. During the 1920s
he typically received $300 for a commissioned portrait. In 1902,
Geroge Raab was appointed curator of the Layton Art Gallery.
He went on to become director of the Decatur Art Institute and
then was associated with Millikin University as acting director of
School of Fine Arts. The artist remained very active in Wisconsin
art including a post as president of the Wisconsin Painters and
Sculptors and a life member of the Milwaukee Art Institute.

George Raab is representative of a generation of Wisconsin
artists who were born in the United States but were highly influenced by the training they received in Europe. Even so, many of
Raab's block print landscapes and cityscapes produced during the
Depression era reflected the changing trends. Numerous examples
of George Raab's work have survived. One of his best, and his
most reproduced painting, is "Veil of Snow" (1910) which is a
scene that depicts snow falling on the buildings across the street
from the Milwaukee Art Institute (Milwaukee Art Museum).

Louis Mayer

(1869-1969)

Louis, youngest of seven children, became a painter and a sculptor after working as a woodcarver and photographer. The artist was a student of Richard Lorenz and Otto von Ernst. Eventually, as several of the young artist descendants of German immigrants did, Louis traveled to Europe and studied art at the Weimar Art School, the Munich Academy, and Dachau, an art colony near Munich. He is thought to be the first young Milwaukee-born painter to study at the European schools. Louis' art career began with his painting and his insistence on precision drawing. He holds a place in Milwaukee art history as a leading player in the formation of the Society of Milwaukee Artists founded in 1900. Later the organization became the Wisconsin Painters and Sculptors. He was the Society's first president. Mayer wrote "Half a Century of Art and Artists in Milwaukee," an important article appearing in the *Milwaukee Sentinel* on April 5, 1903. He eventually left Milwaukee and headed to New York City where he established a studio on 42nd Street. It was here that he primarily began his career in sculpture, finding the studio light not sufficient to pursue painting.

Like other artists, he bought a piece of land and built himself a small cabin. This land purchase ended up to be 800 acres 45 minutes north of New York City in Fishkill, New York. Nonetheless, he still had fond ties to Milwaukee, and he visited frequently. Bouncing to the California coast, he decided to live in Carmel, California, although he kept his home and studio in Fishkill,

New York. After the death of his wife, he remarried at the age
of 87 in 1957.

The artist was considered an excellent portrait painter. He's
also painted landscapes. Mayer used tonal studies, but moved
to more colorful works. A number of exhibitions and awards
rounded out the career. Sculpture was the primary endeavor
for which he is most noted. His work includes many fountain
sculptures, small bronzes, busts of Lincoln, La Follette, Daniel
Hoan, Eugene Debs, Victor Berger, Walt Whitman, and Socrates.
Louis Mayer was an important and influential early artist in the
development of the arts in Milwaukee.

**LEFT: "Albert Schweitzer"
attributed to Louis Mayer
Photo courtesy of Louise
Maynard of Orosi, California**

**BOTTOM: Fountain top
attributed to Louis Mayer
Photo courtesy of Louise
Maynard of Orosi, California**

Adolph Robert Shulz
(1869-1963)

Ada Walter Shulz
(1870-1928)

Adolph Shulz studied at the Art Institute of Chicago and the Art Students League in New York with the renowned artist William Merritt Chase. Shulz later studied in Paris. Adolph Shulz is credited for development of the major artist colony in Brown County, Indiana, where he spent his summers along with his artist wife, Ada. Adolph was born in Delavan, Wisconsin, and he did much of his painting there when taking breaks during his schooling. It was in Delevan that he met his future wife, Ada, who was also an art student at the Art Institute of Chicago. The couple made many trips to Indiana, and finally moved there in 1917.

Adolph Shulz considered Brown County "a fairyland with its winding roads leading the traveler down into creek beds, through water pools and up over hills...picturesque cabins seemed to belong to the landscape as did the people who lived in them." Of course, there was the other side of the coin—the reflections of Indiana native, Felix Brummet, who said,

"You see I don't know anything about painting, but I saw that big red-whiskered fellow over there and I noticed he has this box with small things at his feet. He would look up at the sky and then reach for those little things, then look up again and do something else with those little things. As I said, I don't know nothing about what he was doing but it looked like plum ignorance" *(The Artists*

TOP: Untitled
(Corn Shocks) by
Adolph Schulz
Collection of the
West Bend Art
Museum
LEFT: Ada Walter
Schulz, Brown
County, Indiana
Publication *Our
Brown County*

and Natives of Brown County. Rachel Perry).

Adolph Shulz worked in oil, graphite, and pencil. He is known
for his paintings of architecture, cityscapes, figures, landscape,
portraits, and street scenes. His painting "Nashville Autumn
Street Scene" sold at auction for $41,000 in January 2004.

Ada Walter Shulz is best known for her light bright impressionist paintings of Indiana summers and the children who played

in those summers. She was born in Terre Haute, Indiana, and studied art with John Vanderpoel and Oliver Pennet Grover at the Art Institute of Chicago. Later, Ada studied in Paris at the Vitti Academy. In 1892, she met Adolph in Delavan, Wisconsin. They married and remained there for 20 years. An only child, Walter, became an artist too, but died tragically from diphtheria at the end of World War I after fighting in Germany. Devastated at the death of her only child, Ada put down her paintbrush for a few years, but she returned to painting children as her favorite subjects. Her painting of barnyard animals in the scenery with children is characteristic of paintings beginning in 1925. She used the farmyard of Mary Ann Barnes ("Grandma Barnes"). In 1928, Ada painted "Companions," a painting of Grandma Barnes with a large turkey.

"Sally," as she was fondly known, paid her child models fifty cents in 1925 for their cooperation, as well as children can "cooperate." According to an Indianapolis newspaper, "Mrs. Shulz said Charlotte, one of her models, 'went on strike' one time and wouldn't pose any more because she thought the picture was done—at least it looked 'done' to her" (*Brown County Children: Models for Ada Shulz Paintings*. Rachel Perry). Ada Shulz also told the story of how one mother bribed her daughter to sit for a painting by saying, "Now honey, you just sit and let Mrs. Shulz paint you and when she's through, I'll take you to see the dead cow." It worked.

The paintings of Ada Shulz have uniqueness because of their subject matter. Most artists of the time preferred to paint the hills and landscapes, "as if no one lived there," but Ada Shulz preferred the idyllic scenes of playful children. The artist once wrote, "Children and sunlight were always ringing in my ears. Would they not bring joy to the heart if painted right?" Her delightful paintings are in museums and private collections today. The painting "Mother and Child" sold in December 2003 for $80,000.

Helen Farnsworth Mears

(1872-1916)

The toddler artist supposedly started by using what was within reach—namely pieces of bread. She used the bread to sculpt human and animal figures. To this child, the "don't play with your food" rule was merely an annoyance to be ignored. Her work, "Apollo," was awarded a prize at the Winnebago County Fair when she was 9 years old. Helen continued her artistic interest into her teenage years. At the age of 21, Helen Farnsworth Mears was given a commission by the state of Wisconsin to create a "heroic figure" for exhibition at the Columbian Exhibition of 1893 in Chicago. Helen had been studying at the Art Institute of Chicago thanks to an inheritance from her Aunt Helen Farnsworth. The artist changed her name from Nellie to Helen in honor of her aunt. For the Columbian Exhibition, Helen created a life-sized female figure, "Genius of Wisconsin," draped in a flag and cradling the neck of an eagle, which was later moved to the Wisconsin state Capitol in Madison. The artwork brought her to the attention of world famous sculptor Augustus Saint-Gaudens. She worked and apprenticed with him in New York, Paris, and Italy. Helen studied at the Art Students' League in New York City during the time she worked with Saint-Gaudens.

In 1899, the artist opened a studio in Washington Square and became a very successful professional sculptor. Her commissioned work included: a bronze bust of George Rogers Clark for the Milwaukee Public Museum, a bust of Dr. William T.G. Morton for the Smithsonian Institution, a bas-relief portrait of Saint-Gaudens

RIGHT: "Aphrodite" sculpture
by Helen Farnsworth Mears
West Bend Art Museum

LEFT: "Genius of Wisconsin" 1893 marble sculpture
by Helen Farnsworth Mears, Wisconsin State Capitol
Wisconsin Historical Society Image 7074

for the Peabody Institute in Baltimore, a portrait of the composer Edward MacDowell at the Metropolitan Museum in New York City, and a portrait of her mother, Elizabeth Mears. A monumental sculpture done in 1900 of Frances E. Willard, is located today in Statuary Hall at the Capitol in Washington D.C.

Helen was born in 1872 in Oshkosh, Wisconsin, the youngest of three sisters. Her mother was Mary Elizabeth Mears, an author and Wisconsin's first native playwright. The largest collection of Helen's work is in the Paine Art Center. Other examples are in the Oshkosh Public Museum. One of her most famous works, "The Fountain of Life," was never cast in bronze, and the plaster model has been lost or destroyed. Like many artists, Helen experienced hardship at times. She died in New York in 1916 at the age of 43, reportedly from malnutrition. Many pieces of her work were left unfinished. Her sister Mary, an author who had worked beside Helen in New York, continued to promote the legacy of the artist. Today, Helen Farnsworth Mears is still considered one of the most important female sculptors in the United States. Other works include "The Urn," "Dawn and Labor," "The End of the Day," which was inspired by observation of a New York laborer, "Playing Rabbit," "Reclining Cat," and the erotic "Reclining Eve."

Alexander Mueller

(1872-1935)

Alexander Mueller was another artist who received training from the master Richard Lorenz at the Wisconsin School of Design. He was 17 at the time, and then found employment as a lithographer, engraver, and draftsman in Milwaukee. His foreman at the lithography shop, Albert Otto Tiemann, became one of Alexander Mueller's students and later joined the faculty of Mueller's art school, the School of Fine and Applied Arts. Like the other talented students of Richard Lorenz, Mueller spent four years studying art in Europe in Weimar and Munich. There he ran into the artist Louis Mayer, a fellow Richard Lorenz student from Milwaukee. In Munich, Alexander Mueller had the great fortune of being taught by Carl von Marr, a transplanted artist from Milwaukee.

Artists tend to be innovative and Alexander was no exception. Alexander Mueller is credited with taking his School of Fine and Applied Arts and placing it under the umbrella of the State Normal School, thus developing it into an institution with an enrollment of five hundred students and twenty-two faculty members. It seems people were attracted to the school because of its expansion into applied arts—metalwork, jewelry, embossed leather, textile design, commercial design, and ceramics. Mueller may have been the first Wisconsin artist to apply formal European

Untitled by Alexander Mueller
Collection of the West Bend Art Museum

training to the applied arts of design.

Mueller, dissatisfied with his position at the State Normal School in 1923, made a decision to take his family to Europe and devote his life to painting. The family lived in Munich for five years, and Carl von Marr was then the director of the Munich Academy. Seeking a different climate, the family then moved to San Marino, California. The Depression hit the country, and the demand for art diminished. Mueller's paintings were not selling as well as before. The painting, "Moonlight Scene" (1908), was found at a Goodwill Industries store when artist Philip Miller recognized the work. Nonetheless, many of Mueller's paintings are missing, namely Wisconsin landscapes painted between 1911 and 1923, scenes he painted in Bavaria from 1923-1928, and the California landscapes he painted later in life. Be on the lookout. The painting "Eastern Souvenir" (1898) sold for $8,250 in 1987.

Bruno Ertz

(1873-1956)

The Charles Allis Art Museum in Milwaukee is a work of art in itself. But amidst the grand elegance of this beautiful addition to the planet, one room in particular captures the attention of

Bruno Ertz watercolor untitled Collection of the West Bend Art Musuem

just about every visitor. The bedroom of Sarah Allis, wife of Charles Allis, is home to a collection of the art of Bruno Ertz, famed miniaturist, illustrator, and painter. His expertise was in insects, butterflies, and birds of Wisconsin. The paintings, some as small as 3 x 5 inches, are meticulously detailed. Ertz studied his subjects under magnification as he painted them. Bruno Ertz was a self-taught artist born in Manitowoc, Wisconsin. His parents were German immigrants. Ertz had a studio in the Iron Block in Milwaukee, and later shared a studio in the University Building at the turn of the century.

During the depression, Bruno Ertz worked on the Federal Art Project at the Milwaukee Public Museum. The artist worked mainly in watercolor. His watercolors were collected by

Bruno Ertz watercolor
Courtesy of Charles Allis/Villa Terrace Art Museum

Charles and Sarah Allis, John D. Rockefeller, Baron Lionel Walter Rothschild, and others. Today, the bedroom of Sarah Allis is a conference room at the museum and houses a permanent Bruno Ertz collection. Other homes to the paintings of Bruno Ertz are the Leigh Yawkey Woodson Art Museum in Wausau, Wisconsin, and the Rahr-West Art Museum in Manitowoc, the city where he was born. The artist specialized in photorealism style watercolor and particularly liked to paint insects. Later in life, he switched to birds as his subject. For any student of miniaturist art and watercolor technique, studying the work of Bruno Ertz is well worth the effort. The bees are great.

Emily Groom

(1875-1975)

One of Wisconsin's most influential and noted female artists was Emily Groom. She lived in exciting and dramatically changing times in the world of art. The artist made the study and teaching of art her life's mission. Emily's work, unlike the German influence that surrounded her, favored French Impressionism, and she is particularly known for her landscape paintings of the Genesee and Boscobel area. Capturing skies and the essence of clouds is Emily's hallmark. The artist was the co-founder of the Wisconsin Watercolor Society and a member of the prestigious Wisconsin Painters and Sculptors. Emily was born in Massachusetts, the oldest of six children. Her parents settled in Milwaukee, and Emily began her love and practice of art while attending kindergarten in the basement of the Unitarian Church on Albion Street. She then began taking art lessons in the home of Alida Goodwin.

The young Emily studied at the Art Institute of Chicago in 1894 for two years. Then it was on to the Museum of Fine Arts School in Boston where she found the new freedom of watercolor. Here she studied the works of Winslow Homer, John Singer Sargent, and John Marin. In her essay on Emily Groom, researcher Mary Poser notes, "She felt watercolors were at least as durable as oil. She could produce them faster and sell them cheaper, and thus sell more of them." Emily believed "watercolors are always appropriate in the grandest or simplest of settings," and the watercolor medium posed a challenge of "catching" a certain look.

Downer Wood, Milwaukee. Oil on board c. 1909
Emily Groom
Collection of Lawrence Univerity, Appleton, Wisconsin
(Milwaukee-Downer Collection)

The artist also spent time in New York, England, Scotland, and on the Continent where she perfected her impressionistic style.

Emily retired at the age of 82 in 1957 from teaching at the Layton School of Art and the Milwaukee Downer College. She taught a popular Extension class for 22 years. The woman was as popular as her art. Many art students, some of whom went on to become professional artists, can credit their early, as well as advanced studies, to Miss Groom. Today the artist's oil paintings and watercolors can be found at Marquette University, the Milwaukee Art Museum, the West Bend Art Museum, and many public institutions and libraries. Miss Groom was a co-founder or the Wisconsin Watercolor Society and was a member of the Wisconsin Painters and Sculptors. She exhibited her works with a number of contemporaries who included Robert von Neumann, Alexander Mueller, Gustave Moeller, Jessie Kalmbach Chase, Ada Walter Shulz, Francesco Spicuzza, and many others. Nieces Elizabeth Groom and Helen Johnston are currently cataloging the art of Emily Groom, and have located over 400 of her drawings and paintings.

Merton Grenhagen

(1878-1941)

The famous of the day — governors, state Supreme Court justices, socialites, among others were witness to the painting expertise of Merton Grenhagen (Gruenhagen). The famous

"Tired at Play"
by Merton Grenhagen
West Bend Art Museum

Wisconsin artist was born on a farm near Lake Poygan around Fremont, Wisconsin. He studied electrical engineering and took art classes at the Art Institute of Chicago in his spare time. Apparently, this paid off, because he later received a scholarship to study at the Julian Academy in Paris. Prior to establishing a studio in Oshkosh, Merton taught at the Art Institute of Chicago. He had exhibitions at the Art Institute of Chicago and the Pennsylvania Academy, as well as the Milwaukee Journal Gallery of Wisconsin Art. The artist established an eager clientele in Madison around 1930. While living in Madison, he painted the portraits of many socialites, state political leaders and governors, state Supreme Court justices, and members of the University of Wisconsin faculty and administration.

Grenhagen was strongly in demand as a portrait painter. He was also a member of the Wisconsin Painters & Sculptors and is listed in *Who Was Who in American Art*. His portrait paintings are in the collections of the University of Wisconsin, the Wisconsin State Historical Society, and the West Bend Art Museum. The West Bend Art Museum has a delightful painting titled "Tired at Play," oil on canvas painted in 1906. The colors are as rich today as they were one hundred years ago.

Edward Steichen

(1879-1973)

Edward Steichen was a painter, a lithographer, and nationally famous as a photographer. In World War I, he was a lieutenant colonel and commanded the photographic division of the U.S. Army Air Service in France, accomplishing pioneering work in military aerial reconnaissance. World War II again swept him into action. He served as a lieutenant commander, later a captain, in charge of producing a photographic record of the U. S. Navy at war. After the war, he became director of photography at the Museum of Modern Art in New York, and held that post for fifteen years. His most famous world exhibition was "The Family of Man" in 1955. Considered a classic, his illustrated autobiography, *A Life in Photography* was published in 1963.

Edward didn't exactly start out with all this fame. He was born in Luxemburg, immigrated to the United States with his parents, and settled in Michigan where his father worked in a copper mine. The family moved to Milwaukee in 1889. Edward quit school and went to work as an apprentice for a lithographer. At the age of 16, he began experimenting with photography, and by age

Untitled watercolor by Edward Steichen
Collection of the West Bend Art Museum

18, he had taken a lead in forming the Milwaukee Art Students League,* becoming its first president. At the age of 21, he traveled to Paris in 1900 and took up formal art training. Painting and photography occupied his time, but he was not satisfied with the schooling. The innovative Edward Steichen was the first person to exhibit photographs as works of art in the Paris Salon in 1902. This was a critical turning point in his career, and in the concept of photography as art. He returned to Milwaukee and exhibited his photographic work at the Atheneum; however, this was apparently a rest stop or testing ground. He was soon traveling to New York where he became a founding member of the Photo-Secession and contributed to its journal *Camera Work*.

Edward had attracted the attention of the world famous photographer Alfred Stieglitz, and the two established the Photo-Secession Galleries, a commercial gallery. In 1923, the artist was doing portrait photography for *Vanity Fair* and fashion photography for *Vogue*. Edward Steichen became a renowned photographer of the 1930s. He was recognized for his photography of Hollywood film stars. Maybe on a whim, or maybe as a statement of purpose, the artist burned most of his paintings in 1922 and dedicated his career exclusively to photography. A few of his early watercolors of the Wisconsin Dells are in existence in museum collections. Edward Steichen photos are highly prized by collectors today.

not to be confused with the Art Students League of the Milwaukee State Teachers College organized in 1935.

Jessie Kalmbach Chase

(1879-1970)

It's not been easy for female artists. Not only did Jessie Kalmbach Chase put up with mosquitoes while painting the Door County summers, she ran the hurdles to become a noted Wisconsin artist in her lifetime. Born in Sturgeon Bay, Wisconsin, (Door County area), she spent colder parts of the year in Madison after her marriage. Most of her landscape paintings are of Door County and Madison. She was a *plein air* (French term meaning "open air") artist who spent spring and summer in Door County where she apparently rented the top floor of an old building, the quarry dorm, to use as a studio. Jessie was most concerned with light and shadows and sketched primarily in daylight outside. She

"Picnic Point U.W." by Jesse Kalmbach Chase
Collection of the West Bend Art Museum

"Willow Drive U.W." by Jesse Kalmbach Chase
Collection of the West Bend Art Museum

then retreated to her studio to do the actual painting. It seems her reason for this routine was because 1) she did not want to "copy" nature, and she believed this would have been the temptation if she were to paint in the subject field 2) she wanted to capture light and shadows accurately in daylight, particularly the afternoon, and 3) the blasted mosquitoes came out of nowhere.

Charlie Lyons, former curator of the Miller Art Center in Sturgeon Bay, asked Jessie why she did not sign her paintings immediately. She replied that she knew who painted the piece, so there was no reason to do so. Paintings that left the studio for exhibition or for purchase were signed, however. Seems at this point there was a practical reason for identification. Many of the artist's screen prints and oils can still be found, along with fewer of the watercolors. She specialized in landscapes of the spring and summer while in Door County. Snow scenes were another subject that she liked. Her style varied from a simplified flat pattern adapted from Japanese woodblock prints to an impressionistic style.

Large-scale murals were another interest of the artist. She often used a mixture of cement and oil paint to create a "cement-fresco" for texture. The unusual medium was developed by Olaf Oleson of New York. One of these murals was constructed in 1930 as an arch above the entrance to Madison West High School, Madison, Wisconsin. Other murals were produced for buildings in Fort Atkinson, Sturgeon Bay High School, Madison Public Library, and the Bank of Sturgeon Bay. Jessie was an active member of Wisconsin Painters and Sculptors, was a board member of the Madison Art Association, and participated in other organizations. Her exhibitions were apparently limited to the state of Wisconsin, and she is listed in *Who Was Who in American Art*. The artist is discussed in *Women's Work, Early Wisconsin Women Artists*, a 2001 publication by the West Bend Art Museum. Many of the artist's screen prints and oils, along with fewer watercolor paintings, have survived. Jessie was not actively involved in teaching, but was influential to those artists who sought her opinion. The Miller

Art Museum in Sturgeon Bay is home to several examples of her work. Auction records are scarce. "Birch Trees Along a River" sold in 1989 for $1,662 minus mosquitoes.

Gustave Moeller
(1881-1931)

Born in small town rural New Holstein, Wisconsin, Gustave Moeller was attracted to painting quiet streets and villages. In 1895, he and his parents arrived in Milwaukee where the teenager searched the Milwaukee newspapers for a job that would help him develop his interest and his talent in art. Perhaps luck or perhaps fate, and an ambitious search, landed the boy an apprenticeship with the commercial art studio of Edward Steichen and Herman Pfeifer. Gustave Moeller became one of the first students of the Milwaukee Art Students League in 1896 at the age of 15. His teachers at the school were Alexander Mueller and Richard Lorenz. His interest in art was gaining, and Gustave took classes at the Art Institue of Chicago while he worked as a commercial artist in an engraving firm.

More travel and work were in his future when he left for New York to study at the Academy of Fine Arts and work as an illustrator on the side. The student continued inching his way east and leaped to Europe where he studied in Munich and Paris. He returned to Milwaukee in 1912, again finding work as a commercial artist. Gustave spent the rest of his life teaching art and became director of art education at the Milwaukee State Teachers College, later University of Wisconsin-Milwaukee. Many of the state's well-known artists were his students. The energetic artist founded the Walrus Club, which was a men's sketch club. He was active in many organizations and held offices in the Wisconsin Painters and Sculptors.

As an artist, Gustave Moeller liked painting such areas as Bay-

**Untitled (Alma, Wisconsin) by Gustave Moeller
Collection of the West Bend Art Museum**

field, Wisconsin, a village on Lake Superior; and he particularly like to paint scenes from Alma, Wisconsin in Buffalo County. He worked primarily in oil on panel and watercolor, and his subjects were figure and landscape. In 1931, eight months after his death, the Milwaukee Art Institute held an important exhibition of 165 of his works. Gustave died at the age of 49 from complications of surgery for appendicitis.

Francesco J. Spicuzza

(1883-1962)

"Art is never steadfast—it changes with the times. It must change with the times because it records the times"

Francesco Spicuzza, an important Wisconsin Impressionist, was born in Termini, Sicily. He immigrated as a child to Milwaukee. Francesco was a popular artist about town, and was best noted for his Milwaukee beach scenes done in blue monochromatic

"My Mother at 79"
by Franceso Spicuzza
West Bend Art Museum

pastel. In the biography of artist Spicuzza, written by his daughter, Marguerite Spicuzza Hambling and Joyce R. Newcomb, it was stated that a *Milwaukee Journal* reviewer wrote, "…Spicuzza, of all Milwaukee painters, has evoked Milwaukee as a city by the sea, an inland sea, by his bathing pictures." The painter's subjects included figure, floral, genre (human activity), landscape, marine, portrait, seascape, still life, winter scenes, and Wisconsin landscape. He worked

"On the Pier — Big Cedar Lake" by Francesco Spicuzza
Collection of the West Bend Art Museum

in bright color oil and pursued a painting style akin to French Impressionism. The artist studied at the Milwaukee Art Students League under Alexander Mueller, 1905-1910, and in Woodstock, New York, under John Carlson in 1912. His training began, however with artist Robert Schade, when a wealthy Milwaukee businessman recognized the talent.

Francesco produced hundreds of pieces ranging from smaller, inexpensive works to major works of art. The artist is fondly remembered for teaching at the Milwaukee Art Museum (Milwaukee Art Institute) and in his studio. The paintings have been widely exhibited and have included shows at the Art Institute of Chicago, the National Academy, and by the Society of Independent Artists. A major exhibition of his art was organized and presented at the West Bend Art Museum in 2002. Francesco included his mother's portrait in his exhibitions when the opportunity presented itself because he believed she brought him good luck.

The artist's daughter, Marguerite, notes her father "was considered to be a fair man and a good mediator." This was in reference to the art of politics, and the politics of art, that splashed around public funding of the Milwaukee Art Institute in 1940. A commercial artist of that time made the charge that the institute had "too much modern art, and not enough 'old fashioned' art." The *Milwaukee Journal* titled an article "Art Institute is Called a Chamber of Horrors." The controversy boiled down to a compromise. Francesco's message that the artist must be free to choose subject and treatment of the subject or "there is no art," was coupled with the art critic Thomas Craven's message of "art prospers only when there is cooperation and understanding between the artist and the public for which the art is created." This prompted Spicuzza to compose his "What is Modern Art?" talk, which he used to promote understanding when asked to speak in front of many groups and organizations.

Francesco was an optimist, and an ambassador of the joy and beauty of life and art. A book, *Francesco J. Spicuzza, Wisconsin Impressionist, Clippings of a Life,* by Marguerite Spicuzza Hambling in collaboration with Joyce R. Newcomb, is an interesting illustrated work available at the West Bend Art Museum.

Elsa Emilie Ulbricht

(1885-1980)

I'll say it again. Enough can't be said about female artists, including Elsa Ulbricht. Her art included painting in oil and watercolor. Prints, lithography, pottery, weaving, and bookbinding rounded out her talents. Elsa started out at the age of 23 as a kindergarten teacher from 1907-1909 and trained for that profession at the State Normal School, a teachers college in Milwaukee that had been a project of the Wisconsin Legislature. This teaching experience along with her simultaneous art instruction at the Wisconsin School of Art, which was operated by the Milwaukee Art Students League, catapulted her into a broad lifetime career in art. Her teachers were Alexander Mueller, George Raab, Louis Mayer, and Gustave Moeller, a quartet of artists who under the advice of the famous artist Richard Lorenz had gone to Europe for training. She moved on to receive a degree in art education from the Pratt Institute.

Aside from her own art, she had a long career in teaching art at the Milwaukee State Teacher's College, which ultimately became the University of Wisconsin-Milwaukee where she became the director of the Art Division. Summers off from teaching became summers of teaching at the Oxbow Summer School of Painting in Saugatuck, Michigan, where she served as director and eventually had a home.

The project that ultimately had far-reaching consequences was her work with the Works Project Administration (WPA). This federal agency's purpose was to find employment for workers during the Depression. It was in 1935 that Harriet Clinton, director of the Women's Division of WPA for Milwaukee County, approached Elsa Ulbricht for help in teaching skills and finding jobs for women, many of whom had not worked outside of the home. Elsa took on the monumental task of setting up the project and directing it, all the time insisting that highest design standards

"Old Wash House at the Windmill" by Elsa Ulbricht
Collection of the West Bend Art Museum

be maintained. The limited staff started out with two rooms supplied by the Veterans Administration, but soon expanded to many locations throughout Milwaukee due to tremendous demand. The project employed 5000 women, and included fifty skilled craftsmen hired as instructors and project supervisors. The Milwaukee Handicraft Project turned out useful products that included toys, rugs, and printed drapery fabrics. The goods were purchased by institutions across the country. The artists eventually took on major interior design ventures, studying the interior spaces and then designing the furnishings. The project also hired men with cabinetmaking skills to build furniture.

Elsa's paintings capture light and relaxing settings. She painted landscapes, portraits, and outdoor figure studies. A characteristic of her work is her two-dimensional style of portrait. She was an equally skilled printmaker who was influenced by her association with master printmaker Robert von Neumann. A major retrospective of her artwork, which was organized by Jeune Wussow, a former student, was shown at the Charles Allis Art Library in 1973. The show displayed sixty-eight oils, ten watercolors, and twenty-four graphics.

Elsa was born in Milwaukee, never married, and kept her address at 915 North 28th Street. Her father, a lumber dealer, built the house in 1893. I hesitate to say she had a lot of time actually to "live" at 915. Elsa was not a homebody. She was a busy woman into her ninth decade, and liked to entertain, act in plays, and travel. She was fondly remembered by Alfred George Pelikan as a "liberated young woman of the flapper era who wore her hair bobbed and raised eyebrows by smoking in public." *(German-American Artists in Wisconsin.* Peter C. Merrill)

Georgia Totto O'Keeffe

(1887-1986)

The Diva of Modernist Art—Georgia O'Keeffe—proudly claimed her roots in the young farmlands of the American Midwest. Today she holds the record auction price ever recorded for a painting done by an American woman. The most recent statistic that I was able to locate in a database is:

"Calla Lilies with Red Anemone"   48" x 29.5" oil on masonite.

Auctioned at Christie's in New York on 5/23/2001 for $6,166,000.

Created in 1928.

Another O'Keeffe painting that hit the block that day was:

"Black Cross with Stars and Blue"   40" x 30" oil on canvas

Auctioned at Christie's in New York on 5/23/2001 for $4,076,000

There is no information on when the painting was created.

Artist Georgia O'Keeffe's highest price per square inch is $8,690 for a painting auctioned off on May 21, 1998. The artist is portrayed in approximately 459 books and 141 periodicals.

Georgia is one of the first American Modernists, and is the first woman to gain recognition for that style. Loosely speaking, the term "Modernist" refers to a style and an ideology. In Modernism, the artist depicts the world as he or she perceives it. Thus, it is a breaking away from traditional representational art.

Georgia is known primarily for her southwestern landscapes, and of course, the flowers. Yes, the flowers…she decided that a painting of a flower could not give the viewer exactly the same feeling of enjoyment that she experienced from the flower. She searched for "equivalents" to recreate those feelings that she had derived. Georgia once wrote, "I know I cannot paint a flower, but maybe in terms of paint color I can convey to you my experience of the flower or the experience that makes the flower of significance to me at that particular time."

In 1902, the 14-year-old Georgia was enrolled at Madison (Wisconsin) High School. It was here that she had a significant encounter with a flower. In later years, she talked about remembering passing by an art classroom where a flamboyant teacher in a brilliant colored flowery hat was lecturing. Georgia stood spellbound in the doorway as the woman held a jack-in-the-pulpit plant up for the class to examine. The teacher meticulously pointed out the unique shapes and richness of delicate shades in and about the curvy plant. Up until this day, Georgia had never studied, of all things, a flower, in an art class. This was a commanding revelation that inspired her to paint living things. Drawing from plaster casts or copying pictures had been the usual classroom routine up until this once-in-a-lifetime day. Twenty-five years later, she painted a series of spectacular oils based on that first encounter with an influential flower in a high school classroom. .

The Beginning

November 15, 1887, brought a baby girl who was destined to become one of the world's most famous artists, and indeed, one of the world's most famous women, to Sun Prairie, Wisconsin. Georgia Totto O'Keeffe was named after her Hungarian grandfather, George Totto, a political refugee and count from Budapest, who gave up the harshness of farming and later returned to Hungary, leaving his wife Isabel and the six children to move from Sun

Prairie to Madison. One of the six children, Ida, was to become the mother of Georgia O'Keeffe. It is said that the educated Ida Totto, at age 20, wasn't exactly crazy about tying the knot, but was obedient and fond of Frank O'Keeffe. She married Francis (Frank) because the match was favored by the families and he was interested in purchasing the Tottos' land near Sun Prairie. Frank had halted his education as a young teenager after his father died, and the boy was now obligated to help his mother and brothers run the farm they owned near Sun Prairie.

Georgia was born at home in the small farming community of a few hundred people and was the second of the O'Keeffe children. Her evenutal siblings, Francis, Ida, Anita Natalie, and Alexius, along with Georgia, spent evenings and Sunday afternoons listening to their mother reading classic literature to them. Ida had high expectations for all of her children, and in particular believed emphatically in the education of women.

Georgia, independent from her brothers and sisters, and happy with that arrangement, spent time in the company of her imagination. She recalled building a fantasy household under the branches of one of the apple trees on the 600-acre farm. The little world had a park of clipped grass, trees made of tall weeds, a shingle boat in the dishpan lake, and a doll for which she sewed a wardrobe. Georgia's solitary hours bolstered her imagination, but they also strengthened her inclination to do things her own way, and this was strongly evident throughout her life.

The budding artist ardently studied the illustrations in her mother's books and copied pictures of exotic places from her geography book. It was customary and "proper" for young ladies to learn painting in those days. Mother Ida felt that the schoolteacher had time to teach only the basics of reading, writing, and arithmetic, so she arranged for private art lessons for her daughters from the painter Sarah Mann of Sun Prairie. Every Saturday the O'Keeffe sisters would ride the seven-mile round-trip journey by buggy into the bustling village of 900 people in Sun Prairie for the art lessons. In the evenings, they would spend hours practicing

Georgia O'Keeffe
Photo: Arthur Stieglitz
© 2004 The Georgia O'Keeffe Foundation
Artists Rights Society (ARS), New York

drawing fundamentals.

Sharp-minded and free flying as an eagle, the feisty young O'Keeffe dutifully learned realism at an age when obedience was a childhood requirement. She soon moved on to analyzing the technicalities in her art, and to capturing such fleeting phenomena as the brightness of sunshine and the glow of moonlight on the snow. Georgia's ways were pioneering and insistent. Her mother, Ida, expected her to be an "accomplished young lady" or an art teacher, but to think that a young woman would actually be an "Artist" was practically out of the question in this Victorian era. "I decided that the only thing I could do that was nobody else's business was to paint," said Georgia, recalling one of her black sheep-of-the-family memories.

An account of how she once quarreled with her older brother Francis about the gender of God was another fond memory of hers. She argued that God was a woman. Francis stated she was wrong. Mother Ida was asked to settle the disagreement, and she confirmed that Francis was correct in that God was not a woman. Georgia, confident in her convictions, announced to both Francis and her mother that God was certainly a woman, and that was the final word. Georgia came from a strongly matriarchal family, and perhaps that influence instilled in her the buoyant self-assurance that became her hallmark.

In 1901, Ida enrolled her daughter Georgia, now 13, in an exclusive convent boarding school, Sacred Heart Academy, near Lake Wingra in Madison, Wisconsin. The annual tuition fee was eighty dollars, but Mr. and Mrs. O'Keeffe decided to pay an extra twenty dollars so Georgia could enroll in art instruction. Sister Angelique, the nun who taught art, scolded the teenage Georgia for making her drawings too tiny and dark. Light and large became the order of the day to please Sister Angelique. Georgia was not accustomed to strict rules that the academy operated on, but she managed to respect them, learn from them, and employ her best manners. The daughter of the distinguished Ida Totto was eager to have permission to participate in the classical music concerts, and to do this she had to behave—this included listening to the instruction in art class to lighten her drawings and make them larger. At the end of the year, the nuns awarded her a gold metal for her excellent "deportment."

Departure

Weather in Wisconsin is nothing short of wicked at times. Inescapable frozen winters are severe and cruel. Georgia's father Frank, had lost three brothers to tuberculosis, and he was the only one of the brothers remaining alive in the winter of 1899. Ida had given birth to Claudia Ruth when the bitter cold outside had dropped to thirty-four degrees below zero. Escaping the blow of dropping farm prices and escalating machinery costs, the O'Keeffe's, now land rich, decided to move to Williamsburg, Virginia. They sold the farm in 1903 for $12,000, and bought a nine and a half acre estate in Williamsburg for $3,500. It was a gracious and large estate known as the Wheatlands. The family had few belongings to furnish the eighteen-room house. They brought little furniture with them from Wisconsin and had few valuables other than some jewelry and Mr. O'Keeffe's fiddle.

Georgia, now 15, had departed from Wisconsin and its strongly agrarian culture. Yet the images, the egalitarianism, the closeness to the elements of nature, the intensity and freedom of artistic expression that she coveted and developed, and the sense of importance in education that was instilled in her Wisconsin upbringing, encapsulated her. The cocoon would in years to come open to a butterfly that left an irrefutably permanent and boldly colorful impression on the world of avant-garde art. She would later say, "It is my childhood—I seem to be one of the few people I know of to have no complaints against my first twelve years." Georgia believed that the prairies were the "normal" part of the country, and she found it difficult to talk about America to people who did not know the prairies.

In Williamsburg, Ida O'Keeffe, ever vigilant about her children and their education, enrolled Francis, Georgia's brother, in the

College of William and Mary, sent Georgia to Chatham Episcopal Institute, and hired a tutor for the youngest children. Georgia endured the spartan institute and managed to buck the tradition of wearing dresses with tight-fitting waists and ruffles and bows, fashionable at the time. Then and throughout her life, she wore mostly no-frill black or renditions of it, despite the chatter of her classmates on how they could dress up Georgia. This would have been a challenge, no doubt.

Under the instruction of a talented art teacher, Elizabeth May Willis, Georgia excelled, problematic as she was at times. Sometimes Georgia the student would work intensely for hours or days and accomplish phenomenal results in preciseness and color on projects that seemed to others already completed. At other times, Georgia the pest would dally and annoy the other students in the studio or generate humorous antics. Art teacher Willis, a woman of tolerance, remarked, "When the spirit moves Georgia, she can do more in a day than anybody can do in a week." Georgia spoke with the flat Midwestern inflection, but she wasn't bothered by it, because of course, this was the "correct" way to speak. She received many demerits for infractions of rules, such as getting out of bed after 10 p.m. and would have to spend Saturdays writing some tired expression repeatedly. Finally, after struggling with a spelling test that she had to take six times, at the age of 17, in June 1905 she graduated with her six classmates.

By September of 1905, Georgia was enrolled at the Art Institute of Chicago and lived with her Uncle Charles and Aunt Georgiana Ollie. Another influential woman in Georgia's life was the "autocratic, brilliant, strong-willed" Aunt Ollie who was the sister of Georgia's mother. Ironically, Ollie must have been better at spelling than her niece had been, since she was the only female proofreader at the *Milwaukee Sentinel* for many years. The year Georgia enrolled, there were 900 students at the Art Institute, and Georgia was cast into the competitive lot where a student's work was ranked monthly according to merit. The purpose of the merit ranking was so that students could compare their work to others and learn what qualities are judged most favorably. Although

Georgia had little interest in painting the human body, she was ranked number one in her life drawing class.

Georgia returned home to Virginia in June, but was unable to return to the Art Institute in fall because she had contracted a seriously debilitating case of typhoid fever in Williamsburg. Lucky to have survived typhoid, and quite exhausted from the illness, she began to paint a little by setting up an easel in the yard. Instead of going back to the Art Institute of Chicago, Georgia now cast her ambitions on the Art Students League in New York, where her teacher, Elizabeth May Willis, had gone.

Patsy Paints New York

The year was 1907, and Georgia arrived in Manhattan after a twelve-hour train ride from Virginia. Hotels, saloons, book-stalls, concert halls, and art galleries lined the sidewalks in the bustling crowded city. Georgia rented a room for a few dollars a week near the Art Students League on West 57th Street. She joined the tenacious and exuberant art students as the infancy of the 20th Century began to bring about changes that boldly allowed women's skirts to clear the ground by six inches. Typhoid fever had left Georgia thin, and she held a boyish grace that had a beauty of fine line. During the illness, Georgia had lost her hair, and it had now grown back in soft lush curls. She became known as "Patsy—because her name was O'Keeffe." She was a remarkable beauty.

Miss O'Keeffe bought a notebook upon her arrival in New York, and in the "Yes" column she listed why she should do one thing. In the "No" column she listed why she should not do another thing. She remarked, "The essential question was always if you want to do this, can you do that?" The woman forever believed that, although one may have a number of talents or desires or opportunities, a choice and a focus were ultimately required. Because of her sleek lines and her austere beauty, Georgia was often asked to pose in the portrait class as a model, earning a fee of one dollar for four hours. She needed the money, but by mid winter, she refused to model and instead concentrated on her drive to be a painter.

Georgia took a portrait and still-life class taught by the distinguished painter William Merritt Chase (1849-1916, genre, landscape, portrait, figure; record auction $3,962,500 for "Peonies"). He painted with technical expertise, and in his efforts to lessen the provincialism in American art, he taught the strongest European methods in perspective, foreshortening, highlighting, and shadowing. Chase's friend John Singer Sargent, famous society portraitist, could "delineate a gold watch chain with a single swift stroke of the brush," said Georgia. The vivacious and awesome Chase demanded that his students produce a painting every day, "one on top of the other until the canvas became too thick with paint to continue." One of the art students, Eugene Speicher (1863-1962, portrait, landscape, and still life), asked the lovely Patsy O'Keeffe to poise for a portrait for him. She immediately refused, and he said to her, "It doesn't matter what you do. I'm going to be a great painter, and you will probably end up teaching painting in some girls' school." As fate would have it, Georgia posed for the outspoken Eugene Speicher, and that painting became his first formal recognition as a portraitist. The distinct painting hangs today in the Members' Room at the Art Students League. But, as Eugene reveled in his $50 prize for the portrait, Georgia won the top prize of $100 for a still life of an oil painting of a dead rabbit lying next to a copper pot, painted in the impressionistic style of Chase.

Harder Times

Georgia returned home to Williamsburg at the end of the summer in 1908 and found that her family's financial status was deteriorating badly. It was apparent to her that she would not be able to return to the Student Art League in the fall. Her ambitions and dreams of being a painter in her own right were receding into the shadows of simply making a living. She concluded that she would have to leave Williamsburg and look for work. It was a heartbreaking blow. At age 21, Georgia headed out to the gray coldness of windy Chicago where she found freelance work as a commercial artist sketching lace and embroidery ads for dress advertisements. Illustrators who could speedily meet deadlines were in demand. In later years, she attributed her ability to paint rapidly to the pressure of production in commercial art. After two years in Chicago, she contracted measles that temporarily affected her vision and forced her to give up illustration. Georgia returned to Williamsburg and found her mother was suffering horribly from tuberculosis. Besides the serious illness, Mother Ida was distraught at her husband's business failures.

Georgia's mentor, Elizabeth May Willis was taking a leave of absence from her art teaching position at Chatham, and asked Georgia to fill in for her. By around 1912, Georgia's sister, now a student at the University of Virginia, coaxed Georgia into attending instruction presented by a professor of Columbia Teachers College of New York. She was skeptical, but went anyhow. Arthur Wesley Dow had a revolutionary idea that involved what would be known today as "abstraction." Georgia in later years remarked that his ideas were simple, but could be used to make a very aesthetic decision. "It seemed equipment to go to work with. Art could be a thing of your own."

A teaching job in Amarillo, Texas captured the genius of Georgia O'Keeffe in August 1912. "That was my country—terrible winds and a wonderful emptiness." She spoke of the plains as her spiritual home. With her, she took Dow's much criticized ideas that children should draw objects from their everyday lives instead of copying from a book. Dow saw in this a freedom and freshness of design, which naturally, would be appealing to the maverick Georgia. The Texas Legislature had passed a law requiring that textbooks, including drawing books, selected by the state commission be used in all classes. Georgia refused to concede to this idea, and a battle arose, but by the end of the school year the textbooks had not been purchased by the tough-willed Miss O'Keeffe.

A Changed New York

The pull of New York City and studying with Arthur Dow at Columbia Teachers College was magnetic. Under Dow's guidance, Georgia studied abstract form, decorative patterning, and harmony of color. Probably his most enduring advice that she took to heart was to "fill a space in a beautiful way." Georgia was now 27 years old. In the art world, there had been a change of seasons. Hundreds of European and American avant-garde abstract paintings were on exhibit at the New York Armory. The paintings were as controversial as the pictures photographer Arthur Stieglitz had displayed at his gallery several years ago. Professors from the League were outraged. But Georgia's mentor Dow wrote, "Art is decadent when designers and painters lack inventive power and merely imitate nature or the creations of others. Then come realism, conventionality, and the death of art. The artistic mind is always trying to find new ways of expressing a beautiful idea." Indeed, Mr. Stieglitz's gallery on lower Fifth Avenue was showing the first Picassos and Cézannes in America.

Because her money was in such short supply, even though she lived frugally, Georgia reluctantly left New York and took a teaching position at Columbia College in South Carolina where she essentially became semi-reclusive and blended the chemistry of art and emotion. "Hibernating in South Carolina is an experience that I would not advise anyone to miss," she wrote to her friend Anita. She persistently painted daily, sometimes repeatedly painting the same picture in an effort to capture the emotions that lie hidden beyond the technical ability. Georgia was dissatisfied with her work. She decided to analyze her art with absolute objectivity, paying attention to paintings and drawings she had done to please various professors, and to other projects she completed in an effort to emulate well-known artists. She determined that the images in her mind were abstract and unlike anything she had been taught. Her thoughts were radical and daring. "I visualize things very clearly. I could think of a whole string of things I'd like to put down but I'd never thought of doing it because I'd never seen anything like it," she said later. This turning point would shape the next seventy-two years of Georgia's life, both professionally and personally.

Anita Politzer, Arthur Stieglitz, and Controversy

Georgia's long time friend Anita Politzer, a senior at Columbia Teachers' College in New York, received a roll of charcoal drawings in January 1916 in the mail from Georgia. Anita was amazed at the bravado with which the lines and shapes took on a life of their own. She took the drawings to the famed gallery of photographer Arthur Stieglitz. "Finally, a woman on paper!" was his excited reply. Stieglitz believed that the female experience was "spiritually distinct from that of the male, and that the experience left women more 'advanced' and freer of society's inhibitions than American men." He wanted to show these drawings that were the "purest, finest, sincerest things that have entered [Studio] 291 in a long time." Georgia traveled to New York in March. Arthur Stieglitz decided to display the drawings, without bothering to ask permission of the artist, and was so cavalier in his endeavor, that he even got her name wrong—calling her Virginia O'Keeffe. Georgia was incensed. How dare he show these intensely personal drawings! Georgia dashed to 291 and found that Stieglitz was not there. But the famous drawings were carefully arranged and highlighted by light streaming in from a skylight in the largest room of the gallery.

A few days later she went back to confront Stieglitz. He said her drawings were wonderful and he had to show them. Patrons were aghast that drawings from a female schoolteacher had been displayed on the same walls that supported Picassos and Cézannes. One patron, Mabel Dodge, brought in psychoanalysts to view the work. People were stunned by the naïve sexuality of the drawings. Was it really art, they wondered. Art critic Henry McBride wrote many years later, "Such a scuffling about for draperies there never was! Even many advanced art lovers felt a distinct moral shiver. And incidentally, it was one of the first great triumphs of abstract art, since everybody got it."

Stieglitz loved the uproar. He zealously defended the young woman named O'Keeffe and argued that the energy the exhibit generated would help shake America's puritanical grip and liberate its artists. He delighted in dismissing the critics, and with joy extended the exhibit into July. Georgia had to leave New York to teach summer school at the University of Virginia. Her mother Ida, age 52, had succumbed to a lung hemorrhage as a complication of tuberculosis. Ida was buried along side her brothers and sisters at the Grace Episcopal Church cemetery in Madison, Wisconsin. Georgia was despondent and weary, although she managed to teach classes, resting in bed between the classes. Arthur Stieglitz began to correspond with her, and this eventually helped to lift the artist's depression, as well as confirm her as an artist. Near the end of the summer of 1916, Georgia left for a teaching position in the Wild West — Canyon, Texas. It soon became quite evident that the new teacher from the East brought enthusiasm and new ideas from an intellectual world. "The point was not to teach them to paint pictures, but to show them a way of seeing. There is art in the line of a jacket, and in the shape of a collar, as well as the way one addresses a letter, combs one's hair, or places a window in a house," she said. Georgia insisted that every decision should be affected by what was aesthetically sound.

In April 1917, Georgia's first solo show opened in New York at Stieglitz's 291 studio. Critics were sure to take note, given the commotion her drawings had created in 1916. Henry Tyrrell of the *Christian Science Monitor* published a review that spoke to many. He wrote, "…her strange art affects people variously and some not at all…artists especially wonder at its technical resourcefulness for dealing with what hitherto has been deemed the inexpressible—in visual form, at least. Now perhaps for the first time in art's history, the style is the woman." Georgia left Texas and traveled to New York at the end of her teaching semester. She soon was at 291, and patiently listened in the background as Stieglitz lectured to visitors in the gallery. He nonchalantly turned, and was astonished and exuberant to see the young artist Georgia O'Keeffe unexpectedly standing there. Stieglitz, the famous photographer, soon asked the very photogenic artist with the exquisite profile to model for him. According to critics, this bond resulted in some of the most stunning portraits and work in the history of photography. Of the photos, critic Henry McBride penned, "Georgia O'Keeffe is probably what they will be calling in a few years a B.F. [Before Freud] since all her inhibitions seem to have been removed before the Freudian recommendations were preached on this side of the Atlantic..."

Interestingly, Stieglitz at the age of 13 wrote in his diary, titled "Mental Photography" that his favorite color was black. Ironically, he became one of the world's most famous photographers and loved the black and white medium. Women who dressed in black were a fascination to him. Georgia had long ago begun dressing exclusively in black, with a hint of white at the collar. Throughout her lifetime, styles and fashions of the day did not concern her. Georgia was often asked why she wore black. Her answer was that she was sensitive to color, and that if she dared wear a red dress, she "would be obliged to live up to its flamboyance." The black clothing had a serious matter about it, and this served to broadcast a caution against frivolity or flirtation—to be taken seriously as an artist.

Eventually, Arthur Stieglitz left his marriage of twenty-four years and began living with O'Keeffe. It was a scandalous time, to which neither O'Keeffe or Stieglitz became a slave to criticism and rumors in that Victorian era. In 1924, at the insistence of Arthur Stieglitz, they married, although, unconventional as she was, Georgia couldn't see the point in marrying, since they already had been living together for several years. But it was an intensely romantic relationship as well as a strong business relationship. Stieglitz was essentially the agent of the artist O'Keeffe. When she finished a painting that passed her perfectionist scrutiny, she would release it to Stieglitz. When a patron wanted an O'Keeffe, the patron had to measure up to high standards, and have a good reason for wanting an O'Keeffe before Stieglitz would sell it. An anonymous buyer from France wanted to buy a set of six small calla lily panels painted in 1923. Stieglitz was irritated with the buyer's request, and tossed an unrealistically high price of $25,000 into the arena to ward off the annoyance. The buyer accepted, and the lilies went to France, but only with the agreement that the buyer promise to hang them in his home and not sell them within his lifetime.

Georgia could not tolerate an audience near her when she was painting. She generally would turn a work in progress towards the wall or cover it with a sheet if people were in the room. Having been in New York for a considerable period, Georgia longed for the open spaces of the West. In the summer of 1928, she made a trip to Wisconsin to visit relatives. During this summer, she painted a red barn and silo near Portage. As the year continued, she felt an urge to travel back to the Southwest. It was here, in this land of vast and beautiful space, that an unleashing of unencumbered imagination would beckon her to return every year. Stieglitz was dismayed with these yearly trips that lasted for months, but he believed that "freedom was necessary to sincerity," and he resolved himself to the fact that this was simply Georgia.

In commenting about New Mexico, Georgia once said, "The world is wide here, and it's very hard to feel that it's wide in the East." Aesthetically speaking, in a matter-of-fact way, she said that when you experience New Mexico, "half your work is done for you." A young pianist named Ansel Adams taking pictures for the Sierra Club met Georgia in New Mexico. Subsequently, Ansel was later to meet Stieglitz who exhibited Ansel's work in 1936. The young photographer-pianist, who would become world famous, attributed much of his technical expertise to Arthur Stieglitz in later years.

Fame

Georgia bought a Model-A Ford that afforded her the freedom to roam for miles in search of the perfect desert landscape. By 1939, Georgia O'Keeffe, age 42, was the most famous and most successful female painter in America. She was named one of the twelve most outstanding women of the last fifty years along with Eleanor Roosevelt and Helen Keller. *Life* magazine ran a photographic essay about her in 1938, a year when she was ferociously attacked by critics for using bones that she'd picked up in the desert for subject matter. The steadfast Georgia, not giving any credibility to the criticism, graciously accepted an honorary doctorate of fine arts from the College of William and Mary in 1938. The University of Wisconsin awarded her an honorary doctorate of letters in 1942. Georgia was surprised to have this awarded at the same time the University of Wisconsin was awarding a degree to General Douglas MacArthur. She had been heavily criticized for her pacifist opinions during a time of war. Before the ceremony at the Field House in Madison, Georgia was waiting outside for her Aunt Ollie as Gov. Julius P. Heil walked by her. Later she was irritated at his careless patronizing when he joked in his speech about "the poor little Georgia O'Keeffe" who had to find her way to the ceremony by herself.

Georgia was anything, but "poor" by this time — and contrary to the belittling remarks from the governor of Wisconsin, she could do just about anything "by herself," including being one of the most famous women in the world. She had bought two homes in New Mexico on eighty acres, one being Ghost Ranch which it is rumored, she purchased for $6000, the price of a modest O'Keeffe oil. As one of the most eminent and controversial women in the world, she told a reporter, "I'm loved, but I suspect I'm hated in the same proportion."

Most renowned people who have reached an admired level of achievement more often than not live by a standard and a philosophy. Georgia O'Keeffe was no exception. The artist was a purist. Her paintings were unsigned except for the occasional "OK" that she signed on the back of a canvas. She felt that her style was signature enough. Georgia's paintings were done in series because this was her method of exploring various angles and lights, finally to simplify an object so that it purposefully lost realism. "Nothing is less real than realism—details are confusing," she commented.

"That's one thing that has always kept me working—it's not good enough. It's very good, but it's not good enough." She would tell interviewers that she did not speak in words; she spoke in paintings. "The meaning is in the canvas, and if you don't get it, that's too bad." She is noted for saying that if young artists worked more and complained less, there would be more of their paintings and sculptures to hang in museums and galleries. "You have a chance to get what you want if you go out and work for it. But you must really work, not just talk about it."

Georgia traveled the world studying the art of other cultures. She particularly liked Asian art, specifically Chinese. She declared it the best art in the world because of its dignity, harmony, and craftsmanship. One time she was asked why she traveled so much, and she replied that she wanted to see if she lived in the right place.

The world of academia that included Harvard and Columbia University bestowed many honors on this woman, but she remained ambivalent towards the accolades. She often said she had been happiest when she had the freedom of anonymity. Nonetheless, she refused to undersell herself in the market. Her prices were high and were non-negotiable — a lesson well taught by her husband Arthur Stieglitz.

The art of Georgia O'Keeffe is held in many private collections and is represented in every major museum in the United States. Major awards include election to the American Academy of Arts and Letters in 1963, the Brandeis University Creative Arts Award in 1963, election to the American Academy of Arts and Sciences in 1966, the National Institute of Arts and Letters Gold Medal for Painting, and the Presidential Medal of Freedom in 1977, America's highest civilian honor. The Georgia O'Keeffe Museum opened in Santa Fe in 1977. It is the only museum in the U.S. devoted solely to the work of a woman. Georgia O'Keeffe died in 1986 at the age of 99 in Santa Fe, New Mexico. On the centennial of her birth, a major retrospective of her work was exhibited by the National Gallery of Art in Washington D.C. In 1989, the Georgia O'Keeffe Foundation was established.

Carol Merrill, a perceptive young poet, once remarked, "There's something about that woman. It isn't just charisma, and it isn't just personality. I think it is other levels of consciousness." Well said.

Robert Franz von Neumann

(1888-1976)

As a youngster, the artist liked to watch fishermen working at the docks. His art reflects this interest, and he is noted for paintings and prints showing men at work, particularly the Lake Michigan fishermen. Robert was a painter, a printmaker, a lithographer, and a noted teacher. He was born in Rostock Muklenburg, Germany, and obtained a scholarship in 1910 at the age of 22 to study in Berlin at the *Vereinigte Staatschulen für freie und angewandte Kunst* (translation: United State Schools for Free and Applied Arts). World War I found the young artist serving as a lieutenant in the German Army where he sustained a critical wound and lost his foot. Following the war, he spent another year in Berlin working as a free-lance illustrator and studied painting in Weimar. The artist remained in Berlin and taught until 1925. He and his wife then immigrated to Milwaukee in 1926. Not wasting any time, the artist went to work with a lithography firm and joined the art staff of the *Milwaukee Journal.*

Robert taught at the Wisconsin State Teachers College (later the University of Wisconsin-Milwaukee), the Layton School of Art, the Art Institute of Chicago (visiting instructor), and the Ox-Bow Summer School of Painting in Saugatuck, Michigan. The active artist had several individual shows in Milwaukee, including a show of drawings at the Layton Art Gallery in 1941 and the

Milwaukee Art Institute in 1947, with a major retrospective exhibition in 1972 at the Milwaukee Art Center. He was president of the Wisconsin Painters and Sculptors in 1931 and 1932.

The artist worked prolifically in producing paintings, drawings, lithographs, woodcuts, etchings, linocuts, and mezzotints. Always attracted to the waterfront and shoreline scenes, Robert had a studio overlooking the Milwaukee River. Most of his artwork characteristically depicts labor, which was a common theme of Depression era art. His two children, Robert Von Neumann Jr. (1923-1984) and Angela Von Neumann Ulbricht (1928-) both became professional artists and studied at the Art Institute of Chicago. Angela reportedly lives in Spain.

In 1972, Robert Franz Von Neumann was awarded an honorary doctorate in fine arts from the University of Wisconsin-Milwaukee.

"Boat Scene" by Robert Franz von Neumann, Sr.
Collection of the West Bend Art Museum

Alfred George Pelikan

(1893-1987)

Alfred George Pelikan was a painter, an enamellist, author, and educator born in Breslau, Poland, who immigrated to the United States in 1911. He studied with the Art Students League in New York and at Columbia University, later becoming the director of the Milwaukee Art Institute from 1926-1942, and in addition was art director for the Milwaukee Public Schools until he retired in 1962. He is fondly remembered not only for his art, but also for writing a public school curriculum for art. In 1931, the Bruce Publishing Company published his 123-page book, *The Art of the Child*. A few copies exist today. The artist received early education in Mayfield, Sussex, England, and at Kings College in Oxford. The education was financed by his sister Lillian Leitzel, a celebrated international trapeze artist who died in a performance in Copenhagen.

Alfred Pelikan traveled internationally and studied native art around the world. This no doubt had an influence on his efforts to bring modern art to schoolchildren in Milwaukee. He frequently battled those who opposed the endeavors. Not to be deterred, the artist brought exhibits in from the Museum of Modern Art in New York to the children of Milwaukee. His own work was in traditional landscape painting. Jones Island, Menominee Falls, rural Wisconsin, Mexico, and Maine (marine subjects) were locations for his paintings. Summer trips to Europe also produced a number of paintings and sketches.

He belonged to many organizations including the Wisconsin

Painters and Sculptors, the Royal Society of Art in London, the Academie Latine in Paris, and the International Institute of Arts and Letters. Among his friends were Alfred Stieglitz and Georgia O'Keeffe.

John Steuart Curry

(1897-1946)

John Curry's passion was to paint Rural America, but being a Regionalist was not an easy path to cut. This style of painting was also known as the American Scene School of Painting.

John Steuart Curry, 1938, working in his studio Wisconsin Historical Society Image 11834

John Curry wasn't fond of book studying exactly, so he found himself a railroad job one Kansas summer, earned enough money to buy a suit of clothes, and headed towards the Art Institute of Chicago where he studied for two years. During this time, he swept floors and was a cafeteria bus boy. Later he earned a living as an illustrator, but wheeling and dealing his way through life, he persuaded an art patron to loan him $1000 to go to Paris to study painting at the Academie Julien. In 1928, upon returning from Paris penniless, he painted his first famous work "Baptism in Kansas." It was purchased by Gertrude Vanderbilt Whitney for the Whitney Museum of American Art. The Friends of Art at the Kansas State Agricultural College purchased "Sun Dogs" in 1935 for $500, which was a bargain. The price had been lowered from $1,200 because his mother had attended the Agricultural College, and the Depression had taken its toll when it came to purchasing art. In appreciation, John Curry donated a watercolor and four lithographs.

John Curry was born in Kansas into a long line of farming families. At the age of 19, he attended the Kansas City Art Institute before moving on to the Art Institute of Chicago. From 1928-1936, he lived and worked in New York. While in New York, he was associated with the Art Students League of New York as a student, and later, as a teacher, until he was appointed the University of Wisconsin's first artist-in-residence at the College of Agriculture. His studio was on campus, and he was paid $4,000 per year.

"I was raised on hard work and the shorter catechism. Up at 4 a.m. the year round, doing half a day's work before we rode to town for our lessons," was an attitude that prompted him to stick with it. He credited his mother with sparking an interest in the paintings of the old masters from reproductions of the paintings that she had collected before he was born. John painted a wide variety of subjects. He became one of the best-known realism painters of his time, and painted everything from murals, human activity genre, landscapes, circus scenes, football scenes, animals, floral, portrait, regionalism, seascape, still life, cityscape, to the famous self-portrait. His mediums included chalk, fresco, gouache, oil, watercolor, and printmaking.

John Steuart Curry was a significant regionalist artist and was associated with the National Academy and the WPA Federal Arts Project. In 1934, *Time* magazine proclaimed him one of the three leading regionalist American artists of his era. Thomas Hart Benton of Missouri and Grant Wood of Iowa shared the distinction. His numerous murals included depictions of land settlement and racial justice. The murals can be found today at the Capitol Building in Kansas, at the University of Wisconsin, at the Department of Interior and at the Department of Justice in Washington, D.C.

The artist died in 1946 in Madison, Wisconsin. His widow, Kathleen G. Curry, donated over 900 works to the Marianna Kistler Beach Museum of Art in Manhattan, Kansas. "Preliminary Study for a Mural: Oklahoma Land Rush," went for $175,000 on May 22, 2003.

Carl Robert Holty

(1900-1973)

The artist Carl Holty, was born in Germany, but lived in Milwaukee from the time he was an infant. He was trained by the German artists Mueller and Moeller. Breaking away from traditional art, Carl Holty is described by Porter Butts in his book *Art in Wisconsin* as "... signalizes more sharply perhaps than anyone else the break of the younger painters born after 1900 with the state's dominant tradition. In Wisconsin he is an art personality apart." Not surprisingly, the young painter took himself and his art to New York after serving in the U.S. Army during World War I and spending two years at Marquette University in Milwaukee. In New York, he studied at the National Academy of Design and then went to Munich, Germany, where he was a student at the Academy of Fine Arts and the Hans Hofmann School. After several years in Europe, he returned to Milwaukee, but established his reputation and art in New York where he taught at the Art Students League. Nonetheless, the artist traveled often to Milwaukee and continued to exhibit work in the city in which he grew up.

The artist was an important supporter of abstract art and helped to establish the American Abstract Artists organization in New York. He is likely the first Wisconsin artist to seriously

"Cove" by Carl Holty
Collection of the West Bend Art Museum

study the style and to create significant abstract art including printmaking, as the art form of abstraction spread from Europe to the United States at the beginning of the 20th Century. His influence in this area spread across the country.

Carl Holty worked in gouache, collage, graphite, pen, mixed media, oil, pastel, and watercolor. His styles are listed as abstract and early modern before 1950. Subject areas included abstract renditions of shape, color, and texture. He also produced works in landscape, cityscape, figure, floral, genre, mountain landscape, religion, animals, and human figures. Carl was co-author with Romare Beurden, of the book, *The Painter's Mind*. His painting "Odalisque" created in 1937 sold in May of 2001 for $9,500.

Examples of his work can be seen in several museums.

Marshall Glasier

(1902-1988)

"The mind can never make a drawing; it is the hand that must do it."

— M. Glasier

A true surrealist, Marshall Glasier, was a controversial leader in Wisconsin's jump into European Modernism. But he was in equally notorious company in his circle of artists who included the notables Dudley Huppler, John Wilde, Karl Priebe, and Gertrude Abercrombie, who migrated between Chicago and Wisconsin art scenes. The group informally organized what was known as the Wisconsin Surrealists. Although the group's focus was surrealist art, they "studied" the music of Chicago jazz musicians when Gertrude Abercrombie came to town.

The dream-like fantasy art of the surrealists was inspired by European Surrealism coming out of Paris in the 1920s. In 1947, the group exhibited at the Art Institute of Chicago alongside the famous Salvador Dali and Max Ernst, European surrealists.

Marshall studied at the Art Students League in New York in the 1930s, and he was later represented by the Julien Levy Gallery in New York City. He also exhibited at the Pennsylvania Academy. Some of his works were said to be satirical of the work of John Steuart Curry. The surrealist artists as a group showed defiance of provincial subject matter and moralistic tone. In 1937, Marshall Glasier's work was on exhibit at the Milwaukee Art Institute when it was said the art was "taking an un-American direction." It was a time of suspicion, and the work of surrealists, unconventional as it was and still is, would naturally attract a variety of opinions. Marshall's work is characterized by mythological, allegorical, and Biblical figures in fantasy landscapes. The Madison Art Center's 2000 exhibition, Surreal Wisconsin, featured Marshall Glaiser and his group of surrealists. Marshall had a sense of humor and was a creative maverick.

Gerhard C. F. Miller

(1903-2003)

If you can believe it, there was something missing in Door County — namely an art center. The void was filled when Ruth and Gerhard Miller, along with the work of the Sturgeon Bay Library Board, Friends of the Library, and other interested participants decided enough was enough. In about 1967, the Millers transferred ownership of a building to the Library Board with the idea that the sale of the building would provide seed money to finance an art gallery that was to be a part of the Sturgeon Bay Library. It was agreed that the art center be completed in five years. The Millers' building sold for $54,822.58. Contributions and grants came in that totaled over $600,000. In 1974, the Library Board named this new construction the Miller Art Center. Gerhard Miller's vision of a year-round art gallery in Sturgeon Bay that would be inviting to the public was now a reality.

The artist Gerhard Miller is known for his realism style sometimes described as "imaginative realism," and landscape paintings. His subject areas include scenes from Door County and the area's maritime history. He worked primarily in watercolor and egg tempera. Gerhard taught his students the art of using whatever they might have handy to control the medium. Anything from a knife to a piece of tissue paper would do. When taking on a student, Gerhard encouraged the student to continue developing a sense of color, imagination, and certainly work with persistence.

TOP: "Valdenstein" by Gerhard Miller, Germany, (egg tempera)
BOTTOM LEFT: Gerhard Miller — artist, poet,
writer, teacher, philospher
BOTTOM RIGHT: "Terry's Tree House" by Gerhard Miller,
Door County (egg tempera)
Photos courtesy of Margie Utzinger, daughter of Gerhard Miller

Gerhard Miller, born in 1903, began painting in his childhood in Sturgeon Bay. After a paralyzing attack of polio at age 11, he was told that he would not walk again, but with intense therapy from his father and treatment in St. Louis, he ambitiously overcame this prognosis and walked with a brace. The fated relationship with polio and the awful confinement imposed by the disease enticed Gerhard into cultivating an interest in art. He was slated to run the family clothier business, but painting and drawing were at the core of his interests, and eventually this became his life's work and passion.

The artist was influenced by the work of Roy Mason of Batavia, New York and LaJolla, California. Roy was a member of the American Watercolor Society, the National Academy, and was a leading watercolorist at the time. Gerhard contacted Roy Mason and was then invited to his home, Woodchuck Hollow, near Batavia. "The first contact was a major turning point in my life. First he said I was on the right track, and then he told me not to go near an art school, but to 'just paint a thousand pictures.' Next he gave me a lesson on the three values [color intensity]—the lesson he received from Chauncey Rider, who in turn had gotten it from the Englishman John Sell Cotman. That lesson is still on my studio wall. After that he showed me his method of painting a sky and told me to come back for another critique and lesson in a year. From then on I read everything I could on drawing, painting, composition, and art appreciation." When Gerhard first started working with the medium egg tempera, he meticulously copied the old masters' methods of working, which included painting on wood panels painstakingly prepared so they would not warp.

Gerhard sold enough paintings to build a "travel fund" and eventually made trips to Europe, the Middle East, and South America. During the excursions, he painted and "studied in the best museums in the world." Examples of Gerhard's work are at the Paine Art Center and the Wright Museum of Art. A permanent collection is at the Miller Art Center in Sturgeon Bay, Wisconsin.

Ruth Miller, Gerhard's wife, was an interior decorator and had
formal art training. Her career rapidly expanded to writing and
lecturing. She was the author of several interior decorating textbooks published by McGraw Hill Company and used at the high
school-college level. Gerhard had a business background. The
combination worked well, however Gerhard became the artist and
Ruth, the businesswoman. Gerhard and Ruth wrote several books
including *The Thrill of Castle Hunting,* and *A Spiritual Guide to
the Scientific 21st Century. Levels—Mental, Physical, Spiritual*
and other books include *Miller: His Life, Painting, Philosophy
and Poetry,* and *The Other Side of Door. Philosophical Truisms* was
published most recently. "I must be tough as a boiled owl," said
the artist at the age of 99. He believed that one of his secrets to
long life was to keep on painting, and when the light is gone for
the day, do some writing.

Gerhard's paintings have been exhibited in galleries and
museums all over the United States including the Metropolitan
Museum of Art, the Milwaukee Art Museum, the National Academy and the Knickerbocker Artists Show both in New York. The
artist was inducted into the American Watercolor Society and
the Audubon Artists in 1954. He also wrote for the esteemed
publication *The American Artist.* Gerhard, known fondly as the
"Dean of Door County Painters," taught many a student. As
a mentor, he taught his students never to reach a point where
they think their work is above criticism. However, he believed
that unwarranted praise and destructive criticism have no value,
because they are based on "the current fad in art which has all the
lasting importance of the length of a woman's dress or the width
of a man's necktie." He advised all students of art to 1) find a
well-qualified artist to give a frank critique once a year if the artist is willing 2) correct the weaknesses 3) never stop studying the
museums and the galleries and 4) read whatever you can about the
lives, the works, and the techniques of the great masters. Lastly,
be grateful. His message: a lifetime is not long enough to refine
the knowledge, so keep on working! Gerhard died at the age of
100 in 2003. Ruth lived to be 99.

Gerhard Bakker

(1906-1988)

Gerhard Bakker had the skill, the craftsmanship, and the knowledge to be called the "Jack-of-all-Arts and Master of Many." The title stuck because of his work in watercolor painting, drawing, lithography, etching, and block printing. Never bored, he worked as a photographer, an advertising designer, and an illustrator. The artist used landscapes, architecture, and buildings as his subjects. Gerhard Bakker was born in Solingen, Germany where he studied and taught art at Gewerschule in Solingen. The 23-year-old artist moved to Milwaukee in 1930, and studied art with Gerrit V. Sinclair at the Layton School of Art. Later he taught at the school and established its photography department.

From 1933-1934 he was a part of the Public Works Arts Project, a Depression era project that employed artists. Later Gerhard studied art at the Broadmoor Art Academy in Colorado Springs under the teaching of Boardman Robinson, Ward Lockwood, and Tabor Utley. He returned to Milwaukee and worked as a mechanical engineer for the A.O. Smith Corporation and as an industrial designer at the Baird Company. Eventually Gerhard resumed a teaching career at the Layton School of Art. Bakker was a member of the Wisconsin Printmakers, the Wisconsin Painters and Sculptors, and several other organizations. Examples of his work are in collections at the Wisconsin Historical Society, Milwaukee Art Museum, West Bend Art Museum, Wisconsin Union Art Collection UW-Milwaukee, and the Wichita Art Museum. His advice: "Do the usual in an unusual way."

Guido Brink

(1913- 2003)

Artist Guido Brink began his American experience as a visitor in 1929, working in his uncle's New York stained glass studio. He was 16 years old. Returning to Germany and studying at the Staatliche Akademie in Düsseldorf, the young Guido still felt the pull of life in the United States. He settled in Milwaukee in 1953. Today, he is known worldwide primarily for his metal sculptures that decorate public and commercial buildings. A fountain sculpture at the Milwaukee Zoo, a sculpture at the Kohler Art Center, and a wall relief at the Hyatt Regency Hotel, to name a few, reflect the artist's creativity. His metal figures and creatures are bright and lively and give the viewer a sense of pleasing chaotic balance. The artist's works seem to be influenced by the experience of growing up between two world wars in the battlegrounds of Europe. He was a young art student and a German soldier seeking a mental equilibrium in a torn world.

Guido recalled his experiences in a time of change and innovation in the art world. This revolution included the rise of German expressionism, Neue Sachlichkeit, and Surrealism. Art student Guido Brink and his contemporaries were ordered by Hitler to view the 1937 exhibition of "Degenerate Art" at the Munich Architectural Institute. This had the opposite effect of what the dictator had intended. Hitler was negatively jolted by the unexpected inspiration the "degenerate art" gave to the young students. They admired this new breath of fresh air. The modern art made a firm and lasting impression. But, it was a time of war, and Guido was drafted into the German Army. He witnessed the invasion and the retreat of the German Army on the Russian front. His memories of the battle of Stalingrad and other surrealistic horrors of war are repeated in many of his paintings.

The artist had a major exhibit at the Haggerty Museum of Art in 2002 titled Fifty Years of Painting by Guido Brink. Techno, Biblical, hope, despair, liberation, apocalyptic, inner world, suffering, anguish, and caring are all words that have been used to describe the paintings and sculptures of Guido Brink. He is noted for his brightly colored abstract compositions of reds, yellows, dark blue, and black. Guido taught at the Layton School of Art from 1955-1974. He was instrumental in founding the Milwaukee School of Arts, later named the Milwaukee Institute of Art and Design, becoming its first president. In 1976, he left the school and devoted much of his time to painting and sculpting. His art has strong characteristics and makes a statement in numerous collections.

Phil Austin

(1910-2004)

Artist Phil Austin, a member of the American Watercolor Society, is associated with watercolor paintings of seascapes and landscapes. He primarily worked in the difficult medium of watercolor using a palette of alizarin crimson, vermillion, cadmium orange, cadmium yellow pale, viridian (blue-green), cerulean blue, and ultramarine. Austin attended night school at the American Academy of Art in Chicago for two years, after graduating in 1933 from the University of Michigan. American history was busying itself with a

Phil Austin
Photo courtesy of
Waukeganweb

**"Majesty of the Forest" watercolor
by Phil Austin
Courtesy of Rodin International**

depression and an entrance into World War II at the time Austin was fine-tuning his art. After working at Kling Studios in Chicago for five years, he decided to leap into free-lancing, and he apparently hit the target freelancing from 1950-1966. The artist also taught at Wheaton College from 1963-1970. His commercial clients included the *Chicago Sun Times,* the National Fisheries Institute, Books for Children Press, and United Airlines.

Austin traveled extensively worldwide always taking his paints and brushes along for the ride. Consequently, his art also dotted the world. He painted in all 50 states. One of his paintings was one of six American watercolors recently chosen for the permanent collection in a new art museum in Taiwan. The artist was born in Ellison Bay, Door County, Wisconsin. He died at the age of 94 in Ellison Bay in February 2004.

Edmund Lewandowski

(1914-1998)

Edmund Lewandowski, the child of Polish parents, grew up in industrial Milwaukee where he grew to incorporate this natural part of his industrial heritage into his starkly precise and expertly balanced art. The work of Edmund is characterized by bold, geometrically precise lines and definitive breaks in color. If you look at a Lewandowski painting, you'll see that it is really an exquisitely clever study in angle and perspective with a perfect balance of color. In the mid 1930s when he was a young adult, Edmund became part of the Federal Art Project in Milwaukee. He trained at the Layton School of Art, later taught at the school, and then was president of the institution in 1954. He was a leader and pioneer in the development of American modernism and his style took on an abstract quality in the 1950s. Other examples of well-known precisionists included Georgia O'Keeffe, Joseph Stella, Charles Demuth, and Charles Sheeler.

Lewandowski worked on board, canvas, and paper using gouache, oil, pastel, and watercolor. Although most noted for

"Hull 101"
by Edmund Lewandowski
West Bend Art Museum

"Dry Dock" by Edmund Lewandowski
Collection of the West Bend Art Museum

his unbending industrial form paintings, he also worked in genre, landscape, marine and costal subjects. Major exhibitions include the Art Institute of Chicago and the Museum of Modern Art in New York. Not to be bogged down by administrative duties, the artist completed commissioned murals for luxury liners, and many paintings for private and corporate clients. The mosaic on the west wall of the Milwaukee War Memorial is a Lewandowski work.

Edmund Lewandowski's career took him to South Carolina for a while. He headed the Art Department at Winthrop College in Rock Hill where he remained a professor emeritus. The artist had a passion for art in man-made construction, which fit perfectly, or perhaps is better described as precisely, into the territory of modern art. And although some viewers may find it difficult to think of some modern art as art, a pleasing Lewandowski work takes away the unfamiliarity. The artist noted, "I remember when I was a boy, a good deal of time was spent listening to shoptalk...all of my relatives were engaged in industry...so the depiction of industrial power technology and efficiency has always had a great attraction for me." (West Bend Art Museum article "Edmund Lewandowski: Recording the Beauty of Man-Made Objects and the Energy of American Industry").

Karl Priebe

(1914-1976)

Artist Karl Priebe, like other surrealists, painted the fantasy with the fact. His work flows with nocturnal overtones with dreamlike settings, and fanciful creatures such as unicorns. African Americans are prominent in his later art. The artist associated with jazz musicians Pearl Bailey and Dizzy Gillespie, as well as surrealist artists of the time, such as Marshall Glasier.

Karl studied painting at the Layton School of Art in Milwaukee and at the Art Institute of Chicago. Beginning in 1944,

"Mourning Bride" by Karl Priebe
Collection of the West Bend Art Museum

the 39-year-old Karl Priebe was an instructor at Layton. Prior to this, he worked at the Milwaukee Public Museum as an assistant in Ethnology. The artist was featured in *Life* magazine in 1947.

Although definitely known for his surrealism, Karl Priebe was also a portrait painter. Among his clients were the singer Billie Holiday and the artist Charles Sobree, an African American. Karl had a studio in Evansville, Wisconsin, at one time during his career. He worked in the mediums of casein

"Portrait of a Woman (with turban)" by Karl Priebe
West Bend Art Museum

(protein), gouache, mixed media, oil, and watercolor. His subjects included animal, figure, genre (human activity), and portrait. He exhibited at the Art Institute of Chicago, the Corcoran Gallery, the National Academy, the Pennsylvania Academy, the Madison Art Center, the Charles Allis Art Library, Marquette University, and the Perls Gallery in New York. A collection of his sketchbooks and papers were donated to Marquette University. Works of Priebe can be found at various museums throughout Wisconsin and in other states.

James Alfred Schwalbach

(1912-1984)

Not only was the artist James Schwalbach creating his own art, he also was instructing a classroom of approximately 80,000 potential young artists a week on his radio show.

The radio program "Creative Art" was the precursor of "Let's Draw," a hugely popular show that ran on Wisconsin University

School of the Air for 34 years and was part of the Rural Art Program that began during the Great Depression in 1936. In his writing, "A Brush with History," James Auer, *Milwaukee Journal Sentinel* art critic said it best:

"John Rector Barton, a rural sociologist, and Chris L. Christensen, dean of the University of Wisconsin College of Agriculture, gave it its start, John Steuart Curry and Aaron Bohrod, artists-in-residence at the UW-Madison, gave it its soul. James Schwalbach, host of WHA's "Let's Draw" radio program, gave it its sound. And thousands of eager, if largely untrained, amateur artists and elementary school students kept it energized decade after decade."

Artist James Schwalbach received numerous awards for best educational programming on radio. In addition, he wrote the teachers' manuals that accompanied the programs. It is important to note that James was a talented artist in his own right. Early in his career, he created block prints, and later, around the 1950s moved to painting and serigraphy. The artist of "Let's Draw" awoke many young artists and sent them out the door and into a world of creativity.

Untitled by James Schwalbach
Collection of the West Bend Art Museum

Thomas Dietrich

(1912-1998)

The artist Thomas Mueller Dietrich was known far and wide for his watercolors depicting landscapes, cityscapes, snow scenes, bridges, architectural structures, and people of the Fox River Valley and Door County. Thomas was from Appleton, Wisconsin and was a student at the Cincinnati Art Academy and the Kansas City Art Institute. He was also a student of the Experimental College of the University of Wisconsin, and a student of the Minneapolis School of Art. His style is one of early modern before 1950.

"View of College Avenue, 1882"
Thomas Dietrich, 1912-1998, casein on board (undated)
Gift of Mr. and Mrs. Guy E. McCorison
Collection of Lawrence University, Appleton, Wisconsin

"Morning After Rain (Lake Nebagamon, Wisconsin)"
Thomas Dietrich, 1912-1998,
oil on paper, c. 1930
Collection of Lawrence University, Appleton, Wisconsin

States including the Art Institute of Chicago. The Memorial Presbyterian Church on College Avenue in Appleton, Wisconsin houses a stained glass window designed by the artist, who designed windows for at least seventy churches throughout the United States. His major contributions to Wisconsin art however, are his watercolor and oil paintings of Fox River Valley scenes. Lawrence University in Appleton houses 23 works by Tom Dietrich in their collection. He was artist-in-residence at Lawrence from 1944 to 1974.

Lester Bentley

(1908-1972)

Artist Lester Bentley of Two Rivers, Wisconsin, had an art exhibit at the age of 13, but he had been planning on it for six years prior to that. Early creativity often leads to an exciting life. Lester eventually took his talent on the road and painted portraits of President Dwight Eisenhower, three Wisconsin governors, a United States Supreme Court justice, and president Curtis Tarr of Lawrence University, among other notables. He studied with the artists Carl Buehr, Louis Ritman, Valentine Vedauretta of Mexico, and was a student of the Art Institute of Chicago.

Lester Bentley is known primarily as a portrait artist and mu-

Curtis Tarr, president of Lawrence University, 1963-1969
Painting by Lester Bentley, 1908-1972
Oil on board, 1971
Collection of Lawrence University, Appleton, Wisconsin

ralist. He was part of the Federal Arts Project. He established a winter studio in Greenwich, Connecticut. The artist worked in fresco technique, graphics and printmaking, and oil. The work of Lester Bentley can be found in various museums including the Neville Public Museum in Green Bay, the Elvehjem Art Museum in Madison, and the West Bend Art Museum in West Bend. Some of his work inhabits several churches and the Washington House ballroom in Two Rivers.

Santos Zingale

(1908-1999)

Santos Zingale was born in Milwaukee to immigrant Sicilian parents. His art entails strong statements of social landscapes along with urban and rural settings. He often depicted political and social conditions of African Americans. The artist was troubled by the destruction of the old neighborhoods of Milwaukee, and he captured the streets, buildings, and people in his paintings.

Zingale received a masters degree in education from the University of Wisconsin-Madison and was assistant to the regionalist painter, John Steuart Curry. He also studied at the Milwaukee State Teachers College under Gustave Moeller, Howard Thomas, Robert von Neumann, and Elsa Ulbricht. During the Depression years, he worked on the WPA (Works Progress Administration) painting murals in post offices. Always making a statement through art, the artist joined the U.S. Navy in 1944 where he produced numerous drawings of Navy life. In 1946, he joined the UW-Madison art department.

The artist was known to work in fresco and oil. His subjects include African American figure and genre, human activity genre, travel scenery and architecture. He used a surrealist style and had exhibitions at the Art Institute of Chicago, the Pennsylvania Academy, and the Charles Allis Museum. He retired from UW-Madison in 1978 as professor emeritus.

Aaron Bohrod

(1907-1992)

"I have never been frightened by the bogey of detail. When detail is integrated into a total scheme, it can only serve to enrich the result...in any good painting there is plenty for sensitive people to ponder without asking them to complete, mentally, the artist's intentions about form."
— **Aaron Bohrod**

"The War brought many opportunities to me as an artist. At the age of thirty-five when my war-art period began, I would not have expected that I'd be drafted for active military service. Most likely instead of a gun I would have been handed a broom to sweep up some domestic army barracks (*A Decade of Still Life*, Aaron Bohrod. University of Wisconsin Press.1966)." As a war artist, Aaron Bohrod spent time in the South Pacific, Normandy, England, and Germany during World War II. He was on assignment for *Life* magazine and the U.S. Army Corps of Engineers. Before moving to Madison, Wisconsin, in 1948, his life was in Chicago. In an earlier part of his career, he studied at the Art Institute of Chicago and the Art Students League in New York. Aaron Bohrod credits the influential teacher John Sloan for teaching him the value of the old masters and the richness of painting the reality of urban America. Upon his move to Madison, Aaron Bohrod succeeded John Steuart Curry as artist-in-residence at the University of Wisconsin-Madison.

The artist is well known for his attention to meticulous de-

Aaron Bohrod "Sea Horses" 1963 8" x 10" oil on board
Owner: Private Collection
© Estate of Aaron Bohrod, Licensed by VAGA New York, N.Y.

tail in his still-life paintings. He purposefully instilled mystery, humor, and combinations of seemingly unrelated objects in his later paintings. Studying the paintings, however, one can see that there actually is a relationship between the objects, just as there is a relationship between pieces of a puzzle. Aaron Bohrod worked in a variety of mediums besides oil, including watercolor and gouache. He is known for his landscapes, cityscapes, surrealism without the sinister undertones, and trompe l'oeil (fool the eye) compositions. The artist insisted that the best way to develop "visual vocabulary" was to draw. "I have always believed that if an artist can draw the human figure, he won't have trouble drawing anything," he wrote. (*Aaron Bohrod: Figure Sketches*. 1990. E. Elliot and H. Wooden).

His works are in several museum and private collections. An auction price of $23,000 was listed in 1995 for "Unstringing Tobacco Leaves." The painting "North Clark Street" was sold in

May 2004 for $19,000.

"One of the best artists in America…" declared Harry Saltpeter in his article "Chicago's Gift to Art," *Esquire* magazine, November 6, 1939. "Aaron Bohrod was an American artist who was nationally known in his lifetime. He was the subject of frequent exhibitions and gallery shows in various locations, generally focusing on a particular chronological period of his artistic production. The recipient of numerous prizes and awards (including two Guggenheims and the purchase prize at the 'Artists for Victory' exhibition of 1942-1943 at the Metropolitan Museum in New York), he was both proficient and prolific as a painter, sculptor, printmaker, ceramicist, and as an illustrator. In addition, he was the author of several books on art and an autobiography."

The *New York Times* presented an obituary that described Aaron Bohrod as a "noted realist painter whose paintings could deceive." The artist died in Madison in 1992.

Gertrude Abercrombie

(1908-1977)

Gertrude Abercrombie was as well known in the Chicago jazz arena as she was in the art world where she is described as a surrealist of the 1930s. During that time, she worked on the Federal Art Project. Her friends included Billy Holiday, Charlie Parker, Sarah Vaughn, Dizzy Gillespie, and other famous jazz musicians of the era. They described her as a woman who could take music and transport it to another art form, namely painting. "Bop Artist" Gertrude was never fond of being labeled a surrealist such as Salvador Dali; she claimed she merely painted simple things that were a little strange. In her painting, "Charlie Parker's Favorite Painting," Gertrude portrays the emptiness and tragedy of the lynchings of 3,513 African Americans in one of the darkest segments of American history. Her paintings and sketches have been described as enigmatic, eerie, dreamy, airless, foreboding. She never explained the symbolism of objects in her paintings. The characters in her paintings were often people she knew in life. Gertrude rarely painted men in her work. However, it has been reported that at the time of her divorce, she painted her husband standing behind an empty chair on a balcony, with the chair symbolizing the divorce. Gertrude eventually married jazz musician Frank Sandiford.

Strongly affiliated with Illinois, Gertrude Abercrombie, spent much time in Madison, Wisconsin in association with the Wisconsin xurrealists artists and artist Marshall Glasier. Gertrude Abercrombie's latest recorded art auction was for the sale of "The Queen" for $7000. The painting "Demolition Doors" was estimated at auction for $20,000-$30,000. Gertrude was basically a self-taught artist, with some training in commercial art from the University of Illinois. Her paintings have an attractive simplicity about them and seem to knock boldly on the doors to the viewer's imagination.

John Wilde

(1919-)

Some say his art is surrealism; others say it is magical realism. John Wilde (pronounced "will-dee"), in either case, is known for the fantastic. The newly constructed Overture Center in Madison is graced by his multi-panel work called "The Story of Jane and Joan." But he didn't start out at the Overture Center. The artist's life began in 1919 in Milwaukee. He is a fourth-generation Wisconsinite and likes it here. John Wilde studied art at the University of Wisconsin in Madison and was part of the Wisconsin surrealist movement of the 1930's and 1940's. He was a student of James Watrous, a mentor who taught him classical technique in drawing and painting. Consequently, his paintings had the appearance and romanticism of Renaissance and German art. The artist is definitely known for his detailed fantasy of dream-like landscapes, bones, objects, nude figures, humans, and sometimes renditions of himself painted in for interest, for the heck of it, or to add another mysterious quality to the painting. Surrealist artists have a free-roam license.

World War II interrupted John Wilde's artistic endeavors, but after a stint in the military he soon returned to that love and pursued graduate studies in art history and then finally returned to his work in fine art. Academic life must have appealed to artist Wilde. Beginning in 1948 and for the next thirty-four years, he taught in the art department at the University of Wisconsin-Madison. He retired as professor emeritus in 1982 with the title of Alfred Sessler distinguished professor of art. He is an academician of the National Academy of Design in New York City and a fellow of the Wisconsin Academy of Sciences, Arts and Letters.

The artist sees his world as the stage upon which he paints and draws in a search for himself. The drawings are concise and meticulous with subject matter depicted in surrealism and trompe l' oeil. His work is on canvas, board and panel, and he works in graphite/pencil, oil, and watercolor. The art of John Wilde is held in many public and private collections that include the Art Institute of Chicago; the Pennsylvania Academy of Fine Arts; Butler Institute of American Art in Youngstown, Ohio; Carnegie Museum of Art in Pittsburgh; Santa Barbara Museum of Art; Smithsonian American Art Museum,; Wadsworth Athenaeum in Hartford, Connecticut,; Walker Art Center in Minneapolis; Whitney Museum of American Art in New York City; and others.

Owen Gromme

(1896-1991)

"Is it that a person is merely born into a vision and a mission, or are those ethereal possessions acquired somewhere along life's journey? I've been pondering that question for over a decade now. I thought I had an answer—had it figured out once and for all. But the more I study folks who in some way have made priceless contributions to the planet, whether to humanity, the environment, preservation of a heritage, or preservation of a species; the more I've come to understand that the missionists and vissionists, as I like to call this lot, have, with little exception, found a love of cause. Sometimes this love seems to be imprinted on a child along with a name, other times it is acquired very early in life, and sometimes it happens late, but the seeds for development have been inside for a long time. One of my favorite "missionists and vissionists" is the late Owen Gromme, known by most people for his wildlife art, but also known by many for his crucial insight and dedicated accomplishments in preservation of habitat and species. When I see a falcon in flight, or gaze at the openness of a farm field and spot an endangered Sandhill crane walking with the lanky stance of an awkward adolescent, I know we have someone to thank more so than pure chance. It's true, some will think of a divine Creator as the entity in charge, but I'm talking about a mortal being with a hand in it. I think of the environmentalist, curator, artist, and protector of the feathered."

—Owen Gromme

Owen spent twenty years working on his classic book, *Birds of
Wisconsin*. That's not bad, considering the amazing achievements
he accomplished in his 95 years of life in Wisconsin. He grew up
on the shores of Lake Winnebago in Fond du Lac. The youngster
had grounding in the ways of nature that began with the guidance
of his father who hunted and fished in the area. Owen acquired
an interest in taxidermy, not just for the sake of learning the skill,
but also for the purpose of recording a natural history. The first
entry in a daily journal was dated April 13, 1914. Over 8,000
pages later, he had a collection of volumes filled with sketches and
color notes on specimens, native landscapes, and habitat.

In Owen's life, one thing led to another, as the saying goes.
Owen's taxidermy skills landed him a job in 1922 at the Milwaukee Public Museum. Prior to this, he had worked as a teenager
at the Museum of Natural History in Chicago (now the Field
Museum) under the guidance of taxidermist Herbert L. Stoddard.
He believed that in order to give his employers their money's
worth, he would be a scientist, a painter, a carver, a sculptor, a
lecturer, a writer, a photographer, a bookkeeper, a taxidermist,
and a hunter. He set these standards and goals for himself and
accomplished them. That in itself is admirable, and we could say
this unassuming Midwesterner was an asset to his employer and
had a productive life—well, great, applause and end of story.

No, it was hardly the end of the story. Love of cause entered
the picture. Yes, certainly; he was the all-encompassing museum
man. But the man did not go to work day after day, come
home, kick his feet up, and reflect on what a tough day he had
endured. He spent more than a little time—years, in fact—collecting data on Wisconsin's wildlife, documenting population
fluctuations, and seriously pursuing environmental problems.
Popular today is the use of the word "issues," but Owen didn't
see environmental "issues," a word that rather neutralizes things.
He saw Problems, and called a duck, a duck. His battles were as
lonely as they were lengthy. Owen Gromme began fighting for
stringent and pragmatic wildlife laws in the 1930's. Wildlife laws?

TOP: "Salute to the Dawn" by Owen Gromme, 1972
BOTTOM LEFT: Owen Gromme and crane chick, 1981
BOTTOM RIGHT: Owen Gromme painting
"Salute to the Dawn," 1972
Photos coutesy of the International Crane Foundation,
Baraboo, Wisconsin

What are those? The concept was nonexistent. The curator-artist joined forces with the writer Aldo Leopold in 1935 to fight for protection of herons and bitterns. Hawks and owls were also on the hit list at the time. Owen ferociously battled the Milwaukee Gun Club, which had announced a statewide "varmint hunt" to rid the state of these birds. Owen knew that education was a key, and he relentlessly made efforts to educate the public about the roles of hawks, owls, and crows in the natural order. The *Milwaukee Journal* helped the Gromme crusade enormously, and devoted several articles and columns to the tense situation. It worked. The proposed indiscriminate killing was cancelled. Well, you guessed it. One thing led to another. Owen built and operated Wisconsin's first hawk trapping and banding station at the Cedar Grove site. During the next ten years, the Milwaukee Public Museum staff documented migration patterns of raptors through Wisconsin and recorded baseline data that is crucial to management of these birds today.

The pioneer Gromme was one of the first, if not the first, to notice the scarcity of birds of prey and warblers that coincided with the chemical fight against Dutch elm disease in the 1950's to 1970s. He took the observation, and the plight, and the battle to his favorite means of communication—major newspapers. In addition, the delightful Owen Gromme paintings and prints brought hundreds of thousands of dollars to the naturalist's love of conservation. The sale from prints of his painting of Canada geese titled "Requiem at Horicon Marsh" enabled the Wisconsin Citizens Natural Resources Association to fight the federal government's mismanagement of Horicon Marsh. The feisty Owen took the battle in 1961 to Secretary of State Stewart Udall. The result?

We can see the results of his efforts today from coast to coast and beyond. Many of Owen Gromme's recommendations focused on regulation and management of federal wildlife refuges, and the practices have remained in effect.

The environmentalist-curator-artist-conservationist spent

more than fifty years contributing his time, his creativity, his strong activism, and his resources. The mission was to conserve the habitats, and ultimately the species. The vision was to create awareness and a love of cause in generations to come. Did he accomplish these? As I type this, I'm trying to think how he might have answered the question. The first thing that comes to mind is that he would have said, "I'm still working on it. You can help me, and so can your children, and their children to come."

Owen Justus Gromme was instrumental in founding the International Crane Foundation in Baraboo, Wisconsin. It is largely through his initial efforts that the organization exists. The Foundation is dedicated to saving the endangered cranes of the world. Through ongoing work, the foundation has established community based research and conservation projects all over the world, including concentrated efforts in Africa and China, as well as the United States. The conservation programs are designed to benefit people and wildlife, and protect entire ecosystems through proactive programs. The enthusiastic people of the International Crane Foundation work closely with governments, village leaders, engineers, anthropologists, and restoration ecologists in Africa. China's wetland and grassland communities are coexisting within the bounds of human and wildlife populations. The Chinese culture honors the crane as a symbol of long life and happiness. The International Crane Foundation is working diligently alongside the grateful people of China to insure their ancient symbol remains on the planet and in the culture.

Owen Gromme was a self-taught artist out of necessity. In his museum work, he strove to keep his taxidermy work and the building of his dioramas as accurate as possible. To do this, he had to note the subtleties of color, and sketch subjects for future reference. An important point in his career was an extensive eight-month trip to Africa. During the expedition, he collected 312 mammals, 1390 birds, and thousands of artifacts. He drew over 100 sketches. Again, one thing led to another. He began to dabble with his oil paints on canvas. The paintings have a celestial quality of sorts. They seem to capture a moment in time in which the viewer participates. The artist painted birds, their habitats and behaviors, nesting characteristics, enemies, interaction with other wildlife, and their diets. Owen the artist wanted to "show nature as it really is, and to study and restudy light and musculature and habitat so every one of my paintings will stand up to the scrutiny of knowledgeable people." The artist painted scenes that would "always leave the bird or animal a way to get out of the picture." That's precisely the feeling I experience when I see his dioramas at the Milwaukee Public Museum. I find myself not only looking at the immediate subject at hand, but at the background where I can picture myself hiking into the distance.

It's no secret that a love of cause is helped by a dose of financial vitamins, and the laws of supply and demand. Owen was chosen Ducks Unlimited artist of the year in 1978, and the sale of prints of his wood duck painting Fall Kaleidoscope resulted in $600,000 for waterfowl habitat protection. The artist's vision was a powerful step towards establishing the Wisconsin Peregrine Society, which facilitated the reintroduction of the peregrine falcons in Wisconsin. To this end, he donated the reproduction rights to his 1936 peregrine falcon painting to the organization.

Many might think Owen Gromme had a formal education. Not so. Owen dropped out of high school. He claimed that one of the reasons was that he was distracted by watching the huge flocks of waterfowl on Lake Winnebago from the high school assembly room. Nonetheless, he was unable to escape the notice of educational gurus, and was awarded five honorary doctorates for his environmental work, and his numerous publications that included the heavily illustrated *Birds of Wisconsin* published in 1963 by the University of Wisconsin Press, now in reprint editions.

Owen Gromme worked 43 years for the Milwaukee Public Museum and became Curator Emeritus. The artist retired from the museum in 1965 to continue his art and intense conservation work. He was a member of the Art Commission of the City of Milwaukee, adviser on the Film Committee for Encyclopedia

Britannica, a member of the Audubon Society, the American Ornithologists' Union, the National Wildlife Society, the Wisconsin Society for Ornithologists, Wisconsin Academy of Arts, Science and Letters, the Izaak Walton League of America, and the Seven Arts Society of Milwaukee. His timeless art has been exhibited and collected widely. The artist's numerous dioramas remain on exhibit at the Milwaukee Public Museum. He helped the Leigh Yawkey Woodson Art Museum in Wausau, Wisconsin develop its Birds in Art annual exhibit, which is a major nationwide event to further birds as subject matter in art.

Owen Gromme, the man with a love of cause, a mission, and a vision, fondly referred to as the dean of American wildlife, died on October 29, 1991. Anthony Earl, former governor of Wisconsin said, "During the time I served as secretary of the Department of Natural Resources, I had no firmer friend, nor formidable adversary than Owen Gromme. When he was on my side, we could not be defeated. When he was on the other, I could not win." His beloved causes relevant to the welfare of the planet and all its inhabitants, speak more so now than ever before. The 21st Century has come with a price. But with his legacy, the environmentalist-curator-artist-protector of wildlife is determined to have his say into the future.

On a confusing day I may still ask myself, are people such as Gromme just born with a mission or do they acquire it? But now I conclude there's not a black and white answer, and there seems to be a component of construction and process. About sixteen years ago, a good friend of mine told me to "develop a philosophy." At the time, I thought it a curious statement, but for whatever reason, it stuck with me. And now I believe I know what he meant. Basically, that's what Owen Gromme did. Truly, he developed a philosophy, but he went a step further. He got the ball rolling. One thing led to another. He built a reality rather than just harbor a fantasy.

This quote is from a 1978 commencement speech Owen Gromme gave at Marian College in Fond du Lac, Wisconsin:

"We owe a great deal to those who came before us and it is our duty to pass on to posterity a world morally and physically as good as or better than the one we live in. By every legal means it is our duty to oppose those who out of greed and avarice, or for selfish other reasons, would pollute, defile, or destroy that which means life to every living being."

Author's note: *"Owen Gromme" excerpted from essay written in May 2004 for The Power of Purpose John Templeton Foundation. ©HHLevy 2004.*

Sister Thomasita Fessler

(1912-)

Sister Thomasita Fessler, at age 92, now professor emeritus, has retired, but not really. Her works in sculpting, ceramics, painting, metalwork, and jewelry design are continuous reminders of her boundless energy and dedication to the beauty of art, and the education on many levels that art provides. Sister Thomasita Fessler entered the Franciscan Order at 17. Milwaukee State Teacher's College (University of Wisconsin-Milwaukee) was her next stop. Here she studied art with an eye for the Art Institute of Chicago, and subsequently began commuting to the institution. After cultivating an interest in Egyptian, Minoan, and Etruscan art, she earned a master of fine arts degree. With a mission in mind, the nun with the discipline of a nun founded the art department at Cardinal Stritch College in Milwaukee, and the San Damiano Art Studio. The studio provided an attractive environment for the classes that she offered for adolescents and adults and at the same time was a place for her to focus intensely, and sometimes controversially, on her own contributions to the art world.

The distinctive art of Sister Thomasita depicts a primitive cubist influence, and with the unpretentiousness of a nun, it does away

Sister Thomasita Fessler in her studio
Photo courtesy of James Auer,
Milwaukee Journal Sentinerl

with distracting flourishes. The starkness of her paintings seem to say, "This is the reality; this is the soul." But there are criticisms. Her art occasionally breaks the rules when it comes to traditional religious art. Nonetheless, Pope Pius XII admired it. In 1953, *Life* magazine printed a photo of a nine-foot tall sculpture of Jesus from the St. Cyprian Church in River Grove, Illinois. Letters of disapproval flowed in from every corner. Her answer: "The very violence of their reaction shows the power of modern art. If it were really worthless, they wouldn't bother getting angry about it." Well said.

Sister Thomasita's fans, admirers and appreciative students far outweigh the cynical lot. She has enjoyed and endured a 60-year teaching career, conducted art travel tours to far-off places around the world, and even designed postage stamps. The Turk and Caicos Islands took a leap of faith in 1998 and commissioned Sister Thomasita to design Christmas stamps. You can bet they were not "traditional." She designed eight images of Mary that were nothing short of striking in her primitive style that characterizes the artist nun. Sister Thomasita was particularly attracted to teaching young children and opening creative minds. It is her belief that "children who create, will never destroy."

The artist says, "I tell my students everything they see in the world in nature is God-made. I tell them nature is God's art, and art is man's nature."

The artist has received numerous awards in her lifetime. But the one she is said to be very honored by is one she has in common with the former Israeli Prime Minister Golda Meir. Attorney Dennis McBride, a former student of hers, nominated Sister Thomasita Fessler for the University of Wisconsin-Milwaukee Distinguished Alumna award in 1992. Sister Thomasita's works, including lithographs, are now in gallery collections, churches, and museums around the world.

Ruth Grotenrath
(1912-1988)
Schomer Lichtner

Ruth Grotenrath's art teachers included Robert von Neumann, Gustave Moeller, and Elsa Ulbricht. But perhaps more importantly in her life was the artist Schomer Lichtner who became her husband in 1934. Ruth began as a classic regionalist and then worked into modernism and abstraction influenced by an underlying influence in Japanese art and culture. Ruth's works, many of them floral still life, became increasingly colorful. She was influenced by the styles of Matisse and Van Gogh. Not particularly interested in commercial success, the artist said, "I just want to get down what I'm seeing. You must see poetically." Nonetheless, the artist achieved commercial success and recognition.

Ruth along with her husband, Schomer Lichtner, worked on the Work Projects Administration where she painted murals for three post offices. "Boy Rounding up Stock" (1941) was painted for the post office at Hart, Michigan, "Unloading a River Barge" (1943) was a tempera mural for Hudson, Wisconsin, and another was painted for a post office in Wayzata, Minnesota.

Ruth and husband Schomer Lichtner took the common and mundane aspects and objects that we take for granted and uplifted them into jubilant art. Schomer, still busy in the art world (and the dance) today at age 99, is well known for his whimsical cows and enchanting ballerinas. He is proudly touted as the official artist of the Milwaukee Ballet. So whether he's drawing prancing cows and grazing ballerinas, or the other way around, Schomer finds lightness in life and contends that living into old age has to do with mental attitude.

As the young Schomer Lichtner, the Milwaukee artist studied at the Milwaukee State Teachers College, the Milwaukee Art Students League, the Art Institute of Chicago in 1924, and then at the Art Students League in New York. From 1927-1929 he was a student at the University of Wisconsin in Madison. Schomer completed numerous murals for the WPA (Works Project Administration) for post offices. After they were completed, and the project ended, he continued to paint murals for industry and private clients. He was

"Cow Jar"
by Schomer Lichtner
Photo courtesy of
Schomer Lichtner

also a printmaker and produced block prints, lithographs, and serigraph prints. Typical paintings of the artist depict rural scenes and farm animals, which now have sidetracked to his trademark cows. He became interested in cows when he and Ruth spent summers around Holy Hill in Washington County. The prolific artist has won numerous awards. Several of his drawings have been published in books including the book *Schomer Lichtner Drawings* published in 1964.

Lichtner is official artist of the Milwaukee Ballet and his dancers can be found on many things that can accommodate art—posters, cards, you-name-it. He even kicks up a dance or two now and then.

JoAnna Poehlmann

The artist JoAnna Poehlmann has always lived in Milwaukee, and for 35 years has lived in the same historic residence, but her art draws her into the far corners of nature where insects, plants, and animals become her inspiration. JoAnna uses taxidermy animals that she has collected as models in her work, and takes them along to her shows where they become part of the art compositions. For example, a work titled "Moonrise Over Plymouth Rock," which depicts luna moths, is displayed with the Plymouth Rock chicken. Makes sense to me.

JoAnna has art in every room. She admires and collects the work of Wisconsin artists, many of them her friends. Testing her own artwork by hanging it in her hallway gallery for a while is the way she inaugurates a piece. "If I can live with it, I know it is good enough for someone else to live with." The artist has worked in areas of graphics, printmaking, painting, and illustration from photorealism to the less traditional.

JoAnna has delighted in creating "book art" as a work of art. Book art uses little or no text and does not function as a traditional book. Rather, book art is a three-dimensional work of art, and often one-of-a-kind or very limited edition. The unique art often uses handmade papers, odds and ends, pen and ink, collage, stamps, preserved insects, clay, wood, papier-mâché, and whatever works. JoAnna has fashioned several pieces, including book art that has been published into paperback renditions by various publishers. Titles that she has created or served as an illustrator on include *Eggs under glass (2 dozen)*, *Food for Thought*, *Love Letters*, *Poems for Cat Lovers*, and *Just-Alike Princes*. The Kohler Art Library on the University Wisconsin-Madison campus has collected art books by various artists since the 1970s and has over 650 works including some by JoAnna Poehlmann.

JoAnna is an associate lecturer at the University of Wisconsin-Milwaukee. Examples of her art are found in collections at the Victoria and Albert Museum, London, England; New York Public Library; the Museum for Kunsthandwerk, Frankfurt, Germany; Istvan Kiraly Muzeum, Szekasfechevar, Budapest, Hungary; Permanent Collection-Embrabel, Cabo Frio, Brazil; Walker Art Center, Minneapolis, Minnesota; Museum of Modern Art Library, New York; and Dartmouth College, New Hampshire.

Warrington Colescott

(1921 -)

Warrington Colescott has a sense of humor that bubbles and boils over to his lively painting and printmaking. From his art student days at the University of California at Berkeley and the Academie de la Grande Chaumierre in Paris, to his joining the staff at the University of Wisconsin (1949), to his bold international fame, Professor Colescott probably hasn't lost an ounce of satirical wit. In fact, he's likely compounded the attribute. The artist once commented, "My prints and paintings are narratives, both direct and metaphorical. The intent is moral, if your morality is in my ballpark. The method is satire; comedy is okay, but pretty much anything goes if it fits my drawing concept on paper or copper plate."

Warrington Colescott spent four years in the Army during World War II after earning a bachelor of arts degree at the University of California. He then moved on to obtaining a graduate degree in painting, teaching himself serigraphy, and exhibiting

TOP: "Tchoupitlouas Street
(Chef Emil)" 1998
by Warrington Colescott
Coutesy Warrington Colescott

ABOVE: Warrington Colescott
at work
RIGHT: "An Evening with
Claus" by Warrington
Colescott, 1997
Photos courtesy
of Warrington Colescott

his work on the West Coast. Fortunately, for the University of Wisconsin, in 1949 he took them up on their offer to teach. In 1958, he was chairman of the art department for two years. The early homemade comic book strips of his childhood had indeed given way to humorous sophisticated art in the form of printmaking and etching. Sacrificing accuracy in history is often a subject for his art of wit. He takes a perspective of "what if it would have happened this way," and then proceeds to create images of the Warrington Colescott version—delightfully appealing chaotic twists.

It's all paid off. Warrington Colescott's awards include a Fulbright Fellowship to England (1957), four National Endowment of the Arts fellowships (1975, 1979, 1983, 1993), Wisconsin Governor's Award in the Arts (1976), six University of Wisconsin research grants, and a Guggenheim Memorial Foundation fellowship (1967). His prints and paintings have been in exhibits in the United States, Colombia, Peru, England, France, Germany, Bulgaria, Yugoslavia, Poland, Asia, India, Japan, Russia, Korea, Taiwan, and China. Works are in the permanent collections of the Museum of Modern Art, the Art Institute of Chicago, the Whitney Museum of American Art, the Metropolitan Museum, the Victoria and Albert Museum in London, Bibliotheque Nationale in Paris, New York Public Library, Brooklyn Museum, Philadelphia Museum of Art, Smithsonian Institution, Wake Forest University, Walker Art Center, Minneapolis; Milwaukee Art Museum, and the Elvehjem Museum of Art in Madison. Warrington, along with co-author Arthur O. Hove, wrote *Progressive Printmakers—Wisconsin Artists and the Print Renaissance* (published in July 1999).

Warrington Colescott retired from the University of Wisconsin in 1986 and became the Leo Steppat Chair professor of art emeritus. A fellow of the Wisconsin Academy, and an academician of the National Academy of Design, Warrington was also appointed printmaker emeritus by the Southern Graphics Council in 1992.

"I have a long career as an artist, concentrating on painting and printmaking, with recent work focusing on painting in water soluble media on paper and printmaking in the intaglio media. Narrative ideas have always dominated my expression. I like color and design, but I hate triviality, and the demands I put on myself specify complexity: if you seduce, do it with wit and creativity: if you attack do it with skill: if you educate, do your research. As a satirist I try to have a lot of eye, good hands and plenty of attitude."

Kevin Henkes

(1960 -)

Being a children's book illustrator and writer is not easy. Kevin Henkes has been enjoying the profession for more than 20 years. He notes that writing for children is a tough business. Not a word can be wasted, and the illustrations must carry the story as naturally as the words. Those are just a couple of the reasons it is difficult to write children's literature. Kevin started out in this career at the age of 19 and was talented and persistent enough to find a publisher in New York willing to look at his work. A bit of luck probably helped, but I'm betting that it was mostly the combination of determination and skill.

Kevin was born in Racine, Wisconsin, in 1960, and went to school at the University of Wisconsin—Madison. He currently lives in Madison with his family. Kevin has written and illustrated about 30 books, for which he has won numerous awards. His picture book illustrations use subtle detail and he strives for depth in the story. Kevin often uses childhood problems or worries as a subject for his characters. However, he gives his stories and his characters a hopeful light. As with many authors, his writing sometimes comes from true-life experiences. For example, *Lilly's Purple Plastic Purse* is based on the antics of a child Kevin saw in an airport. She was carrying a purple plastic purse and was driving her father up a wall. You know the type. In recent years, Kevin has written novels in addition to picture books for children. Examples of his titles include *Words of Stone, Protecting Marie, Owen* (Caldecott Honor book), *Chrysanthemum, Chester's Way, Sheila Rae, the Brave; A Weekend with Wendell, Julius the Baby of the World,* and *Lily's Plastic Purse.*

Levi Fisher Ames

(1843-1923)

Levi Fisher Ames literally carved a niche for himself in the world of art. He is fondly remembered for his ability to carve just about anything. Ames was a self-taught artist who created the L.F. Ames Museum of Art, which was also known as the Grand Museum of Art and Natural History Whittled Out of Wood. This Civil War veteran managed to create a collection of over 600 carvings of animals, fantasy and folklore characters, and heroic figures. A carpenter by trade, Artist Ames housed his precious carvings in individual handmade shadow boxes that were hinged to open like a book. Not to be limited by carving animals, Ames found pleasure in carving interesting and beautiful walking sticks,

Untitled Levi Fisher Ames gelatin-silver print (1880-1885) Courtesy John Michael Kohler Art Center

small wooden tools, wooden chains from a tree branch, fraternal logos and symbols, and "hobo art." Hobo art was also known as "tramp art," and it refers to a type of folk art that came about during the Civil War and lasted into the 1930's. The carving methods mostly came from Germany and Scandinavia. Today, tramp art is highly collectible. The most common pieces are frames and small boxes.

Levi Fisher Ames worked in other materials such as shell, stone, and coconut shell in addition to the traditional use of wood. Some of the pieces, including his walking sticks, are detailed with carvings of chains, animals, diamonds, moons, crosses, and trefoils. The shapes represented specific military units in the Civil War, Masonic and fraternal symbols, and logos. It is reported that Ames did not sell any of his work because he believed in order to appreciate the work the collection had to remain intact. The art was gifted as a permanent collection to the John Michael Kohler Arts Center in Sheboygan, Wisconsin. A group of 24-color illustrations portrays the pieces in the book *Levi Fisher Ames: Menagerie* by Leslie Umberger. This inventive legacy of Levi Fisher Ames was presented in its entirety to the Kohler Foundation by his grandson, Howard Jordan.

Top: "The Oryx and Leopard" and "Lion & Buffalo"
(c. 1900); Bottom: "The Jaguar, Native of South
America" and "The Leopard of India" (c. 1890-1915)
by Levi Fisher Ames, *Levi Fisher Ames Menagerie*
Courtesy John Michael Kohler Arts Center

Eugene Von Bruenchenhein

(1910-1983)

"Eugene Von Bruenchenhein—freelance artist, poet, sculptor, innovator, arrow maker and plant man, bone artifacts constructor, photographer, architect, philosopher."
— **Eugene's description of Eugene**

Eugene was probably one of the most curious of outsider artists. He lived his artistic life within the confines of his home--apparently, content merely to produce art for the sake of creating and surrounding himself with a less than usual environment. He was born in Marinette, Wisconsin in 1910, and his mother died when he was 7. His father was a sign painter, and later married an artist-writer who wrote about evolution and reincarnation. She put those thoughts to canvas. Eugene learned about painting from both his father and his stepmother.

Artist Von Bruenchenhein attended school in Green Bay and Milwaukee, but dropped out in the tenth grade to work in the family business that consisted of a grocery, a greenhouse, and a flower shop, later going to work at a bakery. He became rather reclusive in 1959, but indeed, was not idle. It seems the artist had produced thousands of drawings and paintings and managed to cover every inch of his walls with the art, tucking the excess in obscure places. The collection was colorfully abstract and apocalyptic. The extraordinarily creative Eugene produced odd floral ceramic pieces, constructed miniature furniture and towers made from gilded chicken bones, undertook large cement sculptures, wrote hundreds of poems and other writings, and photographed his wife Marie in exotic costumes and settings.

Ruth De Young Kohler and Russell Bowman of the John Michael Kohler Arts Center in Sheboygan discovered the treasured home gallery, moved the entire body of works to the Kohler Arts Center, and held a major exhibition in 1984. Exhibits were held in New York and Philadelphia, at which point the artist's family released some of the works to dealers. I doubt that Eugene Von Bruenchenhein ever had a dull moment.

Adolph Vandertie

(1911-)

Life began for Adolph on May 25, 1911, on a small farm in northern Wisconsin in the community of Lena. The times were hard, his parents divorced, and the six siblings and their mother, moved to Green Bay where the family struggled through the Depression. Adolph spent spare time creating cartoons and riding the rails with the hobos of the era. The hobo whittlers taught him how to carve wood, but the roots of his art can be traced back to his grandfather, who, as a prisoner in the Civil War, had learned carving.

The only thing required to produce tramp art was a jackknife and a stick or a piece of wood. The challenge of creating tramp art could, and did, take a lifetime to perfect. The art was practiced by self-taught artists, and no patterns or written materials showing techniques or styles have been found. The skills passed from hobo to hobo, family to family, and town to town by word of mouth or by example. Discarded wooden cigar boxes, which were usually made of cedar or mahogany or other fine woods, were prime raw material for the hobos. The carvings were produced primarily from the late 1870s to the 1940s when cigar smoking was popular. The U.S. Revenue Act of 1865 required that all cigars be sold in wooden boxes. In addition, the law prohibited reuse of the boxes to sell cigars. This strange law proved to be a boon to the hobo artist.

The trademark of a hobo whittler was the ball-in-cage carving. Adolph created a ball-in-cage design, and that sealed his artistic destiny. By the age of 21, however, the young artist decided to leave his hobo days and pursue a job at a St. Louis brewery. Instead, he married Adeline and they stayed in Green Bay. Adolph began collecting and creating the unusual and beautifully carved intricate "tramp art." His collection grew to some 3,500 pieces. Having a problem with alcohol and tobacco, he eventually used the art as a focal point and ticket to escape from the two addictions. This freedom from alcohol and tobacco rewarded him with the ability and ambition to create numerous outstanding works. In the year 2000, Adolph Vandertie celebrated fifty years of sobriety.

Countless hours of whittling and collecting by Adolph Vandertie resulted in a collection of whimsies, tramp art boxes, frames, astonishing furniture, ball-in-cage pieces, and chains created from single pieces of wood. Much of the Adolph Vandertie Collection of Tramp Art is contained at the Ashwaubenon Historical Museum and the John Michael Kohler Arts Center in Sheboygan, Wisconsin.

From *Hobo and Tramp Art Carving: An Authentic American Folk Tradition* by Adolph Vandertie with Patrick Spielman. Sterling Publishing Co., Inc.:

After the Civil War, the Industrial Revolution exploded across America and, with this rapid industrial growth and the development of the railroad, came the birth and the growth of the world of the American hobo. The true hobo was basically a laboring man of many trades and many talents who wandered the country in search of work.

He laid and repaired railroad track, harvested wheat, cut down trees, mined for gold, herded cattle, built bridges and then moved on. When the Depression hit this country and the times swung from prosperous to destitute, these hard times produced the hobo that we often think of today. By the end of the nineteenth century, it is estimated that more than a million men were on the road, riding the rails, looking for work. It was his constant wandering that made the hobo such a distinct and mythical character.

Adolph Vandertie and the Rail
Photo by Jeff Benzow
Courtesy of *Voyageur: Northeast*
Wisconsin's Historical Review

Mary Nohl

(1914-2001)

The year was 1927 and she was the only girl in the boys' industrial classroom, but not to be outdone by the lot, she won first prize for her model airplane. Perhaps motivated by that claim to fame, Mary Nohl went on to study art at the Milwaukee University School, then enrolled in Rollins College in Winter Park, Florida, and finally studied at the Art Institute of Chicago. In 1937, she received a bachelor of fine arts degree. Teaching in Baltimore and then in Milwaukee was probably a stepping stone to her total immersion into art. By 1943, the artist had built a pottery studio and factory, and for 10 years she designed, produced molds, and mass-produced ceramic wares. The next decade, she fondly referred to as her "silver period," where she produced over 350 pieces of jewelry, which were exhibited at the Milwaukee Art Institute in 1954. Later in 1955, the collection traveled to the Smithsonian Institution.

Art lives outside as well as inside, and Mary began to create her "art environment" in 1964. She built the "band saw fence of friends and relatives in profile" which took over the perimeter of her yard in Fox Point, Wisconsin, along Lake Michigan.

But the unusual attracts usual attention. She eventually installed a fence to keep her art in and the vandals out. In the pre-fence era, thefts of two fifty-pound concrete heads and more than 40 pieces from her "profiles fence" were stolen. In 1973, two driftwood figures were set ablaze leaving two ten-foot pipes standing and anchored in cement. Creativity won out, and the

Mary Nohl outdoor cement sculpture
Photo courtesy of Mike Maggiore Photography

two pipes became front legs of a cement dinosaur.

In 1980, Mary decided, "to renew my struggle with oil paint," and over the next several years, she "re-worked" most of her paintings. Still into outdoor art, the artist created large wood assemblages and installed them on her roof in 1996, which is the same year she gifted her entire collection to the Kohler Foundation for preservation.

In 1997 and 2001, Mary Nohl's art was exhibited at the John Michael Kohler Arts Center in Sheboygan.

Norbert Kox

(1945-)

Norbert Kox journeyed down a destructive and perilous path. But his destination and maybe his fate became one of color, paint, canvas, and a curiosity shop of odds, ends, and thingamajigs. He started life out in Green Bay, Wisconsin, on August 6, 1945, which he notes was merely hours after the atomic bomb was dropped on Hiroshima. In terms of numerology, this gives him a seven in the "life path," which indicates he is a searcher and seeker of truth. As a "seven," he has a clear and compelling sense of himself as a spiritual being whose goal is to investigate into the unknown to answer life's mysteries. As a seven, he enjoys a degree of solitude, is an analytical thinker capable of great concentration and theoretical insight. Coincidently, that is exactly and precisely (I can't say it any more accurately) what his art is about! Personally, I think he planned that "seven" entry onto the planet.

The artist had a childhood and young adulthood plagued by alcoholism and drug use. He dropped out of high school, joined the Army, and served in Germany. Still living on the wild side after departing from the Army, Norb became an Outlaw biker, worked on customizing cars and motorcycles for a living, and rode a Harley. The drug and alcohol problem continued until on his

TOP:
Norbert Kox
Photo by Jodie Wille

RIGHT: "Glory of
the Heavans"
by Norbert Kox.
Courtesy of
Norbert Kox

thirtieth birthday, when a personal apocalypse of sorts led him to abandon the chemicals that were destroying his life and his creativity. The artist says he had a vision that spun his life around and pointed him toward intensely spiritual interests. During the next decade of his life, he meditated, painted and lived as a recluse devoted to spirituality.

The time was somewhere between dropping out of school and doing a stint in the military that Norb taught himself how to paint. In about 1985, those skills were about to flourish when he studied at the University of Wisconsin in Green Bay, and was told that he was an Outsider artist and visionary. By 1988, he had become successful in widely exhibiting his art, and he embarked on painting full time. His work since 1998 uses "Bible codes," described as "equidistant letter sequences" that he extracts from a computerized grid of Hebrew letters. The artist paints "apocalyptic visual parables." His paintings and assemblages are truly his art. They can be disturbing and at the same time intriguing. They dance with surrealism and are fraught with the symbolism of his beliefs and philosophy. They can be outlandish, outlaw-ish, and outside the boundaries of imagination. But one thing is for certain, the work does draw attention, no matter where the art patron's taste is situated.

Norbert Kox has been an artist in one form or another for forty years. For the past seventeen years, his work has gained state, national, and international attention. Articles about his work have appeared in international art magazines such as *Raw Vision* and *World Art*. The art is referred to in several books. In November 2002, the Henry Boxer Gallery in England began to handle his work for the European audience. Success on a canvas, not his riding the Harley, has taken Norb around the globe, from Green Bay to Europe, and possibly to other planets by the looks of his artwork.

Dr. Evermor

(1938-)

I didn't quite know what to expect when I set out to visit
The Land of Evermor. That's "Evermor" with no "e," and that
should have been my first clue. It was a partly gray day as I
drove from Madison along the highway headed toward a target
somewhere between Baraboo and Sauk City. I had heard it was
a place not like anything belonging to this planet. Nearing my
destination and paying semi-attention to my speedometer and
the dullness of spent foliage along the way, I glanced to the left
and saw a peculiar creature on the side of the road just sort of
grazing in tall grass. Then there was another one, and then one
after that—strangest birds I had ever seen. Had I fallen down
the rabbit hole, or was this Oz? Were they ostriches? Were they
graceful Argentinean Don't Cry for Me birds? Well, no, not any
of those, but certainly a related species on which evolution had
really done a number. Thus began the metalliferous expedition
for me. I left the highway, drove on to a gravel road, parked my
car near the woods, and decided I had inadvertently fallen off
the map. But, after all, this was Wisconsin, so I continued on to
The Land of Evermor with hardly a need to travel to far corners
of the world on this particular day.

My first encounter was with the Forevertron. No way can
you miss this cosmic intergalactic ship—it would be like trip-
ping over the Eiffel Tower. The ship is powerfully fueled by
a cargo of fantasy and a man's vision. More on the sculpture

"Forevertron" at the Land of Evermor
Photo courtesy of Bobbi Lane Photography

LEFT: Bug sculture
RIGHT: Dr. Evermor and "Trumpet Bird"
at the Land of Evermor
Photos courtesy of Bobbi Lane Photography

later, but for now, the man is Tom Every, fondly known as Dr. Evermor. No "e." Astronaut Evermor, commanding officer of the Forevertron, came into the art of it all, actually starting as a young boy in Brooklyn, Wisconsin. He was a boy whose heroes were Thomas Edison, Nikola Tesla, Alexander Graham Bell, and George Westinghouse.

The inventive youngster collected what the common human would call "junk." Then he traded it, resold it, and invented gadgets using discarded materials such as toothpaste tubes. So enamored by the possibilities of this rudimentary scrap-salvage idea, young Evermor, age 11, sold a railroad car full of scrap metal. After that, the Brooklyn Salvage Company was born, and was followed by another creation, the Wisconsin By-Products Corporation that processed and recycled by-products for U.S. Rubber.

The ambitious entrepreneur eventually oversaw the dismantling, wrecking, and salvaging of over 350 major industrial sites. The career, which propelled him to all corners of the United States, became a study in contrasts. In the physical world, he was rearranging the industrial landscape with intentional destruction, but simultaneously in his constructive mind, he was building an empire of rivets, pipes, bedposts, machinery, springs, copper drums, and other assorted oddities nobody wanted. This unique obsession of contrasts started as a business and evolved into a serious artistic endeavor. It became Dr. Evermor's dream to revitalize the industrial wastes of a fast-paced society that tended to abandon its unrecognized treasures. Ever the collector was Evermor. Among the things acquired were the decontamination chamber from the Apollo space mission, materials from the Ford Museum, autoclaves in which the moon rocks were processed, musical instruments, carburetors, wiring, an elevator car, generators, scissor blades, a 1927 International Truck, a 1912 generator, metal insignias, spiral staircases, an old ambulance, a discarded bus, and literally tons of you-name-its.

What happens to all this *stuff?* Glad you asked. Back up for a minute. It started in about 1983 with the 400-ton "Forevertron," which mushroomed to a height of three or four stories, grew to one hundred feet in length, and then rocketed right into the Guinness Book of Records as the world's largest recycled metal sculpture. The impressive components of "Forevertron" are mostly 50-100 years old, except for the Apollo decontamination chamber, which is 32,000 pounds and two million dollars worth of steel with a rubber-sealed door. NASA had intended to trash the chamber after the moon mission. Hold your horses, NASA. Collector Evermor got wind of the chamber's fate and made an executive decision to rescue it. And that he did.

At the peak of the "Forevertron" is a copper egg with a glass ball that comes from a hamburger stand. This copper-glass combo is the heartbeat of the star traveler's mission, and it is from this vantage point that he will travel into the depths of the Universe. While earth-bound, however, the "Forevertron", towering giant of artistic vision, is rather hidden from the road. But then take a walk through the wooded area, and the Forevertron majestically arises out of nowhere. It's an odd feeling; believe me. Again there are contrasts—a grand composition of metal design surrounded by a frame of delicate leaves rustling in the tall trees—a companionship of Nature and the Industrial Revolution. Fire up those booster rockets and we're off in this 1890's "Forevertron" rocket ship. Next to Forevertron is the Teahouse, a gazebo atop a metal pedestal-like structure. Of course, this, explains Dr. Evermor, is for Queen Victoria and Prince Albert to witness firsthand the launch of "Forevertron" into the cosmos—a royal perch, one might say. We also have the "Celestial Listening Ear," created from a speaker that once belonged to the Beloit Theater. The Ear has uncanny ability to tune in on messages from the galaxy, and plot astrological bearing points amongst the constellations. The "Overlord Master Control" is the mission intelligence center, and the "Jockey Scale from England" is for weight determination of Astronaut Evermor prior to lift off. The all-important "Graviton" is used for de-watering the starship pilot so as not to put the Jockey Scale into shock. Fret not if thrust power is a worry, since the "Juicer Bug," a giant lightening bug, will accommodate any slack.

Looking around for the Cheshire cat and thinking maybe I really had tumbled down the rabbit hole, I stumbled on to the "Epicurean," which is actually a mega-sized backyard barbeque grill created from a number of discarded objects such as a copper cheese kettle, brewery signs and a brewery keg, just to name a few. The "Epicurean" was made in 1976 for the esteemed Lady Eleanor, the artist and wife of Dr. Evermor. All she wanted was a backyard barbeque—you know the kind. But things got gastronomically out of hand. However, the Epicurean truly does function as a backyard grill, and it's used every year by the Wollersheim Winnery for its Grape Stomp Festival in October. The Epicurean is Dr. Evermor's favorite sculpture because it's "peaceful and elegant; it brings people together." The whimsical backyard barbeque has made its way to various parties, weddings, and events. Lady Eleanor believes the Epicurean is really a history of Dr. Evermor because there are many parts used in its construction that have particular meaning to him.

Moving on to another neighborhood in The Land, all visitors will inevitably run into the Bird Band rehearsing. The "Fiddle Birds" are over 40 feet high and have torsos constructed of stainless steel tanks that were once used in hospitals for polio and burn therapy patients. The avifauna creatures are graceful, spectacular, and well suited for viewing through binoculars, or if you happen to be an owl sitting on a near-by branch, that would work too. Another vital division of the talented Bird Band is the avant-garde "Trumpet Bird" and "Tuba Bird" section. I suppose they could be loud at times. Lady Eleanor found a treasure of discarded instruments on one of her royal outings, and whisked them to their new assignment in The Land of Evermor. Ancient speakers now function as tail feathers. There are 70 sculpture pieces in the "Bird Band," and they delightfully play the First Brigade Band music. I hear the Drum Bird goes wild at times. A flock of "Madagascar Birds," four-toed birds that we thought were extinct by the 12th century are actually in fine form at The Land of Evermor. A favorite stop or pop in The Land is the "Popcorn Stand," which was actually an elevator car in a previous lifetime and came from Elgin, Illinois. It is complete with matching heavy industrial springs for feet that are in charge of the popping effect.

Popcorn is fun, but why all these birds? Dr. Evermor has a certain respect and love for birds because of their non-threatening nature, and their freedom to soar into the heavens with a clear birds-eye-view of the hubbub here on earth. Makes sense, after all, doesn't that same description fit the "Forevertron?" Most people, including me, fantasize about escaping at times, but Dr. Evermor comes about as close to that as anybody I've met. He is an astute alchemist of contrasts who has "turned a negative into a positive," as he would happily say. In 1983, Dr. Evermor suffered from depression. He found himself upset with the human species in general. It was then that he thought about building a time machine because, as he put it, he just "might want to get away from here." Evermor, the Inventor, was so fortunate to have a kind friend named Jim Delaney. Jim, a fellow Wheeler-Dealer Bird in salvage, supplied about a ten-acre chunk of land behind his salvage-surplus business on which Evermor could find the freedom to work on his aerospace project and build the commanding starship "Forevertron." Now the visionary was as free as a soaring eagle to pursue a use for his historical collection of entities from the Industrial Revolution. And so he did!

Philosopher Dr. Evermor desires to use the land to harmonize with peace and tranquility. Besides possessing the gentle voice of peace, however, he is a staunch and loud trumpeter of preservation and integrity. Dr. Evermor does not alter any of the parts or pieces of equipment he uses. They are used "as is." A scissor blade is still recognizable as a scissor blade; a flute still looks like a flute; an Apollo decontamination chamber still looks like an Apollo decontamination chamber. Even in the midst of his wizardry, Dr. Evermor has an energetic passion for leaving some objects such as the 1927 International Truck, or the 1912 compressor with riveted construction and a square gas tank, in pure form. The works are independent examples of machinery art from an era rich in iron and steel that shaped his life and that of his country. These feats of engineering are statements in themselves. Indeed, engineering students visit the park just to see these examples of technology and physics that were primitive but functional starting points, you might say.

Using his artistic eye, Dr. Evermor critiques sculptures brought along by schoolchildren who visit The Land. His insight and interest lend a constructive spin to twists and turns of the fresh three-dimensional artwork. A strong belief in promoting inventiveness and getting minds to "think outside the box" carries his message to "do something creative with what you might throw away." The kids gaze at the "Forevertron," and they listen.

Historian Dr. Evermor tells us that the 7,300-acre World War II Badger Army Ammunition Plant sits across the highway from The Land of Evermor. He has notions, which spark of reality, of moving the "Forevertron" and The Land of Evermor to that location. The ammo plant was declared government surplus and was deserted after the Vietnam War. Not that he'd need all 7,300 acres, Dr. Evermor wishes to keep attitudes and efforts productive, and share the property with others who have ideas on how to use and restore this orphaned piece of land. The region, with its roller coaster past, has brought controversy. Before farming entered the area, the land was part of the Ho-Chunk Nation. In the 1930s, the U.S. Government condemned and appropriated the farmland, despite desperate objections of the families who had cultivated it for decades. During World War II, the Badger Army Ammunition Plant became a source of employment and wages for families in the area. Eventually, the place prompted anger over pollution and gradual deterioration. Today, negotiations between the State of Wisconsin, the Ho-Chunk Nation, conservation groups, and the community are in swing. In February 2004, the chemical dinitrotoluene (DNT), a chemical explosive leftover from the old days, was detected contaminating some area wells.

While the civil squabble surrounding the land on the other side of the road continues, Dr. Evermor pays careful attention, but sticks to his enjoyable creative path, as any serious artist is prone to do. His dream and his welding continue to advance in epic proportions. One of the latest major sculptures can be seen at 211 S. Patterson Street in Madison. The "Dreamkeepers," two gigantic 33-foot-tall birds, named Yon and Beyond, flew to the Patterson Street nesting place in March 2003. I went on a bird-seeking outing in the summer of 2003, and was pleased to find the "Dreamkeepers" watching over the neighborhood. City Watch Birds they must be. Dr. Evermor describes the work as taking two negative pieces of iron in the form of blowers and positively transforming them.

Just as distinguished and fanciful in The Land of Evermor are the honorable "Komodo Dragons," 34 feet long with 50-foot tails, but only a mere six feet tall. They do command a presence in their habitat with musical pieces like Tibetan bells and chimes. Propellers, of which Dr. Evermor has acquired 200, "break up the straight lines," he says. A charmingly mysterious sculpture that reminds me of a colossal valentine is called the "Moon Maiden." Built in 1988, "the Freudian piece," as Dr. Evermor refers to it, represents a lady and a key to her heart. She mysteriously possesses a door from the Apollo mission. Most of the world's doors we probably take for granted, but leave it to a creative soul to claim an Apollo door and incorporate it into the feminine mystique at a sculpture park in Wisconsin.

I found an intriguing part of The Land to be fiercely defended by the "Gladiators," which are little metal guys, designed by Troy, the son of Dr. Evermor. When he was a teenager, Troy created the ingenious sculptures, drew the plans out on paper, collected the parts, and had his father, Dr. Evermor, weld them together. Not to be outdone by the Gladiators, Troy created a Baseball Team complete with coach and umpire. His sculptures are detailed, intricate, and fascinating. Lady Eleanor, an artist in her own right, literally adds splashy color to The Land. In May of every year, she has a painting party that is open to the public. The Lady says, "It's a silly play time where people get to paint an artist's art work, which is a very unusual thing to do." It's a time of year when the energy of spring and the music of the Bird Band are joined by the music of people bands, jolly folks, paint, and food.

The Land of Evermor sells about 800 sculptures throughout the year, and the funds helps to maintain the park. The art ranges in price from $50 to thousands of dollars. I managed to acquire a stingingly yellow Bedpost Knob Bee (that's what I call it). Although the bee is not a challenger to the Forevertron or the functional Waffle Dog, it has nonetheless managed to buzz its way into busy conversations.

Is Dr. Evermor still wheeling and dealing? Some say a scrapped submarine is stored in a clandestine spot. It wouldn't surprise me. He's already got the "all hands on deck" figured out. Dr. Evermor purchased 20,000 aluminum hands from a dismantled plant that made rubber gloves in North Carolina. That ought to be enough to get the sub launched, unless of course the imagination finds other work for those hands. Visit the Land of Evermor, especially if you just "might want to get away" for a day.

"I can buy that for a song and sing it myself"
— **Dr. Evermor**

Dr. Evermor and his work have been featured on the Discovery Channel, National Public Radio's "Savvy Traveler," numerous articles, and in a 2003 documentary film titled "Statutes by the Road," produced by Bob Leff of Video Arts Productions.

In 1999, the nonprofit Evermor Foundation was established to ensure the maintenance of the park. The Evermor Foundation Historic Artistic Sculpture Park is located on Highway 12 south of Baraboo and 45 minutes outside of Madison. No admission fee is charged. Donations are appreciated. It is open year round

Monday through Saturday from about 9A.M. to 5 P.M., and
Sunday from noon to 5 P.M. You can find more information at
www.drevermor.org .

Fred Stonehouse

(1960-)

There is a certain sense of freedom in the surrealistic art of Fred
Stonehouse. I'm apt to say it is refreshing because you get the sense
he's not confined by "the rules," but at the same time the work
comes off as following the rules of what it takes to succeed as an
artist. In a 2002 interview by Janet Roberts, Stonehouse said that
he began this art craze at the home of his grandparents when he
was child. They had a set of encyclopedias that he was drawn to,
and he had a particular fixation with the "S" volume, which had
a picture of Saturn plunging into a sea. The concept triggered a
fascination with the surreal, although he didn't have a label for it
back then. "I took my favorite orange crayon and 'enhanced' it
[the S volume]." That pretty much set the ball rolling.

The artist graduated with a bachelor of fine arts degree from
the University of Wisconsin-Milwaukee in 1982. In the beginning of his schooling, it was a toss-up—art or auto mechanics.
He liked tinkering, but disliked it even more, so art became the
bigger draw. Much of his art is in acrylics, and his subject matter
varies, but he is closely associated with figures and the human
head. South American and Mexican folk art are influential in
his work, as are his impulses, feelings, and connections he makes
to objects and whatever pops into his head. Some of his work is
humorous and provocative, and is known to poke fun at life on
the dark side.

Stonehouse is drawn to the work of early Renaissance art, the
work of artists such as Van Eyck, and the Northern European and
Northern Italian painters. He carries some of the technical aspects

through to a lot of his work. The Fred Stonehouse paintings are on exhibit internationally, and his work can be found in several galleries including some in Milwaukee. To see a Fred Stonehouse painting gets you to wondering—dark side, light side, escapes to somewhere unfamiliar. My main simplistic criterion for judging any work of art is a question. Does this piece pull you in? With a Fred Stonehouse painting, I'd have to answer in the affirmative.

Fred has remarked that "firsts" are always memorable. To that end, he fondly remembers his first show in New York in the 1990s, his first show in Chicago, and the sale of one of his paintings to the singer and film star Madonna.

Robert Randall Burkert

(1930-)

Nancy Ekholm Burkert

(1933-)

Two artists in this family have graced Wisconsin art for many years. Robert Randall Burkert, born in Green Bay, is a retired art professor from the University of Wisconsin-Milwaukee. His active art participation is noted in the lithographs, prints, and serigraphs he has produced. Robert was one of the well-recognized exhibitors at the Elvehjem Museum of Art in Madison's exhibit titled 150 Years of Wisconsin Printmaking in 1998. A small part of his art is on display at the General Services Administration building in Washington, D.C. These pieces include "English Garden," a print, "Moonlit Tree," a lithograph, and "Spanish Hills," a serigraph.

Familiar to many connoisseurs of children's books is Nancy Ekholm Burkert, wife of Robert. Nancy was born in Colorado and moved to Wisconsin at the age of 12. Her career as an illustrator has been incredible. For years, I've admired the illustrations that she created for the Roald Dahl classic *James and the Giant Peach.* The original drawings are now in the collection of Harvard University. Nancy used her children as models for her illustrations. Other books she illustrated include *Snow White and the Seven Dwarfs,* a 1973 Honor Book for the Caldecott Award and a 1972 *New York Times* Notable Book; and *Valentine and Orson,* which received the *Boston Globe* Horn Book Award and a special citation for creative excellence. A book, *The Art of Nancy Ekholm Burkert* (Bantam 1977 by Michael Danoff, former curator at the Milwaukee Art Museum) expertly depicts her talent with pencil, brush, and ink. Danoff says, "Burkert works in a tradition of artists for whom book illustration is one of the fine arts like painting or sculpture. Each of the drawings she makes is, in its own right, a fully realized work of art. Her drawings are not a secondary accompaniment to words, but a primary and integral part of the book experience in which she is an equal partner with the writer."

Nancy's concerns for peace were promoted in exhibits that she organized in connection with artists of books for children in New York and Milwaukee. The Bread and Books program was founded by Nancy in 1990. The program provides books for children and families who use Milwaukee's free meal programs.

Patrick Farrell

I stared at a Patrick Farrell oil painting and I was pleasantly confused. Was I actually seeing a superb photo or was this the pinnacle of realist tradition? I honestly lost track, and found myself saying, how can anybody pull this off so well? Obsession with perfect accuracy is his forte, his gift, and his drive. It hasn't been easy for Patrick. For reasons beyond anybody's understanding, at least on this planet, life has declared War on Patrick a number of times. Yet, he prevails. Why? It's the Obsession and it's the Artist. Simple as that.

Patrick Farrell, 2004
Photo by James W. Schroeder

By studying the paintings, one might think Patrick has gone to the most prestigious of art schools. But that is not the case. Patrick is self-taught. He did not finish high school. Thrust into the world of make-it or break-it at the young age of 17, Patrick left his childhood where he grew up in a mobile home the size of a matchbox. Today, his paintings are represented by outstanding galleries in Washington, D.C.; Chevy Chase, Maryland; New York City; and Martha's Vineyard in Massachusetts; San Francisco; and Charlotte, North Carolina. Nationally, his work has been on exhibit at the Ameri-

TOP: "Fruit in an Oval of Silver" oil on linen 15" x 28" by Patrick Farrell

LEFT: "In Pink with Diamonds" 10" x 8 " oil by Patrick Farrell Photos by James W. Schroeder

can Academy and Institute of Arts & Letters, National Academy Galleries, the World Trade Center in New York, the Oklahoma Art Center, and the Butler Institute of American Art. The ultra-realism paintings have distinguished more than 30 solo exhibitions, and just as many international group exhibitions.

A fire of unmerciful proportion attacked the artist's exquisite Milwaukee studio and house in 1978. One might unknowingly say, well at least he had his health. Not so. The hands of time caught up with the young Patrick in 1980 by means of a devastating heart attack. He underwent heart surgery and outran the moment. In 1995, while still in his 40's, he underwent angioplasty for the heart condition. The war continued, with yet another battle shortly after the angioplasty. This time it was emergency surgery for an abdominal aortic aneurysm and a life-threatening, out of control pulse rate. I've heard it said that the reason optimists live longer than pessimists live is because they keep trying. Patrick is definitely a case in point, or perhaps a case in paint. I don't think this fortunate outcome is a matter of luck. It's a matter of obsession to live, and to live now, in the face of adversity. This same ruling passion is captured and reflected in the superior mastery of the artist's brush, his sense of design, and use of light and color.

When the serious health conditions dominated the scene, Patrick did a reassessment of his life and made some critical changes. No smoking, no caffeine, and a diet that is counter to the American lifestyle. The toll was greater than that however. He cancelled major shows in Milwaukee and Washington D.C., and postponed several commissioned paintings. Patrick has had to exit stress. It has meant using the "no" word and judiciously accepting projects with careful scrutiny. The near-death events married the artist to a reflection of his life. In a 1998 interview by James Auer, *Milwaukee Journal Sentinel* art critic, the artist says, "This summer while relaxing in the backyard, I was reflecting about my life and the events of the last year, its highs and lows. In December, I had won a major art award at the National Arts Club in New York. Then a few weeks later, I developed health problems. As I sat there, recovered and feeling strong again, a thought went through my mind. As I looked at the garage and reminisced about my modest beginnings and the trailer home I grew up in, a trailer house that would easily fit into this garage, a smile filled my face. All in all, I think I've done pretty well for a kid who didn't finish high school and taught himself how to paint pictures." Auer describes Patrick as "street smart, self-made; a spunky survivor."

Patrick Farrell is primarily known for his still lifes, and secondarily his landscapes, portraits, and movie star themes. Speaking of movie star themes, I mentioned to Patrick that I like to wear my sparkly elegant "Marilyn Monroe earrings" for lively occasions. He then sent me a photo of his 1991 Marilyn painting "In Pink With Diamonds" (oil 10 x 8). The image will be included in the high profile book *Marilyn in Art* compiled by Roger G. Taylor of the United Kingdom, to be published in 2005. The first *Marilyn in Art* was published in 1984 and it is now a collector's book. Since Patrick concentrates on meticulous definition of images in his paintings, collectors of his paintings have come to expect this perfectionism.

Patrick has had three retrospective showings beginning in 1989 at the Appleton Art Center, Appleton, Wisconsin. The next retrospective was in 1992 at the Wisconsin Academy of Sciences, Arts, and Letters in Madison. His latest was a ten-year retrospective at the Anderson Arts Center, Kemper Center Inc. in Kenosha in 1996. It's been rumored there may be another retrospective in the works.

Patrick credits his mentor and friend the late Aaron Bohrod for his generosity of time and technique that helped him achieve the ultimate results in his paintings. Bohrod's valuable advice included using panel with an egg-shell finish. Patrick expertly carries on the beauty of this blend. However, he found that working on linen allowed him to use a heavier dose of oil paint and achieve the same amount of detail by using larger brushes. A prime example of an oil on linen painting is Patrick's "Apple of My Eye."

The painting reminds the connoisseur of a Bohrod *trompe l' oeil* composition, but at the same time, the work is uniquely a Patrick Farrell. "Apple of My Eye" is inspired by Lucas Cranach the Elder's painting "Adam and Eve," which resides at the Uffizi Gallery in Florence, Italy. A grocery list for apple pie ingredients, an early painting of an apple, and an "apple of my mother's eye" fifth grade photo of Patrick all fit naturally into place. I am compelled to say they fit logically into the painting, because somehow, the longer I think about what's captivating about this painting, the more these simple components take on a logical life of their own. Just as there is a depth to the painter, there is a multilayer depth to his paintings.

Patrick says one of his most difficult works thus far was the 15 x 28 inch oil on linen, "Fruit in an Oval of Silver," painted in 2002. Painting the likeness of silver objects with all their reflections is definitely a challenge, but Patrick captures the nuances perfectly. The Marilyn Monroe earrings with all their facets would fit into the "challenge" category here. What's around the corner for Farrell? He says he has a desire to work on fewer and larger paintings now, thus a switch from board to canvas or linen is unfolding. His audience and his collectors are likely to see some exciting new works if the past predicts the future. Recent exhibitions include Best of Realism 2004 at the Marin-Price Galleries in Washington D.C./Chevy Chase, Maryland, and the 20th Anniversary Exhibition-Patrick Farrell Featured Artist 2004 at the River Edge Galleries in Mishicot, Wisconsin.

Patrick is included in *Who's Who in American Art*. My observation is that he's also included in everybody's book titled *Beating the Odds*. The late Margaret Fish Rahill, director and curator of the Charles Allis Art Museum, once wrote, "Patrick Farrell is in two inseparable ways his own oeuvre...on his own at hardly 17, he has made himself an artist of distinction and a man of taste...." This is not a statement of opinion; it is a statement of immortal fact.

Evelyn Patricia Terry

Evelyn Terry told me that from the time she was a very young child, she'd always be drawing something—not doodling—drawing. In her memories of the fourth grade, she notes that she was jealous of a friend, a boy who could draw characters and flip pages to show animation. Evelyn reflects on this mild conflict as a dichotomy that would serve to sharpen her awareness as her art career developed. Later in high school, Evelyn drew pigs and frogs for students who requested her help. Evelyn, an African American, was born in Milwaukee, went to North Division High School, and has lived in Milwaukee most of her life. As she began college at the University of Wisconsin, Evelyn's mother, Jessie Mae Terry, encouraged her daughter to become a cook because "there's always a job for a cook." Alternatively, careers in education or social work looked like they could be promising, according to advisers. Well, none of this happened.

Evelyn Patricia Terry

Evelyn describes herself as withdrawn, introverted, and miserable for a period during high school and the first three years of college. She attributes this to a frustrating lack of direction. In

"Pandora's Box Series: The Judgment and the Exit"
by Evelyn Patricia Terry
30" x 40" pastel, 1995

her junior year of college, as fate might have it, an insightful home economics professor, Jean Stange, took note of Evelyn's talent and pointed her in the direction of art. Art? What's that? Evelyn had not considered it, actually did not even know it existed, but nonetheless, she discovered art as a career path in her junior year at the University of Wisconsin-Milwaukee and decided to pursue a bachelor's of fine art degree. Her training, however, took her on to the School of the Art Institute of Chicago (SAIC) were she earned a master of fine arts degree. At one point, Evelyn, after having developed a career as an artist, asked her mother about the notion of directing Evelyn toward the study of art when she was a child. Evelyn's mother replied that in her day, kids who drew things were made to sit in the corner. Art as a profession was not understood or encouraged—the only goal was to get a job.

After her art education, Evelyn, as a professional artist, pursued galleries and consultants who in turn pursued corporate and public collections to purchase her work. Today her work is in approximately one hundred collections. Her list includes Blue Cross & Blue Shield of Wisconsin, Quad/Graphics, Wisconsin Gas, GE Medical, Firstar Corp,, SC Johnson, and the Hyatt Regency Milwaukee. She has also pursued involvement in public art. "Giving Gifts" is a twelve-part public art sculpture piece that represents Milwaukee's ethnic legacies, and it is located by each of the elevators in the new parking structure at Mitchell International Airport in Milwaukee. The project was completed by Evelyn and welder George Ray McCormick, Sr. in November 2002.

Evelyn's works have been shown in various Wisconsin galleries. In Milwaukee, the galleries have included those owned by Dorothy Bradley, Katie Gingrass, Judith Posner, and Bill Delind. Additionally, during the last several years, galleries carrying her work have included Cissie Peltz, Bilhenry Walker, Calvin Greer of Greer Oaks, and numerous college galleries. In Madison, she has shown her work at M.B. Perine, the University of Wisconsin, and most recently at Grace Chosy.

Always dedicated to the cause for awareness of art, and most notably African American Art, Evelyn has written a book that has been seven years in the making. *Permission to Paint, Please!* is an illustrated coffee table book that features approximately 230 African American artists connected to Wisconsin and their contributions to American art. The book is to be released in September 2005 from the University of Wisconsin Press. The book has received support from over one hundred donors, and grants from the Wisconsin Sesquicentennial Commission and the Helen Bader Foundation.

Evelyn is an explorer. She had no black role model early in her art career, and she thought she might be the first black artist. Then Evelyn discovered a book in the library on African American artists. Shocked and puzzled, the artist questioned one of her professors as to why black artists were never mentioned in the art history or studio classes. He replied that it was because their work was "stylized." So Evelyn attempted to avoid creating whatever was perceived as "stylized" work. Then she took a class on African traditional art, and the instructor remarked that the African art was so great because it was "stylized." This contrast was a turning point for Evelyn. She reconstructed her belief system and decided to free herself from other people's perceptions and ideology, instead concentrating on things that worked for her, believing that ultimately would lead to the most fulfilling work.

Faraway places and people became an interest for Evelyn as she advanced to seek direction and inspiration from successful African American artists. She crossed the country attending several art conventions and visiting many notable artists in Boston, New York, and Washington D.C. These notable artists included Samella Lewis of California, publisher of the *International Review in African American Art,* and Margaret Borroughs, founder of the DuSable Museum in Chicago, authors David Driskell, and Faith Ringgold. She has been inspired by the work of American artists Arthur Saunders and Margo Humphrey, and English artist Francis Bacon, as well as Picasso's tremendous output and the constant evolution of his work.

Evelyn received awards, grants, fellowships, and commissions including the Milwaukee County Arts Fellowship and the McKnight Fellowship for her installation work. After the terrorist attack in September 2001, her known art world took a downward spiral and this affected her sales. Since 1985, she has maintained a studio as artist-in-residence at Lincoln School Center for the Arts. As an instructor, she emphasizes drawing skills and instructs students on painting multicultural murals that depict cultural artifacts and diversity.

Evelyn has been a professional artist since 1981 after working as a draftsman at the Milwaukee Metropolitan Sewerage District. Her work ranges from non-objective abstraction to figurative realism and utilizes printmaking and pastels as her major media. Evelyn's themes include relationships (sex), race, and religion. She has a fondness for using the subject of watermelon in her artwork because of the fruit's formal qualities and its symbolic connection with the lives and history of African Americans. Originally, the connection between the African American culture and the fruit was a spiritual one.

"I avoid being the art Nazi — someone who thinks only one kind of art is 'right,'" says Evelyn. She believes that no artistic authority exists whose judgment can determine what's good art and what's not good art. The problems lie in the artist who believes he or she is the authority and that others have to acquiesce. Evelyn Patricia Terry, the person, is energetic, ambitious, and strives to mentor utilizing her philosophical outlook on life. She has two children. Talleah E. Bridges, who has a master's degree in broadcast journalism and a career in the film industry in California, and Fondé Bridges, a writer who published a book titled *101 Simple Suggestions for Better Living*.

Michael Riddet

(1947-)

Michael Riddet's art has seen its way to over forty museums in the United States and beyond. The works were featured at Christie's South Kensington Galleries in London, England, and in the book *Best of Wildlife Art* published by North Light Books. The artist was the winner of the Wisconsin Waterfowl Stamp competition in 1984, 1992, and 2003. He is represented in the permanent collection at the Leigh Yawkey Woodson Art Museum, and his paintings have been selected for the museum's Birds in Art exhibition for eleven years. Selections of his works have been issued as limited edition reproductions. In 1996, Michael was awarded the Society of Animal Artists (New York) award of excellence and elected into the organization.

Indeed, the accomplishments are impressive. But there's always more to the story. Michael's family emigrated to the United States in the 1920s, returned to England during the Depression, and settled for a second time in the United States in 1956 when

Michael was 9 years old. The young artist-to-be entered the fourth grade only to be teased for his use of the King's English. He says that his fourth grade experience "was a bit harrowing." The teacher was not even a comfort. She ridiculed a completed art project of a roadrunner made from scraps of fabric, and then commented on how ""bad" it was to another teacher. Hurtful as the lightening bolt event was, it was also a springboard for the young boy. Michael commented, "It was then that I told myself I was going to be an artist and that I would someday show her what I was capable of."

Within a year, a more insightful art teacher appeared and encouraged Michael's parents to purchase a set of encyclopedias so the boy could become familiar with the world that surrounded him. Michael's interest and talent in art soared. His aunt sent him a gift of "a complete set of oils in a wooden artist's box" and a copy of John James Audubon's *Birds in America*. The focus in art spanned from elementary school through high school where he took mandatory and elective art courses. Michael painted in his bedroom studio and explored the woods to learn more about his subject matter.

The artist collected butterflies while he was a high school student in Illinois, but decided at the time, that this probably was not a fact that he wanted spread around. Later, he found out that others were collectors, too, but again, none wanted to make it headline news. Nonetheless, Michael's interest in butterflies and wildlife pulled him toward the study of biological sciences. But at the same time, remaining committed to his art work, the adventurous high school student decided to seek an opinion on a couple of his paintings by venturing into the studio of Charles Vickery, a renowned artist. Not long after that encounter, Michael began associating with Vickery and his friends at their Saturday morning gatherings. They encouraged him to show his art at the shows. His art began selling. This factor probably gave him the confidence to experiment and move from landscape to wildlife art and to switch from oil on canvas to watercolor and illustration

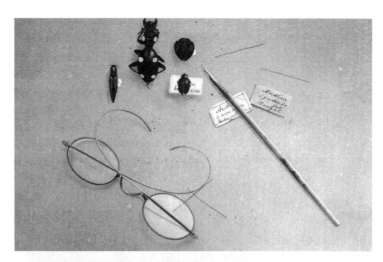

TOP: "The Collector" by Michael Riddet Photo courtesy of Michael Riddet

BOTTOM: "Under the Trees" by Michael Riddet Photo courtesy of Michael Riddet

board. During his college years, Michael continued to expand his art endeavors, and described his early work as "objective, realistic, and detailed."

After graduating from Roosevelt University in 1969 with a biology degree, Michael found a job as an associate industrial engineer, then an artist for a wildlife art company that went out of business, and finally he took a job as a security guard working evenings. He noted that he was a guard "with a paintbrush in one hand and a revolver in the other." The income from his paintings far exceeded his income as a security guard. Then Emmet Blake, the curator of birds at Chicago's Field Museum of Natural History found him, as did the *Chicago Tribune Magazine*, which featured the artist in their article "Birds of the Midwest." One thing lead to another and Michael was offered a job as an artist and naturalist at a forest preserve in DuPage County near Chicago. His reputation grew exponentially.

Faithful to his familiar mediums, the artist one day daringly tried out acrylic paints at the suggestion of his wife, also an artist. The result: "My watercolors went into the drawer, where they still remain. Acrylics are a remarkable medium." An exhibition of 54 premier wildlife artists in 1978 at the Leigh Yawkey Woodson Art Museum brought the Canadian, Terence Shortt, an artist with the Royal Ontario Museum in Toronto, to town. Michael Riddet met Shortt, who seriously recommended that Michael pursue painting full time. A fork in the road was now in front of Michael and his wife—should they stay with a secure job with their employer; or take a risk, head to the great unknown, and seek a living in the art world. Fifty acres in southwestern Wisconsin, one decision in 1979, and an unrelenting desire to capture creative compositions with his brush, provided the answer to this life-changing question.

So where is this artist headed? In 1996, Michael started painting in trompe l'oeil, more commonly known as "trick the eye," or "fool the eye." The style is a study in precision. He says, "I look at each new work as a personal challenge to fool me as I walk past the easel. I've even gotten my golden retriever involved. In a recent piece, I painted several North American moths sitting on a hieroglyphic tablet, the largest moth being an underwing, about two-and-a-half inches long. As I had placed the finished painting on the floor to get a look at it, my dog lunged forward and attempted to snap it up. Much to his surprise, there was nothing to retrieve. So far, he is my best critic." Once the work passes the dog's instinctive inspection and the sharp eye of the artist, Michael Riddet's work is represented by Winstanley-Roark Fine Arts in Dennis, Massachusetts, and Holland & Holland, London, New York.

Charles Dix

The artist's Moonwalk Gallery in Delafield had been a prime tourist attraction for around thirty years. It is surrounded by five acres of gardens that harmonize with the 6,000-square-foot gallery. Nature had her way with the land, however, and the property was plagued by uncontrollable flooding over the years. Charles Dix dodged the puddles, but decided to uproot and plant his plans for a new spacious gallery, called Oak Pond, on nineteen acres that appear to be ruled by a rather spirited kingfisher. Nonetheless, this abstractionist artist is creating and fitting into his new natural surroundings. Charles Dix is known for his serene watercolors that take a hint from nature, and for his flashy depictions of galactic subject matter.

Charles is mostly self-taught. He began painting in 1957, and today his paintings characteristically depict the interplay of colors and colors transposed. Space exploration and intense interest in the cosmos blend with his adeptness at color. Early work was done primarily in watercolor. In the 1960s, he was using acrylics. Later paintings portray astral vistas and solar explosions, and "frag-

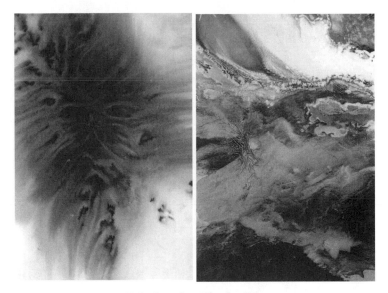

Paintings by Charles Dix
Photos courtesy of Charles Dix

ments of forgotten civilizations." The paintings are uncanny in that they are quite similar to later photographs taken by Voyager I, Voyager II, and the Hubble telescope. The artist continues to find vision, inspiration, and fascination with all of the unexplored universe, as well as "cosmic forces that battle with inexplicable objects." He pioneered the use of bronze powders suspended in various bronzing fluids and used them as a painting medium and in combination with other mediums.

Charles Dix has had a long career exhibiting in many juried shows and competitions and has won numerous awards. His 40" by 30" acrylic "Night Bridge" was reproduced and featured on the cover of *Art Calendar,* a business magazine for visual artists in June 2000. Corporate and other collections that own his pieces include Allis Art Library, Alverno College, Bank One, Bergstrom Art Center, Bradley Collections, Elvehjem Art Museum, Marquette University, Miller Brewing, Milwaukee Art Museum, Milwaukee Public Library, Milwaukee Symphony, Rahr West

Museum, University of Puerto Rico, University of Wisconsin-La Crosse, Wustum Museum.

The visionary artist finds that a love of travel unleashes the painting spirit. He has enjoyed travel to New York, London, Paris, Puerto Rico, and other parts of the globe. In his travels, he has collected stones from areas of Mexico, and uses these in his silver design work in jewelry. Now he has Oak Pond and its wildlife to inspire new creativity and a new gallery, all major events. The title of a recent work is telltale. "Event Horizon," a watercolor painting was accepted for the 83rd annual exhibition of the National Watercolor Society held in Brea, California in 2004.

Harvey K. Littleton

(1922 -)

"I was born very early in the morning on June 14, 1922, and I was named Harvey K. Littleton, which my father said meant 'high cost of living'."
— Interview by Joan Falconer Byrd
(Archives of American Art, Smithsonian Institution)

"But we injected among the art students people with degrees in chemistry, people with degrees in psychology, people with degrees in sociology, people with degrees in economics, people with degrees in damn-near-anything, who decided they wanted to take art. In 1970, 70% of our graduate students at the University of Wisconsin had come to art with other degrees. I always use Fritz [Dreisbach], because Fritz in 5,000 years of glassmaking was the first glassmaker who handled the blowpipe with five university degrees on his back"
— Interview by Joan Falconer Byrd, March 15, 2001

On May 15, 2004, Harvey K. Littleton received an honorary doctor of fine arts from North Carolina State University in Raleigh. On May 2, 2004, he received the Wisconsin Visual Art Lifetime Achievement Award at the West Bend Art Museum in West Bend, Wisconsin. Not that the artist runs around collecting awards, but he's piled up a bunch of them over the years. Harvey K. Littleton is called the father of the studio glass movement. Today he lives in Spruce Pine, North Carolina. He started out as a potter, but in 1959, he was intrigued with the possibility that glass could be a versatile art medium. The idea caught on, and in 1962 the Toledo Museum of Art invited Harvey to lead a glassblowing workshop. He demonstrated to his students that glass could be melted and mixed, blown and worked by the studio artist. This was a revolutionary concept, since up until this time glass was industrially mass-produced and structured through the labor of designers and craftsmen.

Harvey Littleton was a ceramics instructor at the University of Wisconsin in Madison beginning in 1951. The artist had a farm outside of Madison where he created a glass studio and offered a graduate course. From 1964 to 1967 and 1969 to 1971, he served as art department chairman at the university. The artist retired from teaching in 1976 to work full time on his art. He moved to Spruce Pines, North Carolina, set up a glass studio, and continued to develop techniques.

The artist was born in Corning, New York. His father was a physicist who worked for the Corning Glassworks and invented what is known in the industry as the Littleton Point, which is a way to determine what is a glass and to differentiate one type of glass from another. It was the idea of Harvey's father to use glass as a cooking utensil for ovenware, so he sawed off the bottom of a Corning battery jar made of borosilicate glass, gave it to Mrs. Littleton, Harvey's mother, and she baked a cake in it—magic—the first Corning ovenware was born. Corning has a square one on display in its museum today as the original, but Harvey's mother said it was actually round, that she fed the dogs in it, and that eventually the dogs broke it.

Part of Harvey's interesting life was that of a soldier drafted into World War II. He had been attending the University of Michigan for industrial design at the time he was drafted, which meant that instead of graduating in 1943, he had to postpone graduation until 1947. He served with the 849th Signal Intelligence Unit in North Africa. During this lengthy tour of duty, the young soldier received a commendation from the chief signal officer in Europe for inventing a decoding device. Because of this award, Harvey was sent to England at the end of the war where he entered the Brighton School of Design. After returning to the states, he received a master of fine arts Degree at the Cranbrook Academy of Art. He pioneered the printmaking technique of vitreography, which was later used by his friend and printmaker Warrington Colescott. Harvey has invited painters, printmakers, glass artists, and sculptors to his studio in North Carolina to create vitreographs at Littleton Studios.

Harvey K. Littleton's art has been in solo exhibitions at the Art Institute of Chicago (1963) and the Museum of Contemporary Crafts in New York (1964). His work is in collections at the American Craft Museum in New York City, the Cooper Hewitt National Museum of Design, the Smithsonian Institution, the Corning Museum of Glass, the Detroit Institute of Art, the Los Angeles County Museum, the Metropolitan Museum of Art, the Museum of Art in New York City, Renwick Gallery, and the White House.

Tom Uttech

(1942 -)

Tom's paintings say something about the artist. He has a fascination, no, probably an obsession with the nuances of nature. When I see one of his paintings it gets me to thinking about my own childhood of trampling though the woods and the swamp over broken twigs and curious vegetation, delighting in all the seasons, especially the spring. These days Tom works at his art full time and paints in his barn-studio in rural Wisconsin. He has a relationship with the land, the botany, the bird life, the creatures, the darkness and the light of his surroundings.

The artist is known throughout the United States for his landscape paintings. His paintings pull in a mystical aura, and it is amusing to see a wispy string of light secretively swirl through the branches of the trees. What is that? That's what makes the painting unusual—this captivating blend of surrealism into what one might think is a typical woodsy landscape. Tom grew up near Wausau, Wisconsin. Always interested in nature, he took that part of him into his study of art. His interest in art began at an early age, and he recalls that at about 3 years old, he remembers seeing a red-winged blackbird portrayed in a yellow field of June hay. The image became imbedded in his mind and created a vortex of interest that spun out to all of nature, and especially birds. He joined a Wausau bird club in high school and took field trips to the home of world famous ornithologists Frances and Frederick Hamerstrom. The influence of their way of life and their devotion to wildlife made a life-long impression on Tom.

Knowing that art was his passion, Tom entered Layton School of Art in Milwaukee in 1961. He experienced the magnetism of two poles—conforming to the expectations and the trends of the art world; or indulging in landscape art, which was not popular at the time. It was a struggle for years. He entered graduate school at the University of Cincinnati and became involved in pop art and superheroes. In hindsight, he says his work "went to hell." But he managed to pull himself from the abyss and spent more time just pretty much living the landscape. Quetico Provincial Park in Ontario, a wilderness spot that is beyond words, proved to be a spiritual place for the painter and helped guide him back to the purity of his art in painting landscapes, only with a mystical surrealism bend. Tom taught painting at the University of Wisconsin-Milwaukee until he made the decision to devote himself to his own art. His art has been extensively exhibited and is represented by several galleries in Wisconsin and in New York.

Dean Meeker

(1920-2002)

Dean Meeker is synonymous with serigraphy (original silk-screen color print). He learned the technique while he was an art student in Chicago and working for a print shop. In 1946, the artist became an instructor at the University of Wisconsin-Madison and shared his knowledge in the form of teaching a course on

Dean Meeker
Photo courtesy Bobbi Lane
Photography

serigraphy. This was an innovative move that led to another innovative development—the invention of the Meeker-McFee press. John McFee of the UW engineering department collaborated with Dean Meeker. The artist was invited in 1957 by the Art Institute of Chicago to present a one man serigraphy show. A Guggenheim Fellowship to continue development of techniques in combining serigraphy and etching was awarded to him in 1959.

Dean Meeker had a dedication to teaching art, and in 1960 he was named professor. He wasn't good at remembering students' names when he'd run into them on the street, but he'd ask them to describe their work, and then he'd put two and two together. "He was a real innovator. I think he was the first person to ever exhibit serigraph at the Museum of Modern Art in New York," said Philip Hamilton, a UW art professor of graphic design (article October 11, 2002, by Amy Silvers, *Milwaukee Journal Sentinel*).

The artist set up a print studio on his property in Dane in 1962. Around 1970 Meeker started doing sculpture so he needed a second studio. A third studio was in the works when he converted a garage to a welding studio. The works of Dean Meeker include an estimated 10,000 prints and hundreds of sculptures. They are in more than 100 museum collections, including the Milwaukee Art Museum, the Art Institute of Chicago, the Whitney Museum of American Art in New York, the Library of Congress, and the Bibliotheque Nationale in Paris.

Dan Gerhartz

Interviewed October 2003, Kewaskum, Wisconsin

How long have you been working in professional art?

I have been working professionally as an artist for about 15 years, beginning around 1987. My dad is a music teacher, and my mother was a stay-at-home mom. I was blessed with neat parents who were supportive and encouraging. Strict too, but it was good in the end. I attended high school in Kewaskum, and had an art teacher who was influential in my career. He was fun; wry sense of humor, great teaching style. It was a fantastic learning environment because he taught the fundamentals of art well and made it interesting. After I had a solid foundation, I went on to art school. At first, I wasn't confident about going to Chicago, and thought I might get blown out of the water, but nonetheless, I charged ahead. I studied at the American Academy of Art and met a core of students, who to this day have remained in close contact. We have given each other critique and encouragement all these years, and we do the best we can with that.

Another person I met was Richard Schmid. He was very generous towards me, and actually kind of re-taught me how to "see" the subject. We didn't spend a lot of time together, but when we were together, the teaching and learning was concentrated. During that period, a retrospective show of John Singer Sargent came to the States and I absorbed it as best I could. I was also able to travel to Sweden to see an Anders Zorn retrospective. Those events were immensely informative and influential for me.

In 1988, I married Jennifer, who has always played a major part in my development as an artist. As a physical therapist, she's got a great eye and has anatomical knowledge, but she also possesses an outstanding sense of design. It's innate. She can look at a piece, and if there is a problem, she has no hesitation in saying, "This just isn't working."

Looking around your fantastic studio, I see a lot of art in an Impressionist style.

Yes, that's what I'm doing now with these subjects. I also have an interest in landscapes. What truly excites me is harmony and design. Whether that includes a landscape or a still life is not important. What I see from day to day that I can create from is important to me. Art that triggers an emotional response is my ultimate goal. I believe that the emotional response is accomplished by harmony and design. The human element always adds something, and I do use the human form quite a bit.

When I look at a human figure, the skin tone is what speaks to me. There is so much depth to skin. Opulent blues and greens, and everything in the skin can be captured and is exciting. There's so much beauty.

What would you say your personality is like, such that it drew you into artwork?

...Besides completely off the wall? I don't know. Artists often

TOP: "Carefree" 48" x 60" oil
Dan F. Gerhartz, 2004
BOTTOM: "Hinda Feet" 96" x 72" oil
Dan F. Gerhartz, 2004

have a particular stereotype, and I think there is some truth to that…flighty…zone off and you're on another tangent or planet. I think it fits, and yet some people use that as an excuse (myself included on occasion). But it can be an asset; it's a trait that seems to travel with creative thinking. I was never pegged with that characteristic when I was growing up. As a Wisconsin kid, I liked to hunt, fish, and play baseball. I remember my high school teacher, John Bainger, pointing out to me that I noticed a lot of things—nuances. Now, noticing nuances is exactly the driving force in what I do. As I live, I continuously notice the beauty that is in the creative world around me. I try to find little tweaks. Take for example, this quaking aspen tree branch that I have in the corner of my studio. There are absolutely stunning designs in the leaf patterns—every one of them—look at where the small twigs twist around. The designs appear chaotic, yet I am convinced there is some extremely high math going on there that I don't presume to understand. What creates the splendor is fascinating! Really, there is art in everything. God wasn't just joking around. It's the truth. We can find art in rocks or tree bark—explosions of color.

Where are your paintings, and what prices have they sold for?

The paintings are in collections throughout the United States and Japan. Primarily, I sell out of a few galleries, and they are located in Scottsdale, Arizona and Santa Fe, New Mexico. I've shown in some galleries in California and in New York. The prices vary a lot. Smaller pieces are in the $2,000-$3,000 range. Large paintings are usually $20,000-$30,000, and some are higher. I've sold up to $65,000 to a buyer on the coast of California. It really does vary considerably. I typically don't work on commission.

Museums?

I have not pursued that route extensively. To concentrate on museum work has to be an active quest, and it's a job in itself. That would be nice, but truthfully, right now I would rather paint than concentrate on getting my work into collections. This oil, titled "Hinda Feet" (oil 96" x 72"), I'm saving for some reason, but I'm not quite sure why. I'd like to see it out in a public place where people can see it and enjoy it hopefully. Maybe that sounds arrogant, but it's meant to be a wish of generosity. I like to see museum collections that reflect the best art for that particular

museum. That can mean not following trends, and not following the biggest name. A good eye for art is what is important.
At times, I've seen pieces of art on the wall that I can't imagine
uplift anybody. Why is that even there?

It looks like you work primarily in oils. Do you ever work in acrylic?

Yes, I work in oils mostly. I have worked in watercolor and
pastels. I haven't worked in acrylic in such a long time. I don't
know; it might be fun. It depends on how you use it. I don't
have an aversion to it; it's not taboo. It's easier to clean and
doesn't have an obnoxious odor. It's also a little less toxic. But
nonetheless, there is a certain and definite depth that you lose in
acrylic painting and it's primarily in the dark colors. In oil, you
get those deep rich darks that you can travel half a mile into. It's
very hard to get that effect using acrylics because there is a flat-
tening effect. In oil, you can really feel the texture, and it builds
up and stays. When acrylic dries, it flattens out and you lose out.
Certainly, with acrylics, the drying time is fast, and sometimes
that can be an advantage. I like the surface texture that an oil
painting gives. That's important. Oil is the old standby. It is
classic and it's ageless.

Do you produce prints of any of your works?

Yes, we have produced very high quality prints, and they are
quite limited. Half the run is on paper and half is on canvas. I
also work with a publisher who does some smaller prints, and
these are mass-produced. It's a little different; I'm glad to be doing
both really. We just came out with a calendar too. The signed
prints are limited to 195. In the last five years, the print market
took somewhat of a dive with the economy the way it is, but we
don't really rely on the print market for income. I'd rather sell
the originals. I haven't paid a lot of attention to the up and down
prices of prints. It is a way for people to enjoy art, however, and I
think that is extremely important. I think of it in the same sense

Daniel F. Gerhartz

as I like Tiffany, even though an original is out of my reach, but there are people who are doing some darn nice work with his designs. I'm so delighted to have some of their work—just to be able to enjoy it.

Is there anybody in history who has inspired your painting?
Largely, there are several. I've always like the work of Alfonz Mucha (Czech) and Nicholi Fessin (Russian). I love his work. Carl von Marr, whose work is displayed in the West Bend Art Museum, was born in Milwaukee, but he spent most of his life in Germany. Von Marr could do everything from beautifully academic paintings to impressionistic pieces that are striking. The museum in West Bend is a "jaw breaker." It's fantastic! This museum is a "must experience" place. I have artists from around the country who come to visit, and I take them to the West Bend Art Museum. They can't believe the phenomenal place exists.

I like John Singer Sargent, as I mentioned earlier, and painters in that realm. There are so many to talk about. Joaquin Sorolla and Jules Bastien-LePage (French) come to mind. I enjoy the school of naturalism work, which came out just prior to impressionism.

In a general sense, what do you think is the most important fundamentally? Drawing ability?
I think drawing is very important. When you say drawing, that means accurate proportions, accurate values, meaning light and dark and using that scale accurately. True relational edges are important, so that the edges work as we see them. This takes training and practice by the eye—to see the form, the abstract

form. I find it important to look at it abstractly, and paint it as abstractly as you can, and then use your anatomical knowledge to pull it all together. I've had students sometimes rely on anatomical knowledge too heavily, and then the pieces turn out looking too cartoonish. They over- delineate muscle insertions, origins, and bony prominences. The human figure starts to look grotesque, not accurate; not how we see it. I try to paint "light," in other words, as light falls upon objects. If you can capture the light, half the work is done.

So do you subscribe to the teaching that the light source must come from the left hand side when you're doing a project?

No, it doesn't matter. I say to students to paint everything. Don't lock yourself into just one thing, because avoiding that tendency will help your eye to stay fresh. In other words, avoid developing a formula about how things "should be." That's when your work gets into trouble. Too much formula means you're not looking; you're not paying attention! I love backlight, and that can be from any direction.

Tell me about your teaching.

I teach principally workshops of about twenty students, two or three times a year. Usually I travel to Arizona and New Mexico to teach them. I've taught some out of my studio. Occasionally, I'll mentor an individual student when I can. A lot depends on how much that individual student truly wants to dive into art. That motivation is incredibly important. It can't be a fleeting desire. If someone aspires to do very well in art, there must be a strong passion for it. Serious art takes an incredible amount of self-discipline. You've absolutely got to stick with it.

What do you think about "modern art?"

Personally, it leaves me empty. It leaves me cold and emotionally bankrupt. The American public, and probably people worldwide, don't trust their emotions anymore. Everybody can feel if a piece of art moves you or not. It's like music. Some music moves you, and other music you can do without, or it doesn't matter what you do with it. Generally, people feel like they have to give an excuse, because they've been so brainwashed. They think if they don't like a particular piece of art, they are ignorant, or they think that you, the other person, don't know what art is. For starters, that's complete arrogance at its height—not to mention, it's just so wrong-headed. On the other hand, individuals have individual preferences no matter what kind of art we're looking at, and that in itself is what can give art richness.

Do you think your background and growing up in this area of Wisconsin influences your art at all?

I'm positive it does. The light in particular influences me strongly. I'm drawn to art that seems to have the same type of light—a lot of European art. French and Russian art have this quality in particular. It resonates in my soul and is all around me so strongly that I can just feel it. I know it affects my heart in an emotional way. When I travel around the nation or in foreign countries, I love coming back here—to this radiance—to these trees. It's home, but it's also home in an artistic sense. It's peaceful but so alive with a harmony and design that includes the natural elements I love. I've been to the desert many times, but it's taken a number of trips to kind of warm up to it to the point where I can envision art from that perch. When I travel to a different place, I have to picture how I would process it from an art perspective.

What are you best at as far as your work goes?

Best at? I haven't really thought about it. One thing I would like to do is to become continually more sensitive to design. Learning in art, as in many things, is the work of a lifetime. To key into how God wired me to be a designer, and to do that without emulating others, and to do that without trying to be unique is my challenge. C.S. Lewis hit the nail on the head when he said, "Even in literature and in art no man who bothers about originality will ever be original. If you simply try to tell the truth without caring two pence about how often it has been told before, you will, nine times out of ten, become original without ever having noticed it." When I see people in some of the college art classes try to be original, the art comes off as false and cold, but when they just simply tell the truth over and over again, their originality blossoms. Claude Monet, for example, when I think of where he started and where he ended up...very original work, and yet I don't believe he overtaxed his mind thinking about it. He just captured the light repeatedly, and that became the progression in his work.

In painting, I strive to explore different emotions, and to capture them on canvas in a way that doesn't diminish the emotions, and yet people can live with it. I think of contrasts, such as a dominance of hope with an element of despair, or the other way around—dominance of despair with a fragment of hope. Emotion has to be painted without sweeping it out so much that you have diluted the sensitivity of pain and loss. It must be painted effectively. I'm drawn to those contrasts in art and in music, and I try to capture that piece of magic. Thank God, I have not had to live through a lot of turmoil, as I've talked about, but maybe there will come a time.

Do you paint exclusively in your studio?

I paint in my studio with set up scenes and hired models. I also paint on location. As you can see in this issue of *International Artist* (March 2002), these paintings of mine were done on location. When I'm in my studio, I always have music playing as I paint. Usually I listen to classics or ancient choral music. The music helps me to focus. To work from life is the best way for me.

Do you ever work from photos?

Generally, I do not work from photos except in using little

children or animals in the painting. Even then, I still try to work as much as possible from life. It always turns out better—so much more interesting. I can't say enough about the light being a huge factor. To use photos causes such a loss of dimension. Your eye can't travel to the side and behind, and to all the angles if all you use are photos. That sense of depth and air is lost.

What's your advice to those studying art?

Study, study, and then study. Did I mention study? Paint from life as much as you can. Study the Masters, and even copy the Masters. For years, there has been a taboo on copying, but that is quite ridiculous. That's how we discover, and grow and learn. Think of classical pianists not playing any music written by Mozart, Beethoven, or Chopin because it would be labeled "copying." But that's how we learn! And learning is always the key. It is precisely the same in art. Keep uplifting yourself this way. The world is a big place, and that's your canvas. Most of the major movements in art came about because somebody copied the style of somebody else.

What are your goals?

My goal is to continue—to capture emotions more effectively, to create art that moves people to the Creator, not to me. I want to have people look at the art and be moved to a sense of beauty and wonder and awe—not at any human artist—but so they can capture a sense of God and the magnificence of all that is created to transcend our human condition. That's what I strive for now. I'm glad you asked, because it's good to remind myself of that. Why am I doing this, and who is supposed to get the glory here—Dan? It's hard as a human not to go there. But take a walk in the woods, and look at the splendor around you. Then it's natural to think of a Creator who has it so precisely mapped out. I recall a time I was on the coast of California painting. The panorama I was working from was just breathtaking. I was painting by a roadside, and there were people around who were saying,

"Oh, nice painting." I was grateful, but I wanted to thank the Creator for this scenery. There's a superb Designer whose work is a heck of a lot more impressive than my work is. Even one-celled organisms have engineering and design. It's truly amazing! Everybody has a gift, and we must seek to find out what it is and how we can best use it. That's the plan.

Before you began working in your present endeavors, what were you doing?

When I went to art school, I really did not know someone could make a living at this as I do today. When I graduated from college, I went to work as a commercial artist as an illustrator. I was terrible in that I had a hard time generating the excitement and the enthusiasm to see a piece of work through when it was someone else's idea. Paint a flower for this Kleenex box—what? Based on what I just said, I should have not had a hard time doing it, but it was tough. For the most part, I am grateful to get out of it when I did. I wasn't married at the time, and neither did I have any financial burdens—mortgage, car payments. I generated enough work so that I was able to interview with galleries. It took a long time, several years in fact, but as I emphasized before, I worked at it.

How would you compare yourself to an architect?

From an artistic design sense, I could compare myself to an architect. However, an architect seems to me to be a good combination of right and left-brain. I remember seeing a Far Side cartoon that portrayed an artist with the whole left side of the brain caved in—that would pretty much fit me. We just had an architect work on the house, and it was pure joy. I'm guessing he was more right than left-brain.

If someone wants to see examples of your work, where would you direct them?

Legacy Gallery in Scottsdale, Arizona, and the Meyer Gallery in Santa Fe, New Mexico…some work is online, otherwise here at the studio. I've just about completed a Web site. My work has been in several publications.

What is the easiest part of your work—the most satisfying?

The initial emotional response that is triggered in me is the most rewarding. It creates this giddy excitement, and you want to combine the harmony with the thrill. When I have a client who has acquired one of the paintings, and I know it is a good match, it creates a bright spot in my life. It's fun working with people too. I have a Thursday night group that gets together and paints from a model in the studio. Painting for me is a form of worship, not a form of worship of the flowers or of the trees or of the birds. To look at the creation on canvas and to be in awe as I'm painting really aids the process. The art is kicked to another level when this happens. I think it makes a difference. There are times when you paint and you are not hyper excited, but the discipline of actually doing it, spending time with the subject and observing all that you can possibly observe, puts you in the position of being inspired. Often for me this process is set in motion by taking walks, being around people, observing nuances of movement, or hiring models for particular settings.

Final comments?

Yes. I have advice for students. Study intensely and paint from life. Get a portable easel (French easel). Paint all kinds of light—whatever inspires you—but be sure to paint from life. Animals and children are hard because they are always moving, but still try to paint from life. Photographs can be used to complement the painting. Use the photo just for drawing and then key into the creativity and the beauty of your live subject. Get *good* critiques from people you can trust to evaluate honestly and accurately — not pats on the back. Study the masters and copy the texture, harmony, and composition. It doesn't matter what medium you use. I've seen stunning works from color pencil. When I paint oil, I usually tack a piece of canvas or linen onto a board and then stretch it after the fact. That way you can get the design the way you want it. For the very large pieces, I stretch the canvas ahead of time.

Work on permanent materials. That is critically important, so research this. Use acid-free materials. Put a barrier between the oil paint and the surface so that the oil doesn't rot the canvas in 50 or 100 years. I prime canvases with rabbit-skin glue and either an oil or a lead priming. This is archival and has been proven to withstand the test of time. The canvases that you buy in art stores are probably fine, and often use acrylic priming. I don't prefer acrylic priming, but it works. There are so many different ways to prepare a canvas. *The Artist Handbook of Materials and Techniques* by Ralph Mayer is what I recommend. Everything you can imagine is in that book, and the author tells you what's permanent and what's not.

If you're doing work on non-archival materials, there is really nothing you can do to make it last as if you had used archival materials to begin with, but it will still probably last 50-100 years. If you're selling art, you really must pay attention to the materials that you use, and definitely, the work has to be done on archival materials. Brushes are a matter of personal decision, but get the best you can afford, and remember that you don't have to have the best of everything to create great art, and in fact may not even need it. Find paints that are light-fast. They aren't necessarily expensive, but there are certain colors that fade faster, such as the alizarins (reds) and so on. Do some research. Bottom line—create art that lasts—everything else about your work is a personal choice.

My words of wisdom: Continue to learn. Capture things from memory in your own mind and make a mental note or do a quick sketch of the harmony-design that really moves you, and then use that to set up a composition—something from life. The all-encompassing glow of a sunset is fantastic. I can't invent this;

I have to go to nature to capture it...and that's when the brushes and the colors come alive.

Lee Weiss

(1928 -)

On June 10, 2004, I paid a visit to the home of Lee Weiss of Madison, Wisconsin. The home of an artist is a treasure and a world apart no matter how sparse or how grand the surroundings. I was immediately absorbed into her private collection paintings. The nuances of light and texture in the paintings are perfect. The one question that I use when viewing any piece of art in any medium is this: Does it pull me into it? It's always a simple yes or no answer. The paintings of Lee Weiss not only pulled, but they operated with an aura of magnetism about them. They have that quality of look at it once, look at it twice, look at it a thousand times, and you'll always find something new. I asked Lee about this phenomenon and she said, "That's what keeps it from being an illustration. A painting has a depth that makes it a painting." She's not knocking illustration; she's defining a painting.

OK, so how does the artist achieve this immortal effect? As Lee explained, she is one of the few watercolor artists who paints wet-on-wet (wet brush-wet paper), and she does so by directly layering colors and allowing a calculated bleeding of water and color into the work. "I began layering in different colors and discovered I got wonderful color separation, because some pigments are lighter in weight than others and tend to pull away in different directions." Additionally, one of the techniques she sometimes uses involves painting on both sides and flipping the paper onto a slick-surface Plexiglas. The watercolor paper then picks up the paint sitting on the Plexiglas surface from the previous flip maneuvers. The results take on a natural tone and seem to capture bits of color in natural places. Lee uses various watercolor papers depending on the technique. The flipping and layering procedure works well on paper with a random texture. She often uses hot-pressed paper (a smoother paper), and seldom uses standard rough watercolor paper because the texture is too uniform. Lee uses no fugitive (not lightfast) colors.

"I look for textures and then develop them into subject matter. I don't go back to a subject until I have something new to say about it." When she talks about "texture," the artist refers to things like the grittiness or smoothness of a rock, water flowing, water that incorporates sunlight as it slightly ripples over pebbles in a shallow pool. "I look up through a tree rather

Lee Weiss

than at the tree" is how she describes painting the relationship of light as it beams amid the tree branches or bounces off the leaves. The artist mixes colors with the knowledge that when they dry they will produce "glowing" areas as the pigments pull apart. By keeping the painting surfaces wet, she is able to "lift" pigment out with her brush. She never uses a sponge, tissue blotter, or paper towel.

Lee usually does not paint on commission. Instead, after she produces a painting, and when she thinks it suits a particular client's request regarding color or natural subject, she contacts the client. The artist does not complete more than one painting in a week, and paintings may take several weeks to complete. About every five or six years, she keeps one of her paintings so that she has a record of her progression through the years. The majority

TOP: "Ridge Rocks"
32" x 40" watercolor
by Lee Weiss

BOTTOM: "Nested
Pebbles" 1987
40" x 30" watercolor
by Lee Weiss

Photos courtesy
of Lee Weiss

of her paintings are large, usually 30"x 40" with an occasional six-foot masterpiece. She says she frames her work under acrylic Plexiglas because according to a curator, the material allows the work to breathe, thus no foxing or moisture buildup. The painting can be put flat upon the surface. Lee does not allow her art to be reproduced in prints, although there have been a few limited exceptions. She believes that having prints on the market devalues the originals, and the art becomes commonplace. How many Mona Lisas do you want to look at?

Lee attended the California College of Arts and Crafts (CCAC) in Oakland when she was 18. The experience taught her color theory, drawing in perspective, life drawing, design, and most importantly "how to see." She became a successful interior designer in the Bay Area while putting her first husband through pre-med and medical school.

Later, Lee married Len Weiss, a widower with two little girls. With her, she brought two daughters of her own into the marriage. When she had the strength and energy that outpaced the toddlers, the artist resumed her painting at night. Around 1957, Lee decided to observe a few sessions of a class taught by Eric Oback, with a friend of hers who was enrolled at the time. She enrolled herself for the second semester. "What Eric made me do was change my perspective. I was no longer painting to save my sanity." He enthusiastically encouraged her to "Go home and paint!" The message was profound. Now I was painting because I am a painter." The four daughters at home were under the age of 6 at the time.

Two years later, Lee was taking private instruction from Alexander Nepote, who set up monthly aesthetic problem solving for his students. He taught her that any quadrant of a painting must be interesting in and of itself, and that it should entertain the eye as well as the mind. She maintains that concept today and critiques her own work in this way. The artist was competing and exhibiting in the Bay Area by 1959. In 1962, she and the family came to Wisconsin when her husband Leonard Weiss took a position in the economics department of the University of Wisconsin-Madison. She packed with her, seventeen awards, including two best-of-show and ten first place awards from California.

Why watercolor over other mediums?

"I love the spontaneity and the fluidity," she said. "Watercolor suggests things far more beautiful than what's in the head. Heavier mediums like oil and acrylic are not as appealing to me. They are good mediums to use in covering up mistakes, which is something I don't like to do with a painting. To me the work then becomes too 'studied' and not natural; there's no mystery. Watercolors give me feedback."

The day I visited Lee, she had a work in progress and another work that was completed and in the process of stretching. I asked her, "How do you know when a painting is finished?" Her reply: "Tough question." She has had to take framed paintings apart when she later decides the painting is not finished. There may be a corner that's just not right, or some other perceived flaw. Occasionally a painter can go too far and ruin a painting. She discards some of her works when she feels the necessity. Other times she will take an about-to-be-discarded work and experiment with it. Working on these "failed paintings," as she refers to them, can lead to discovering new and alluring techniques. The artist does not use sketches or paint on location. She likes to use what she calls the "remembered image." Although some artists use a "paint from life" approach, the remembered image has the advantage of mysticism and the mind's eye. This is most appealing to Lee because it provides the "spirit" and the "thrill" that she cherishes.

Lee has taught workshops in the past, but prefers to jury exhibitions and shows now. She is currently the Chair for jury selection for the National Watercolor Society.

Her works are included in at least 31 corporate and 34 public collections, including collections of the National Academy of Design in New York; the National Air and Space Museum at the Smithsonian Institution; NASA Museum in Cape Canaveral;

Florida; the National Museum of American Art at the Smithsonian Institution; the National Museum of Women in the Arts in Washington D.C.; and the Phillips Collection at the Phillips Gallery in Washington D.C. to name just a few.

"What is it that attracts you to painting?" I asked her.

The artist didn't hesitate for even a second before she replied, "Refuge, joy, career, art, encouragement—I am the luckiest person I know. There have been some rough spots in life—loss of a child, a husband with a lingering illness prior to his death."

Lee is an ambassador and has juried for VSA (Very Special Arts) of Wisconsin, a group that promotes the art of children and adults with disabilities. She has many other projects going, including a painted work for use by the Governor's Commission.

My final words: One painting is worth a thousand bubbling intrigues. Lee's succinct wisdom: Painting takes a tremendous amount of self-discipline. Keep at it. Be open. See what your experience is teaching you and go further with the "ah-ha."

Claggett Wilson

(1887-1952)

The year was 1935. A stage set designer named Claggett Wilson designed the set for a production of Shakespeare's "The Taming of the Shrew," starring Alfred Lunt and Lynn Fontanne. After the shrew was tamed in 1938, Alfred Lunt and Lynn Fontanne hired Claggett to paint a "single mural" in the main house at their summer home in Genessee Depot, Wisconsin in Waukesha County. Claggett stayed for more than two years and essentially turned the estate, later known as Ten Chimneys, into an extraordinary art project. It's obvious to any visitor touring the inviting residence of the "First Couple of American Theater," that Claggett Wilson had done what Lynn Fontanne had asked him to do. The actress instructed him to "make it look lived in," because living in a model house would be "like sitting nude forever in the center of a huge white dinner plate."

The Ten Chimneys project became a major work of the artist. The estate has both English and Swedish influence throughout. When you first arrive at the main house at Ten Chimneys, the first thing you'll encounter is an open gate crafted in a dogwood pattern, which is a Swedish design meaning "welcome." Walls in the house have everything from classic English floral design to rosemaling depicting the Scandinavian influence, to Claggett Wilson murals, and collections of silk embroidery. The walls, ceilings, and floors tastefully have become the gallery—the structures themselves are the paintings. Wallpaper cutouts, some enhanced by paint here and there, adorn several walls. The sconces and other unique light fixtures have half shades to "shed light on the players" as would happen on a stage.

Wilson's paintings have been described as whimsical, clever, and flirtatious. Some probably even tell a tale. One of the techniques he used to simulate features in a room was trompe l'oeil ("fool the eye"). Look at the alleged crown molding carefully and you'll see. It's not really molding; it's painting that utilizes grisaille, which is a painting done entirely in shades of gray or another neutral grayish color. Finished work in grisaille imitates the effects of sculpture. Nonetheless, it all fits perfectly with the room décor and the "stage set."

Themes used by the artist include pastoral, Biblical but not religious, with some figures dressed in modern-day clothing. Cherubs, swans, cupids, and other motifs are repeating themes. In the corners of the dinning room ceiling are painted renditions of Antoinette, Lynn Fontanne's sister. The conservators believe the paintings depict Antoinette in a timeline of inebriation. A bathroom in the cottage has capriciously cartoon-ish figures of an elephant and his true love who happens to be a petite redhead. The Helen Hayes bedroom has a "Taming of the Shrew" influence. The artist also blended the practical necessities of the house with his painting. For example, on the wall above the radiator in

Set designer Claggett Wilson in 1939
Main House Drawing Room, Ten Chimneys
Estate of Alfred Lunt and Lynn Fontaine
Photo courtesy of Ten Chimneys Foundation

the spirited entryway is painted a tray with tea and scones. The tray looks as if it is resting on the radiator. Murals of costumed people painted on the wall, as if they were a backdrop for a stage set, offer the visitor cheese and wine. Need a dash of marble wall or a marble column in any room? No problem, Claggett had a paintbrush that could construct the desired illusion. The stage was always set with the most articulate of plans.

Claggett Wilson, born in 1887, became one of America's first Modernist painters. He taught painting and drawing at Columbia University in New York. He then enlisted in the Marines in 1917, becoming a lieutenant. Claggett served in the Indian Head Division as Brigade HQ Chief, and later as aide-de-camp to Brigadier General Wendell Neville. Lt. Claggett Wilson was wounded twice and was awarded the Navy Cross, Sliver Star, and the Croix de Guerre. While in Coblenz, Germany, in 1919, Claggett painted war scenes of what he thought was the "war to end all wars." The Marines had no official artists in World War I; however, Lt. Wilson is recognized as one of the finest artists to record pictorially the experiences of the Marines in the war.

Alexander Woolcott, *New York Times* drama critic, and former *Stars and Stripes* reporter, published 24 of the Claggett Wilson paintings in his book *The War Paintings of Clagett Wilson* (1928). Following the "war to end all wars," Claggett became a stage set designer and mural painter in New York. Today his works are in several museums including the Metropolitan Museum of Art in New York City.

The artist's significant Wisconsin connection is, of course, his artistic sovereignty at Ten Chimneys. As of June 2004, the estate is the 35th National Historic Landmark in Wisconsin, and only the 10th related to theater and arts out of 2,365 landmarks throughout the country. The estate opened for tours on May 26, 2003. With the purchase of the 54-acre Lunt-Fontanne estate in 1996 for the purpose of preservation, the late Joseph W. Garton, fought to save the historic residence and its priceless memorabilia from imminent destruction and encroaching condominium development. His visionary actions were timely. A developer with other intentions had tried to purchase the property, but failed. I believe that was destiny.

The history of actor Alfred Lunt is a destiny that meshes well with the arts. His mother, Hattie Sederhom, encouraged Alfred's interest in theater and acting. The young actor was born in Milwaukee to a lumber family. He lived in Milwaukee and in Sweden for a time. Alfred went to Carroll College, where he was a student of Mary Nickell Rankin, whom he regarded as having a major influence on his pursuit of acting. Of that experience he said, "She was the substance of my education." Mary Rankin developed the curriculum for the Department of Oratory and Dramatic Literature at Carroll Academy and College in Waukesha. Alfred Lunt acted in twelve plays under her direction. At the age of 21 in 1914, he bought three acres in Genesee Depot, 30 miles west of Milwaukee. Eventually, the property increased substantially to well over 100 acres. With an inheritance, Alfred built a house for his mother and sisters.

In 1919, Alfred Lunt had two great breaks. He starred in the play "Clarence" and met Lynn Fontanne, an English-born actress who was starring in the play "Dulcy." The actor and actress were married in 1922 by a justice of the peace in New York City after grabbing two strangers off the street to act as witnesses for them. Alfred notified his mother, Hattie, with a telegram that said, "Have made an honest woman of Lynn." Impulsive as the simple marriage may appear, Alfred and Lynn were married for 55 years, and only separated with the death of Alfred in 1977.

Ten Chimneys became a place where the soul could find some of the intangible luxuries of life. Alfred's mother Hattie was quoted as saying, "You can do without the necessities but you can't live without the luxuries." It was a favorite place of relaxation, rejuvenation, and creativity for actors, writers, and artists of the day. The recognizable personalities who were frequent guests at this summer home, included Helen Hayes, Laurence Olivier, Alexander Woolcott, Katherine Hepburn, Charlie Chaplin, Noel

Coward, Edna Ferber, Hal Holbrook, and countless others. Actress Carol Channing is quoted as saying, "What the Vatican is
to Catholics, Ten Chimneys is to actors."

The rooms of the main house are eloquently decorated as if
they are a stage set. And, just as in building a stage set, when it's
done, it's done. The house, its rooms, the furnishings, and the
memorabilia are miraculously still the same as when the couple
lived there. Most of what was in the house during the lives of the
couple remained with the estate when it was purchased in 1996.
In fact, it feels like the residents have just stepped out for a walk.
The dinning room chairs, designed in needlepoint to depict the
twelve signs of the zodiac, were stitched by Lynn and Helen Hayes.
Plates are displayed on one of the walls. The Lunts subscribed
to the adage that if there's a plate hanging on the wall, there's always room for one more. Alfred had studied at the Cordon Bleu
Cooking School and loved to prepare superb cuisine in his large
kitchen. Today the kitchen can still be seen in its 1950s update,
which was the last time it was remodeled. The personal address
book, with phone numbers and addresses of the actors who visited
Ten Chimneys, still sits on the kitchen counter.

The drawing room is sprinkled with Claggett's angels and
cherubs. Possibly this is in reference to "The Celestials," as Alfred
and Lynn, were referred to as the "greatest English speaking actors
of the time." On a wall in the drawing room is where Claggett
signed his work. The room also has a small table where Lynn
played solitaire to settle her nerves before a performance. No
one was to disturb her during that hour. The Steinway grand
piano is a painting in itself, and has six legs instead of the usual
four. The piano was painted white and highlighted with other
paintings by Claggett to coincide with the subject matter in the
room. When Noel Coward visited, he did not like to play on a
boring black piano. Clagett's colorful but tasteful painting was
a sure-fire cure for dreary black.

The flirtation room is a curiously small room with six exits,
reminiscent of a stage with several avenues of quick escapes.

The room has a couch for two, is decorated with peach and reds, and was used as a cozy tearoom at times. A nonfunctional fireplace that's only a prop sets the mood, just as it would in a stage design.

From 1922 to 1937, Alfred and Lynn lived in the cottage, which fondly became known as the "henhouse," while Alfred's mother and sisters lived in the main house. The cottage has a strong Swedish décor. Alfred did much of the rosemaling on the walls himself, and made sure that every corner had a fireplace, or a hutch, or something to prevent trolls from hiding in the spaces. Look closely at the wall and you'll see pencil lines used in the drawing plan for painting. After all, an audience wouldn't see pencil lines on a stage anyhow. Some of the walls are covered with painted canvases done in the style of the itinerant artists of Sweden in the 17th and 18th centuries. Even the kitchen door is a work of art. It's not just a door; it's a painted grocery list of items with the words painted in Swedish. In 1938, mother Hattie moved into the henhouse, and Alfred and Lynn moved to the main house.

On the property is a 17th Century Swedish log house that was used as a studio for practicing plays, colluding on scripts, and often entertaining guests who had come to indulge in artistic endeavors. The log abode is a playhouse of sorts and has an inside balcony accessible by ladder for the actor to ascend to his or her oratory platform. On the property sits a stone chicken coop and a stable where Franklin resided. The horse was named after Franklin D. Roosevelt because FDR was able to get the actor and actress travel visas to Europe where they continued to perform during World War II. The couple pursued their acting during the winters, spent summers in Wisconsin, and made sure this arrangement was part of a contract with the Theater Guild.

Alfred Lunt and Lynn Fontanne were the purity, the excitement, and the royalty of live American Theatre. They had little interest in starring in movies, finding the process tedious and not to their liking. However, they made one movie together, The

Guardsman in 1931. The film was a critical and commercial success, thus creating a stir in the world of film production. The couple turned down numerous film contracts including a 1932 offer for $1 million from a studio to do a two-film production. Lynn said to the studio king, "We can be bought, but we can't be bored." That lack of the boring-mundane carries across to the art and the creativity of Ten Chimneys, thanks to the work of Claggett Wilson, the art of Alfred Lunt, and the creativity of the First Couple of the American Theater. To quote, Sean Malone, president of The Ten Chimneys Foundation, "Their choices were more about theatricality and whimsy than opulence." Ten Chimneys isn't about hero-worship or nostalgia in a time capsule. The more you live, the more Ten Chimneys speaks to you." Precisely, that is what an artist strives for—art that speaks to you.

In 1958 the Lunt-Fontanne Theatre in New York City was dedicated with the opening of "The Visit," the last play in which the couple performed. "Beauty and the Beast" is currently playing at the theater. The Lunts received the Presidential Medal of Freedom, Emmy Awards for "The Magnificent Yankee," Lifetime Achievement Tony Awards, and the Kennedy Center Honor. In later years, Lynn Fontanne was asked if she could name her favorite award. She replied that Alfred was her favorite, and that she missed him every second of every day. Lynne Fontanne died in 1983, six years after Alfred.

Architecture
and Design

Louis W. Claude
Edward F. Starck

To walk about Madison and not see an example of Claude and Starck architecture would be tricky. The architects built more than 175 buildings in Madison. Louis Claude, an ambitious young man from Baraboo, Wisconsin was a student and associate of architects Conover and Porter, who were the principal designers of the distinctive building on the University of Wisconsin-Madison campus, known as Science Hall. In addition, Claude worked in Chicago and had a working acquaintance with Frank Lloyd Wright throughout much of his career. Louis Claude decided to open his own firm in 1895 on West Main Street in Madison. Joining him was Edward Starck, a student who had been working in architectural offices and knew the construction trade. The combination worked well in this partnership that ended up to span 32 years and a repertoire of design and construction.

The two artists of functional design originally planned houses, but soon branched out into commercial buildings, banks, apartment buildings, and schools. They designed forty Carnegie libraries throughout the Midwest. Besides having a colossal representation in Madison, the architects are credited with the Watertown Main Street commercial historic district, the Columbus Public Library, and the Kilbourn (Wisconsin Dells) Public Library, to name a few. In Madison, the William Collins house, now a bed and breakfast inn, at 704 E. Gorham St., and Lincoln School at 728 E. Gorham St. are good examples of their designs. Stucco

**Claude and Starck design, east-facing side of Lincoln School
Gorham Street, Madison. Photo: HH Levy**

**Claude and Starck design, Collins House Bed& Breakfast
Gorham Street, Madison. Photo: HH Levy**

and half timbers lend a distinctive look to some of the Claude
and Starck buildings.

According to the National Register of Historic Places, the
multi-talented and flexible architects used the influence of Itali-
anate design, art deco, and Queen Anne, as well as the Prairie

School style. The designers liked to use leaded glass, but to be more functional (and perhaps more flashy) than the Wright leaded glass designs, they added colored borders for greater transparency. These two remarkable artists contributed a grand combination of daring design and exquisite craftsmanship that has easily endured into the 21st Century. The team of Claude and Starck dissolved in 1928, and neither one of them individually achieved the same level of success.

Arthur Peabody

The architect Arthur Peabody started designing his UW build-ings in 1906, and kept up the work until 1940. The campus can thank him for designing or overseeing the construction of Barnard, Birge, Sterling, Lathrop, the Field House, the Memorial Union, the Carillon Tower, Mechanical Engineering, old Camp Randall, the Stock Pavilion, Agricultural Engineering, and other buildings.

Peabody used the craftsman influence in his buildings to give the space openness and a feeling of welcome. He was fond of red tile roofs, which he used on several of the campus buildings. Good examples of the red tile roofs can be seen at the Lakeshore dorms. Peabody chose a Georgian and Renaissance Revival style for Bascom, North, and South Halls, again paying attention to open space.

Arthur Peabody's masterpiece is the Memorial Union. His idea was to tempt the mind to visualize an Italian lakeside pal-ace. The Memorial Union, on the edge of Lake Mendota on Langdon Street, has a green tile roof, which was chosen for its unifying influence. One well-known guy in town by the name of Frank Lloyd Wright commented in 1932, "Yes it speaks Italian, extremely bad Italian, and very difficult to understand." Well, I guess we can't please everybody; especially those who have no use for Italian palaces. Keeping design in the family, Arthur's daugh-ter Charlotte, a landscape architect, designed the Union Terrace

University of Wisconsin Madison Memorial Union 1944
Architect: Arthur Peabody
Wisconsin Historical Society Image 13277

complete with sunburst chairs. The chairs, as anyone who visits the Terrace might guess, have become a hallmark.

Arthur Peabody's mission was to find and build a common theme or a blending of architecture that would tie the campus together instead of constructing hodgepodge, whatever-will-be buildings. His buildings have remained one of Madison's treasures; however, time and need for other structures may see some of them disappear.

George Edwin Bergstrom

George "Edwin" Bergstrom, in collaboration with architect David J. Witmer, was the chief architect who designed and refined the Pentagon, just across the Potomac River from Washington D.C. George Edwin Bergstrom's roots are in the Neenah, Wisconsin area. As a young boy, he immigrated to the United States with his parents and an older brother, Dedrick Bergstrom. George's son, G. "Edwin" eventually moved to the East Coast, as did the rest of George's family.

The Pentagon had to be hurriedly built due to a need for office space for the United States military. World War II was at the doorstep. Architect G. Edwin Bergstrom was directed by Brigadier General Somervell to present him with a basic plan and architectural perspective in five days time. The building was to provide office space for 40, 000 people. Nothing like a little deadline to make your day. On July 22, 1941, the plan was on the general's desk, and by July 28, it had been approved by the House. It was approved by the Senate on August 14, 1941. President Franklin Roosevelt signed the bill on August 14, 1941. Construction began on September 11, 1941. It was completed by January 15, 1943, one year and four months later. Preliminary drawings and drafting took 34 days. This was a project of absolute unprecedented magnitude. Eventually, 327 architects and engineers, along with 117 field inspectors were summoned to the task. Work ensued 24 hours a day, employing 15,000 people working three shifts. New drawings were issued daily, and this reportedly consumed 15,000 yards of paper per week—all this without computers.

The pentagonal design of the building was configured to fit the shape of the road that existed at the location. It was really an "accidental" design of sorts. An early plan shows a square building with a corner cut off to accommodate one of the roads—an uneven-sided skewed pentagon. To make better use of the space and land, Bergstrom proposed a true, equal-sided pentagonal shape, which was eventually adopted. Today, the Pentagon is unquestionably one of the most widely recognized buildings in the world.

Alexander Eschweiler

(1865-1940)

Alexander C. Eschweiler was a popular and widely recognized residential architect. He was born in Boston of German-American heritage. Several German American architects were significant in the architecture of 19th century America. Eschweiler was commissioned by Charles Allis, the first president of the Allis-Chalmers

Manufacturing Company, to build the mansion in 1909. The Allis-Chalmers Company was a world leader in the manufacture of farm implements and a large producer of armaments during World War II. Charles Allis was a director of the First National Bank and the Milwaukee Trust Company. He was also the first president of the Milwaukee Art Society, and a trustee of the Layton Art Gallery.

Alexander Eschweiler used Jacobean and Elizabethan design in the Charles Allis mansion. His work is characterized by taut, smooth surfaces of brick and stone in dark colors. He used steeply pitched rooflines with gabled pavilions. The interiors feature walnut and mahogany paneling. The property on Prospect Avenue on Milwaukee's East Side was willed to the city in 1945 upon the death of Mrs. Allis. Today it is the popular Charles Allis Art Museum.

The Hotel Metro, another Eschweiler project, stood vacant since 1992 and has recently undergone a $7 million renovation. The makeover retains the 1937 Deco feel with its "Art Moderne" design. It was originally the John Mariner Building. The structure

Charles Allis Mansion
Architect: Alexander Eschweiler
Courtesy of Charles Allix/Villa Terrace Art Museums

was the first commercial building in Milwaukee to feature central air conditioning. The architects of Eschweiler and Eschweiler gave it a streamlined wraparound façade to prompt a reminder of the elegant passenger trains, such as the Hiawatha. The style was leaning towards the budding notion of merging form with function. Today a visitor to the Hotel Metro in Milwaukee will find distinctive oval columns with walnut veneers and chrome trim in the lobby to match the period décor.

Other works of Eschweiler and Eschweiler include the James K. Ilsley House, Elizabeth Black residence, Milwaukee Gas Light Company West Side Works, Milwaukee-Downer College buildings (UW-Milwaukee), Wisconsin Gas Building, Wisconsin Telephone Building, and the Milwaukee Arena.

Ferry and Clas Architects

Alfred C. Clas, architect
Wisconsin Historical
Society Image 10524

The Pabst Mansion was the first joint commissioned project of the architects George Bowman Ferry and Alfred Charles Clas, who had merged their talent and individual architectural practices in 1890. The mansion at 2000 W. Wisconsin Avenue in Milwaukee, is a historic house museum today that is one of the highlights of Milwaukee architecture. The project was finished in 1892 and became a fine example of Flemish Renaissance architecture. It was described as the "jewel" of Milwaukee's famous avenue of mansions called the Grand Avenue. Captain Frederick Pabst, of German heritage, was 57

Captain Frederick Pabst Mansion, Milwaukee, Wisconsin
Architects: Ferry and Flas
Photo courtesy of the Pabst Archives and Pabst Museum

years-old when his mansion was completed. By this time, he was a beer baron, a real estate developer, an accomplished sea captain, a philanthropist, and a patron of the arts. The finished mansion had thirty-seven rooms, twelve baths, and fourteen fireplaces. The 1890's became known as the "Pabst Decade" in Milwaukee.

The firm of Ferry and Clas designed some of the most prominent commercial, residential, and public buildings in Wisconsin over the next twenty-three years. These included the Milwaukee Public Library, the Steinmeyer and Mathews Brothers Buildings, the Milwaukee Central Library, Women's Club of Wisconsin clubhouse, Gustave G. Pabst Mansion, Milwaukee Theater Auditorium, old U.S. Coast Guard Station, Northern Trust Bank, the Cudahy Tower, and the Wisconsin State Historical Society building. A nationwide competition had been held to find a design for the State Historical Society of Wisconsin building. Ferry and Clas won the competition and completed the building in 1900 at a cost of one million dollars. The Historical Society was the most expensive structure built by the state of Wisconsin at the time.

Many of the Ferry and Clas drawings and renderings were donated to the Captain Frederick Pabst Mansion by George B. Ferry's grandson, William P. Ferry. The partnership of the architects designed well over 300 buildings by 1913 when the partnership dissolved.

Keck and Keck Architects

William Keck and his brother George Fred Keck formed the architectural partnership of Keck and Keck in 1945. William Keck (1908-1995) was born in Watertown, Wisconsin and studied architecture at the University of Illinois. He graduated in 1931 from the school and joined older brother George who was already an established Chicago architect. The two architects are well known for their "House of Tomorrow," a glass and steel structure designed for the 1933 Century of Progress Exhibition in Chicago. William had to leave his career for a time to serve in the military in World War II.

Keck and Keck were pioneers in passive solar architecture and avant-garde modern design. The architectural partnership was awarded the First Illinois Medal in Architecture from the University of Illinois in 1980. William Keck discussed the "House of Tomorrow" in an interview for the Art Institute of Chicago, and noted that at the time they had difficulty securing loans on any "modern" designs. Fred decided to "go as far out into left field as he possibly could as a design, and then bring them back to earth enough to show what could be done to help sell the idea to banks…We got plenty of publicity out of that. Of course, the newspapers said, 'If you live in a glass house, don't throw stones,' and all that kind of headlines." The apartment building at 5551

S. University Avenue in Chicago, which the architects designed and lived in, has been designated a Chicago landmark. William Keck was elected to the College of Fellows of the American Institute of Architects in 1969.

Brooks Stevens

(1911-1995)

In the 1930s the profession of "industrial designer" was born. Prior to this, engineers determined the appearance of a product. Brooks Stevens noted that engineers, understandably so, were more concerned with utility than with "eye appeal." Therefore, he set about to style the manufacturer's product to give it appeal in the marketplace. He was one of the country's first industrial designers, and mostly noted for his automotive designs such as the Willys-Overland Jeepster, the Studebaker Gran Turismo Hawk, and the Excalibur. Other noted designs were done for motors, toys, packages, appliances, bikes, planes, trains, and clothing. The Miller Brewery logo, for example, is a Brooks Stevens design.

Probably his most endearing design was for a rendition of the Oscar Mayer Wienermobile. "There's nothing more aerodynamic than a wiener," said the designer. The original idea for the Wienermobile came from the Oscar Mayer Company in 1936. Brooks Stevens was commissioned in 1958 to redesign the vehicle. He said that his main contribution was simply "to put the wiener in the bun." Before the Stevens design, the promotional vehicle was a low truck with a giant hotdog riding atop it. Stevens decided that a fiberglass version would give it a sculpted look, thus we have today's sculptured Wienermobile.

At the age of 8, Clifford Brooks Stevens was hit with a severely crippling case of polio. It was predicted that he would never walk again, and his right arm was non-functional. Brooks' father, William, was instrumental in defying the odds. He encouraged his son to draw by supplying him with sketchbooks. William then helped the young Brooks Steven build model planes and boats, and challenged him to ride a bike and then swim a mile in a pool. Throwing in the promise to buy Brooks a Model T when Brooks succeeded in swimming the mile, William Stevens was pivotal in his son's remarkable rehabilitation. Much effort went into the swimming challenge, but Brooks said that he finally got the car. William Stevens had instilled great motivation in the young man.

In 1929, Brooks enrolled at Cornell University to study architecture. He returned to Milwaukee in 1933 to work as an inventory manager. While at school, he spent much of his time drawing cars instead of buildings. He recalled the opinion of his professors by saying, "If I spent as much time on the bank building as I did on the cars that I drew on the rendering in front of the building, I could have been a good architect." As an inventory manager, the ambitious Brooks Stevens was restless until he started to redesign some of the product labels for his employer, the Jewitt and Sherman grocery supply firm. That move was a stepping stone. He soon won an award for redesigning the company logo for Cutler-Hammer, and the career began to take flight.

Brooks Stevens opened his own design firm in 1935 at 340 North Milwaukee Street. By1940 he had over fifty industrial accounts. In 1937, he married Alice Kopmeier and designed and built a home in conjunction with Fitzhugh Scott, Jr. Today the home in Fox Point, north of Milwaukee, stands as one of Milwaukee's most significant examples of modernist domestic architecture. Brooks and Alice lived in the home for fifty years.

Stevens was a clever salesman. Nearly immediately, when he started his firm, he began to deliver slide show lectures on "Industrial Design and its Practical Application to Industry." The main point: Design will pay for itself many times over. With World War II in the spotlight, he converted military manufacturing into civilian consumer products. The army Jeep became the station wagon, and then a snappy little touring car called the Jeepster. The ambitions of the designer lead him to seek com-

Brooks Stevens 1958 design, Oscar Mayer Weinermobile™ Kraft Foods Inc. Courtesy of Kraft Foods Inc.

missions from high profile manufacturers in Milwaukee such as Miller Brewing, Allen-Bradley, Outboard Marine Company, and Harley Davidson. The new train, Olympian Hiawatha, with its Sky Top glass lounge, operated by the Milwaukee Road, was a Brooks Stevens design.

Stevens was the only Midwestern founder of the Society of Industrial Designers and was the first to be honored in a museum retrospective at the Milwaukee Art Institute. In 1954 he delivered a speech to an advertising club in Minneapolis, and impulsively, the night before, came up with the catchphrase "planned obsolescence" as a description of the industrial designer's mission. The phrase has an enormous impact on design theory today, and remains forever a controversial topic of discussion. To illustrate, in 1954 when the designer was asked to name his favorite design among all the firms with whom he contracted, he responded, "none, because every one would have to be restudied for the tastes of tomorrow. Would I change anything now that I did in the past? Hell, yes! Everything! Because it's all outmoded." At the time of his retirement and turning over of the management of the design company to son Kipp, Brooks Stevens had been instrumental in designing over 3,000 products for 600 clients. He also had a reputation as a speaker whose speeches, ranging from car design to planned obsolescence to politics, were informative, funny, and always interesting. Many of the staff became successful independent designers. Brooks Stevens' contributions range from the original concept for the SUV to the wide-mouthed peanut butter jar.

This essay was complied from information from the Milwaukee Art Museum exhibit in 2003. The Michael Lord Gallery, the Milwaukee Institute of Art and Design, and the Milwaukee Art Museum have created exhibitions and publications for preserving Brooks Stevens' contributions to design.

George Mann Niedecken

(1878 or 1871-1945)

George Mann Niedecken, interior designer and artist, was born in Milwaukee, studied art at a young age, and his earliest training came from the great artist Richard Lorenz at the Wisconsin Art Institute. Other students at the time were George Raab, Jessie Schley, Louis Mayer, Alexander Mueller, and Carl Reimann. The ambitious student went on to study at the Art Institute of Chicago, then in Berlin and in Paris. Probably one of the greatest influences on the artist was the Czech artist Alfons Maria Mucha. When George returned to the Midwest, he brought with him the Art Nouveau style from Paris and incorporated it into designs for tapestries, mosaics, art glass, and furniture. Another huge influence on Niedecken was the Arts and Crafts movement that began in Victorian England by William Morris, as a revolt, actually, against cluttered and over-decorated furnishings of the

Victorian era. George was a collector of Japanese prints and Chinese ceramics. Simplicity of Japanese art appealed to the artist-interior designer.

Around 1904, he began working with Frank Lloyd Wright in Oak Park, Illinois. He painted murals and provided custom-made furnishings for eleven of Wright's houses, including the Dana, Coonley, and Robie houses. In 1907 the Niedecken-Walbridge Company, an interior decorating and design firm was formed in Milwaukee, near the Bresler Galleries. He remained president of the firm until 1945. George Niedecken was the first president of the Wisconsin Painters and Sculptors and was a trustee of the Milwaukee Art Institute.

Aside from interior decorating and design, George Niedecken was known as a muralist. His subjects included floral, genre-human activity, still life, and decoration. A small work, "Spring Landscape," sold in 2003 for $3,500.

Marshall Erdman

(1922-1995)

"Baby," said the famous Frank Lloyd Wright to Marshall Erdman, "how would you like to be famous?"

Marshall Erdman started out in Lithuania as Mausas Erdmanas in 1922. His nickname at the time was "Goldene," which means Goldilocks. In Yiddish, the word also means someone who "does good work with his hands, in a manner that everything he touches turns to gold," oftentimes a builder. How coincidental. The teenager immigrated to the United States at the age of 16 to live in Chicago with his mother's brother, Ben Braude. Marshall's mother, Bayla, had died eight years earlier, and Marshall was never to see his younger brother and father again. The Nazis took their horrific toll in Lithuania, killing more than 130,000 Lithuanian

Marshall Erdman and Frank Lloyd Wright
inside of their first prefab house, 1956
Photo courtesy of Dan Erdman

Jews; among them were 10 year-old Nonas, and Marshall's father, Jonas.

In 1940, Marshall, at the age of 18, entered the University of Illinois and majored in architecture. He took one architecture class during his time at the University of Illinois, and ultimately it would jump-start a career. However, the world was at war, and there was a military interruption in Marshall's plans. In 1943, Marshall joined the U.S. Army, and immediately was granted United States citizenship. He served in France with the 63rd Engineer Combat Battalion.

Returning to America, he took advantage of the G.I. bill and got a degree in political science at the University of Wisconsin. He also ended up with fellow student, Joyce Mickey of Washington D.C., as his wife. The couple lived in a basement apartment at 514 North Carroll Street in Madison, with a lease contingent upon the handyman skills of Marshall to install a gas stove, a kitchen sink, an icebox, and a bathroom shower. With no shortage of skills, he also built the furniture — all good practice for what was about to happen to him.

The couple saved their money and bought a lot for $1,000 at 509 North Meadow Lane in Madison. They took the other $2000 in savings and the two literally began building a house that Joyce designed. Much to their surprise, Marshall and Joyce were able to sell the house before it was completed. Sold! The sale brought in a quick $14,000. The next day the entrepreneurs bought two more lots. Marshall, at age 24, had suddenly found his career. By 1947, they built six houses, and established Marshall Erdman & Associates. Marshall attracted much attention when in 1948 he decided to build quality housing for World War II veterans who had children and household incomes of less than $3,000.

A questionable, albeit intriguing, project on the table was about to take root. In 1945, a church called the Unitarian Meeting House had sold its spot in downtown Madison to Manchester's department store for $105,000. The Unitarians, eager to build another meetinghouse, hired Frank Lloyd Wright in 1946 as the architect to come up with a design for the four acres they had purchased in 1947 on University Bay Drive. The price of the land was $21,500. Not everyone in the congregation supported Frank Lloyd Wright. Some were nothing short of hostile. Wright's estimates to build the structure went from $60,000 to $75,000, a considerable difference. This didn't include the landscaping, furnishings, or Wright's fee.

Harold Groves, a member of the building committee, mentioned that there was a young builder named Marshall Erdman, who, along with Joyce Erdman, was building houses in Madison. Joseph Mire, a member of the governing board of the Unitarian Society, purchased an Erdman house in 1949, and was impressed with the experience of buying a house from the young Erdman, and the affordability of the house. Marshall was 27 years old. As the story goes, Wright wasn't interested in "amateurs," so he sent the plans to major firms in Chicago and New York. Supposedly, the bids came back ranging from $500,000 to $1.2 million. At that point, Wright called Mr. Groves and asked to meet Marshall. Eighteen months later, Marshall Erdman, along with the substantial efforts of volunteer labor, had gone through the $75,000, and the structure still lacked a roof. Wright was angry. Marshall Erdman had cashed in his life insurance policies and secured mortgages in order to finish the building. In the end, the total came to $213,000 according to records. On the subject of Wright, Marshall said, "He opened doors that never would have been open to me without his association."

That was the beginning of the beginning. The young firm of Marshall Erdman & Associates reported $175,000 worth of business in 1949. By 1950, the firm reported $675,000 in business. The company records listed as projects homes, apartment buildings, stores, warehouses, and a church. Marshall's empire expanded exponentially year after year.

Prefabricated houses with the Wright stamp of approval took off like wildfire. Marshall and company were just the ones to

Unitarian Meeting House, Madison, Wisconsin
Marshall Erdman and Frank Lloyd Wright
Photo: HH Levy, 2004

take on the challenge and perfect the concept. The wheeling, dealing, and construction continued, but Marshall had mind-expanding ideas that went beyond business. In 1961, the Peace Corps called on Marshall as a consultant. The appointment came from Sargent Shriver, and Marshall traveled to Puerto Rico to build a Peace Corps training site that would house 150 Peace Corps volunteers. When it came to the needs of the Peace Corps, Marshall was perceptive to say the least. Regarding the project, he said, "The whole thing is a crude set-up. This is not intended to be designed as they have it at home. It's to give the volunteer a taste of what he can expect." When he arrived at the building site, Marshall decided against uprooting precious trees, and instead scattered tents in the natural setting. He then built kitchen facilities, a mess hall-classroom, and bathroom facilities. "Part of what I learned from Frank Lloyd Wright was to make the most of native materials—to build a building without destroying a site." In 1962, the Peace Corps people again tapped Marshall on the shoulder and asked him go to Gabon, West Africa to help in a school construction project. Thirty schools and a hundred houses later, the project was fairly complete. Marshall was particularly proud of the schools that he constructed. The buildings were functional without frills, used native materials in the construction, and employed relatively unskilled labor from the native population. Marshall had ordered plants placed around one of the early schools, but he was quickly corrected by a superintendent who was not particularly keen on the landscaping due to the likelihood of snakes nesting in the bushes.

Life continued, as did the building boom for Marshall Erdman & Associates. Although the company built many commercial buildings, a reputation for the construction of medical buildings and clinics blossomed. The Marshfield Clinic addition built in 1975 was a doorway to a specialized area of building structures for group medical practices. In 1995, the Mayo Clinic's Midelfort Clinic in Eau Claire was completed, and Marshall commented that it was at the time, his company's finest building. Marshall won numerous awards, his designs have won the approval of millions of people, and he remained throughout his life, an astute businessman who lived for the day. His projects employed hundreds of people. Marshall was fond of using the adage, "just a little common sense," and this adage speaks to us through the countless homes, commercial and medical buildings, churches, and schools that he leaves as his legacy to thousands of people.

I exuberantly refer the reader to the book Uncommon Sense—The Life of Marshall Erdman *written by Doug Moe and Alice D'Alessio (2003 Trails Custom Publishing, Trails Media Group, Inc.) In my short essay, I used information from that book, and I highly recommend that you read more about Marshall Erdman.*

Frank Lloyd Wright

(1867-1959)

"The architect must be a prophet...a prophet in the true sense of the term; if he can't see at least ten years ahead don't call him an architect."
        — **Frank Lloyd Wright**

Empire builders come in different forms. Frank Lloyd Wright possessed the philosophy, vision, style, and ambition to build, both literally and figuratively, his empire. To visit a Wright-designed commercial building or residence is to experience the weaving of natural terrain and space and light into a flowing unobtrusive design. The destined-for-fame architect was born in Richland Center on June 8, 1867. He began his career at the University of Wisconsin-Madison working for Professor Allan Conover in the department of engineering. Wright spent two semesters studying civil engineering at the University and assisted the architect

Frank Lloyd Wright and Olgizanna Wright in Crosley car, 1948
Wisconsin Historical Society Image 1904

Joseph Lyman Silsbee in the construction of Unity Chapel (near Taliesin). Wright was 18 years old at the time, and he worked for the professor in order to help his family financially after his parents divorce in 1885.

Moving from Madison, the young Wright left for Chicago to work primarily at a drafting job with the architectural firm of Adler and Sullivan. He became an apprentice to Louis Sullivan and worked under his supervision for six years. Sullivan, a proponent of developing an American tradition in architecture, wanted to steer away from a European tradition and style. The senior architect coined the adage, "form follows function," which Wright later refined to "form and function are one." This concept strongly influenced the young and impressionable Wright. "Buildings, too, are children of Earth and sun." as he once said, probably exemplifies his idea of "organic architecture." He described what he meant in poetic terms as "organic buildings are the strength and the lightness of the spiders' spinning, buildings qualified by light, bred by native character to environment, married to the ground." The architect wanted to make a visibly obvious break from traditional and classic constructions. "Classicism is a mask and does not reflect transition. How can such a static expression allow interpretation of human life, as we know it? A firehouse should not resemble a French chateau, a bank a Greek Temple and a university a Gothic cathedral. All of the isms are imposition on life itself by way of previous education."

The young Frank Lloyd Wright married Catherine Tobin and built a home in the Chicago suburb of Oak Park (the Frank Lloyd Wright Home and Studio).The year was 1899, and Frank was 22. In 1893, he left his association with Louis Sullivan because Wright had been accepting commissions for "bootleg" designs for houses. But blessings sometimes come in strange packages. It was after this departure, that Wright built his own architectural practice in Chicago, and his career, solidly based on a foundation he had gained under Sullivan, started to take shape and become his own. The first notable structure from his practice that incorporated space, light, and openness, was the Winslow House built in 1893 in River Forest, Illinois. The "Prairie Houses" were born in short time. The houses took the form of the prairies on which they were built. The structures were long, low, had low-pitched roofs, deep overhangs, no attics or basements, and lengthy rows of casement windows emphasizing the horizontal style. This was a trend gaining strength in the Chicago architectural community, and it became known as the "Prairie School." Wright emphasized simple line and use of native and natural materials.

Wright's structures during this period included the Martin House in Buffalo, New York; the Robie House in Chicago; the Larkin Building in Buffalo, which had the first metal furniture; and Unity Temple in Oak Park, Illinois, which employed the use of poured concrete, an innovation at that time. It is reported that Wright took off to Europe in the year 1909 with Mamah Borthwick Cheney, the wife of a client, and left his practice and life behind in Oak Park. Two important portfolios were developed while he was in Europe, Ausgefurhte Bauten und Entwurfe in 1910, and Ausgefurhte Bauten in 1911. No matter what was going on in his personal life, Frank Lloyd never seemed to lose track of his goals and visions of design in his architectural life. The European publications brought international recognition to the 44-year-old Frank Lloyd Wright.

Finding comfort in a return to Wisconsin, Wright returned to the land and began the planning and construction of Taliesin, near Spring Green. Taliesin is a Welsh a term meaning "shinning brow." His mother was Anna Lloyd Jones whose Welsh family had settled the valley near Spring Green. Taliesin is an estate that includes Wright's personal residence, Taliesin, the Romeo and Juliet Windmill (1896), Hillside Home School (1901, 1932, and 1952), Tan-y-deri House (1907), and Midway Farms (1930's and 1940's). Today, Taliesin remains a popular tourist destination where visitors can experience the design concepts and tour the estate.

Upon his return to Wisconsin, Wright's recognition brought him significant commissions for an entertainment establishment in Chicago called Midway Gardens and a design for the Imperial Hotel in Tokyo, Japan. But tragedy was not far behind in 1914.

The "airplane house," Madison, Wisconsin
Designed by Frank Lloyd Wright
Wisconsin Historical Society Image 25211

A servant at Taliesin started a fire in the living quarters, killing Mamah Cheney, her children, and four other people. Wright was in Chicago at time working on Midway Gardens. The tragic event brought sorrow to Wright, but he endured and rebuilt Taliesin. The sculptor Miriam Noel came into his life and the couple married. Wright continued work on the Imperial Hotel which was six years in the making (1915-1922). He designed the structure to be earthquake-proof. Indeed, the hotel was one of the few buildings that remained standing after a devastating 1923 earthquake leveled much of Tokyo.

Diligently pursuing his love of design, Wright developed the plans for California residences such as the Hollyhock House and the Millard House. Millard represented his first use of the "textile block," a type of concrete block design. More problems plagued Taliesin again in 1925. This time an electrical fire due to lightening destroyed part of the residence, and Wright rebuilt for the second time. Not letting this impede his work, Wright traveled to Arizona in 1928 to work on the Arizona Biltmore Hotel. In Arizona, he built a camp for himself and his assistants and draftsmen. This became known as Ocatilla, a precursor to Taliesin West.

The Depression and the stock market crash essentially shut down business for a period. Wright again persevered. He turned to lecturing, and this consequently enhanced his exposure to the country. In 1932, he published *An Autobiography and The Disappearing City*, and established the Taliesin Fellowship, a school for apprentice architects that is presently known as The Frank Lloyd Wright School of Architecture.

Wright was a man with a "practical" sense of humor. "I have black and blue marks in some spot, somewhere, almost all my life, from too intimate contacts with my own furniture." He also scoffed at the idea that his designs might be "out of style." After all, the year was 1936. "Why I just shake buildings out of my sleeves." In a way, he was right. In 1936 he received commissions for the S.C. Johnson Wax Administration Building in

Racine, Wisconsin; Fallingwater house in Mill Run, Pennsylvania and Jacobs I , one of the "Usonian" houses. Commissions were pouring in for the 70-year-old architect.

The S.C. Johnson Wax Administration Building was completed in 1939, and it attracts tourists and architects from around the world today. The building is presently used as the world headquarters for SC Johnson Wax. More than 200 sizes and shapes of the Cherokee red bricks were used to form the angles and curves of the design. Many unusual features are inherent in this building. For example, slim dendrite-form columns support the roof, and glass tubing is used instead of conventional windows.

Fallingwater is a remarkable house, and even that's too common a description. Bruce Pfeiffer, director of Frank Lloyd Wright Archives, remarked that Fallingwater is "unquestionably the most famous private residence ever built." The *National Geographic Traveler* designated it "Place of a Lifetime." The house was built in 1935 for the Edgar J. Kaufmann family as a vacation home. Wright received the commission in 1934 after the family had purchased a 1600-acre tract of land. The family wanted the home near the waterfall. Wright went a step beyond and designed the house to rise above the waterfall, thus brilliantly incorporating his concept of organic architecture into reality. The house is constructed of sandstone quarried on the property and completed in 1939 with a guest and service wing. Fallingwater, owned by the Western Pennsylvania Conservancy, is the only major Wright work to come into the public domain with its setting, original furnishings and artwork intact. It is a popular tourist destination.

Wright was a planner and a doer, not only on a large scale, but also on a pragmatic scale. The solution was the Usonian home. These low cost homes included radiant heat, which was conducted through hot water pipes in cement slab floors, sandwich walls made of boards and tarpaper, his signature open floor plan, and of course, the carport (another Wright invention). The homes came to be as popular as his Prairie houses. "Usonian Automatic" was a house that could be "owner built."

Madison, Wisconsin, is home to Monona Terrace Community and Convention Center, which opened in July 1997 after 60 years of battling. In 1938, Frank Lloyd Wright approached the city with the idea of building Monona Terrace in an effort to build a structure that would house an auditorium, armory, boat harbor, train station, and city-county building. Political obstacles and disagreements arose over the next several decades. Frank Lloyd Wright died in April 1959 — 21 years, and eight designs after the original proposal. Five referendums, ten lawsuits, ten pieces of state legislation, and more than four thousand newspaper articles were ignited by the design and the commitment to the project. Wright was paid $250 for the plan. Finally, in the 1990s Taliesin architect Tony Putnam was hired to work with the city of Madison planning committee to get the show on the road. The dramatic and sweeping piece of architecture was completed at a cost of $67.1 million.

Another interesting structure in Madison is the Unitarian Meeting House at 900 University Bay Drive. It was commissioned by the First Unitarian Society of Madison in 1946, and members of the society supplied labor by hauling stone from a nearby quarry, building furniture, and finishing the interior. Two additions were designed in 1964 and 1990 by Taliesin Associated Architects.

The year 1955 was significant for the architect. The University of Wisconsin presented him with an honorary doctor of fine arts degree. Wright also stayed in New York in an apartment for a period while he worked on the Guggenheim Museum building. Always being one to want surroundings conducive to his creative mind, he redecorated the apartment with black and red lacquer furniture and peach colored carpet, now calling it Taliesin East. In 1957, Wright was handed 59 new projects, 35 of them were projects for public buildings. Curiously enough, one of the designs was for the house of Marilyn Monroe, which was never built.

At age 90, Wright wrote *A Testament* in which he made his "final statement concerning the place of his work and his art in the 20th century," according to Bruce Brooks Pfeiffer, Wright archivist. It is amazing that in 1958, at the age of 91, a batch of thirty-one new commissions arrived, and the busy architect now had 166 projects sitting before him. He kept right on working, and wrote the book *Living City* as he continued to supervise the construction of the Guggenheim Museum.

Frank Lloyd Wright designed more than 1,100 projects in his lifetime, with almost one-third of them created in his last decade. When asked which of his buildings was the most beautiful, his reply was, "The one on my board right now." Yes, along with his creative vision, came the humor and curtness of his practical remarks. He once remarked, "Early in life I had to choose between honest arrogance and hypocritical humility. I chose the former and have seen no reason to change." Apparently, a client of his called to complain about a leaky roof and the fact that rain was leaking onto the dinning room table. "Move the chair," was the architect's advice. He was also a man with a worldly view and worldly advice. "Tip the world on its side, and everything loose will land in Los Angeles."

As I was writing this essay, I took a rather broad view of the architectural achievements and decided that the designs somehow looked distantly familiar. At first, I couldn't pin it down—what was it that was familiar? Then in talking to a friend of mine one day, it suddenly dawned on me that various structures, with their simple unobstructed paths and lines, really resemble a Japanese style, only "thicker." My friend laughed and said, "You know, I never thought of it that way, but now that you mention it, you're right. Put that in the book."

Creativity Continues...
A Few More
of the Many

Alex Jordan Jr.—builder of the House on the Rock
Alfred Lunt—actor, rosemaling
Alfred Sessler—UW professor; graphite artist, worked for Works Projects Administration
Ammar Nsoroma—painter, mixed media, murals, pastels
Amy E. Arntson—painting, Lake Mills
Andrew Gordon Balkin—printmaker; founder of Andrew Balkins Editions
Anne Miotke—watercolorist, adjunct professor of fine arts at MIAD in Milwaukee
Anneliese Steppat—fiber artist
Armin O. Hansen—illustrator of children's books, painter
Arthur Thrall—printmaker, stylized calligraphy
Babette Wainwright—African American self-taught painter, ceramic sculptor
Barry Carlsen—painter known for mysteriously illuminated landscape
Bill Nichols—retired professor of painting, large landscape
Bob Nolen—colored pencil
Calvin Greer—African American self-taught wood turner
Carol Emmons—sculpture, professor of art UW-Green Bay

Catlin, Theodore Burr—19th Century Green Bay painter, fresco

Charles "Chick" Peterson—Door County watercolorist

Charles Frederick Keller—early painter of animals, figures, landscapes

Charles Lyons—Miller Art Center curator, painter Door County

Charles Munch—oil painter and painting conservator

Charles Radtke—Cedarburg woodworker

Charles Sumner Frost—architect railroad buildings

Charles Thwaites—lithographer

Charlie Tupa—architectural artist

Charlotte Partridge—prominent art instructor, Layton Art Gallery and Associated Artists

Chrystal Denise Gillon—African American printmaker, assemblage

Clary Nelson Cole—African American printmaker, instructor at UW-Green Bay

Constance J. Glowacki—watercolor, Janesville

Cynthia Jackson—African American ceramist

Dan O'Neal—realism oil painter, uses objects with unexpected relationship

Daniel Leon Schatz—early portrait and mural painter

David Giffey—Muralist who employs iconic themes

David Kahler—Milwaukee Art Museum architect, collaborated with Santiago Calatrava

Della Wells—self-taught, pastels, collage, active in promotion of artists of color,

Dennis Nechvatal—painter of figures and landscapes

Dona Look—contemporary basket craft

Doug Haynes—watercolor, Madison artist

Dudley Crafts Watson—early artist of landscape, floral, marine, still life

Dudley Huppler—surreal figure painter of 1930s, English professor UW-Oshkosh

E.B. Warren—one of Wisconsin's first art teachers

Edward Townsend Mix—architect; National Soldier's Home, Milwaukee Club, others

Ellen Baxter—one of the "rural artists" self-taught, Wisconsin Rural Art Program

Ellen Raskin—Illustrator, writer, designer, children's books

Elwood Warren Bartlett—early artist, self-taught engraver and illustrator

Erhard Brielmaier—early Milwaukee church architect

Frances Myers—sculptor, printmaking, abstract style

Frank Tenney Johnson—popular early Western painter from Oconomowoc

Frankie B. Cole—African American photographer

Franz Rohrbeck—Panorama painter American Panorama Co., late 1800s.

Fred Berman—known for painting and photography. professor emeritus UW-Milwaukee

Fred Smith—Concrete park sculptures in Phillips, Wisconsin; began around 1950

Frieda High—African American mixed media artist

Friedrich Wilhelm Wehle—early Milwaukee portrait and religious painter

Gary John Gresl—mixed media assemblage, past president, Wisconsin Painters and Sculptors

George McCormick—African American woodcarver, metal work, painter

George Peter—painter for the American Panorama Co., art director, Milwaukee Public Museum

George Pollard—portrait and celebrity painting, realism

George Ray McCormick—Milwaukee artist

Gerald Duane Coleman—African American self-taught quilter, painter, assemblage

Gerrit V. Sinclair—early painter cityscapes and working-class neighborhoods

Gloria Adrian—watercolor, woodworking

Gregory Coniff—photography, lawyer

Gustav Stickley—early furniture designer and manufacturer

Hal Rammel—designer of musical instruments, drawing, photography

Hans John Stoltenberg—early rural landscape painter of snow and trees

Helen R. Klebesadel—large feminist watercolors, Madison artist

Henry Koch—Milwaukee architect; Pfister Hotel and other Milwaukee buildings

Herman Michalowski—panorama painter

Howard Thomas—early painter who used earth as pigment source

Jacqueline A. Richards—African American painter, drawing

James Reeve Stuart—portrait painter, Confederate Army, UW Artist in Residence

James Watrous—mural painter (Paul Bunyon), UW instructor, activist

Janet Moore—botanical watercolor

Janie Gildow—colored pencil

Jean Kavanaugh—early 20th Century painter of floral and still-life

Jean Marie Salem—African American installations artist

Jeffrey Stolz—watercolor, costume designer

Jens Jensen—famous landscape architect

Jerry Butler—African American painter

Jerry Johnson—African American watercolorist, art director

Joe Sambataro—schooling in Wisconsin; painter, many portraits

John Balsley—sculptor, professor

John Marr—engraver, sculptor, father of Carl von Marr

John Mominee—printmaker, artist-in-residence Center for the Arts, UW-Platteville

John Nicholson Colt—abstract style painter

John Sayers—Milwaukee still-life painter

John Shimon & Julie Lindemann—photographers

Joseph Friebert—Milwaukee lithographer and painter, former pharmacist

Joseph Rozman—watercolorist; *Who's Who in American Art* since 1976

Josephus Farmer—Milwaukee African American painter

Josie Osborne—mixed media assemblage

Kathryn Ward—African American self-taught painter

Kathryn Wedge—watercolor, Neenah artist

Ktinsley—African American self-taught assemblages

Laverne Kammerude---painter

Leo Steppat—bronze sculptor, abstract and realism, animal subjects

Lois Ehlert—Milwaukee illustrator of children's books

Lois Ireland—self-taught painter

Lucia Stern—self-taught painter and sculptor, mixed media

Maginel Wright Barney—illustrator, sister of Frank Lloyd Wright

Marco Spalatin—abstract artist originally born in Croatia, master printmaker

Margaret E. Brewster—watercolor realism

Mark Mulhern—painting figurative expressionist style

Marlon H. Banks—African American watercolorist, oil painter

Martha Glowacki—sculpture, co-founder of Sylva Designs

Martin Tullgren and Herbert Tullgren—architects; Astor Hotel, others

Mel Kishner—painter

Mona Webb—"Queen of Williamson Street," Madison African American artist

Monique J. Isham—watercolorist

Monique Passicot—colored pencil

Muneer Bahauddeen—ceramist, murals, public art

Nancy Mladenoff—painting, drawing, fabric arts

Otto von Ernst—early painter and art instructor

Patrick Turner—African American assemblage, collage, pastel

Paul A.Siefert—Folk art, naïve, landscape and architectural subjects

Paul Donhauser—potter, writer of notable book on pottery, UW-Oshkosh professor

Pauline Jacobus—pottery, Pauline Pottery, Edgerton

Peter Brust—lead architect for Milwaukee Public Library and Milwaukee Museum

Peter Whitebird— Chippewa, painted life and culture of the Ojibwa tribe, late 1920's

Portia Cobb—African American installation artist

Prophet Blackmon—African American self-taught painter

Randall Berndt—director of James Watrous Gallery, Overture Center

Raymond Gloeckler—printmaker, humorist

Reginald Baylor—African American painter

Reverend Josephus Farmer—African American self-taught wood carver and sculptor

Reynaldo Hernandez—African American painter of murals

Richard Lippold—early sculptor, painter, abstract expressionism

Robert Holty—early painter

Robert Koehler—early painter, first Wisconsin artist to interject social questions into artwork

Robert Merrill—Beaver Dam artist taught first art classes at Wayland Academy

Robert Schultz—draftsman, student of Wilde's, had retrospective at Yale University

Russell Barr Williamson—Milwaukee architect

Ruthanne Bessman—origami paper folding

Sally Hutchinson—paintings that study geometry, color, and texture

Sarah Aslakson—painter, Argyle

Sera Kohlman—metalsmith

Sid Boyum—Madison sculptor in cement

Simon Sparrow—African American outsider artist of collage, folk art

Sonya Clark—African American fiber artist

Sonya Lyster-Baime—watercolorist, Milwaukee

Steve Ballard—mixed media assemblage

Steven Kozar—landscape painter, Madison

Susan Cressy—early Milwaukee painter and art teacher

Susan K. Cressy—early painter, Milwaukee Female College art instructor 1894

Sylvester Sims—African American self-taught painter

T.L. Solien—painter, printmaker

Tamlyn Akins—painting, Black Earth artist

Terrill Knaack—wildlife oil painter, student of Owen Gromme for seven years

Thomas Lidtke—sculptor, director of West Bend Art Museum, researcher

Tony Putnam—Taliesen architect

Trenton Baylor—African American sculptor, woodwork, assemblage

Truman Lowe—Native American artist, sculptor

Virginia Huber—watercolor, collage, drawing

William Christian—African American painter, drawing

William J. Blackmon—Milwaukee African American painter, prophet

William Weege—lithographer

William Wehner—German-born entrepreneur who started panorama company

Winifred Gordon Brown—African American metalsmith

Zane Williams—photographer, featured in many publications

Places to Visit

Appleton
Appleton Art Center
920-733-4089
Outagamie Museum / Houdini Center
920-733-8445
Wriston Art Center Galleries—Lawrence University
920-832-7000

Ashwaubenon
Ashwaubenon Historical Cultural Center Museum
920-494-0362

Baraboo
International Crane Foundation
608-356-9462

Beloit
Wright Museum of Art
608-363-2677

Fond Du Lac
Windhover Center for the Arts
920-921-5410

Genesee Depot
Ten Chimneys
262-968-4110

Green Bay
Green Bay Galleries University of Wisconsin
920-465-2916
Neville Public Museum of Brown County
414-448-4460

Madison
Elvehjem Museum of Art
608-263-2246
Madison Museum of Contemporary Art
(Overture Center for the Arts)
Wisconsin Historical Society—816 State Street
Wisconsin Historical Society Museum—30 N. Caroll St.
608-264-6555

Wisconsin Union Galleries, University of Wisconsin Memorial Union
608-262-5969
Overture Center for the Arts
608-258-4141
Olbrich Botanical Gardens
608-246-4550
DeRicci Gallery –Edgewood College
608-663-2800

Manitowoc
Rahr-West Art Museum
920-683-4501

Marshfield
New Visions Gallery Inc. (Marshfield Clinic)
715-387-5562

Milwaukee
Charles Allis Art Museum
414-278-8295
Patrick and Beatrice Haggerty Museum
414-288-1669
Milwaukee Art Museum
414-224-3200
Milwaukee Institute of Art and Design
414-276-7889
University of Wisconsin-Milwaukee Art Museum
414-229-5070
Villa Terrace Art Museum
414-271-3656
Captain Frederick Pabst Museum
414-931-0808
Milwaukee Public Museum
414-278-2728

Ten Chimneys
(Genesee Depot—west of Milwaukee)
262-968-4110

Neenah
Bergstrom-Mahler Museum
920-751-4658

Oshkosh
Allen Priebe Gallery University of Wisconsin-Oshkosh
414-424-2235
The Morgan House
920-232-0260
Oshkosh Public Museum
920-424-4731
Paine Art Center and Arboretum
920-235-6903

Plymouth
Gallery 110 North / Plymouth Arts Foundation
920-892-8409

Racine
Charles A. Wustum Museum of Fine Art
262-636-9177
Racine Art Museum
262-638-8300

Richland Center
Frank Lloyd Wright Museum and German Warehouse
608-647-2808

Sheboygan
The Bradley Gallery of Fine Arts – Lakeland College
920-565-1280
John Michael Kohler Arts Center
920-458-6144

Spring Green
Taliesin
Frank Lloyd Wright Estate
Toll free 877-588-7900

Stevens Point
Edna Carlsten Gallery
University of Wisconsin-Stevens Point
715-346-4797
Smith Scarabocchio Art Museum
715-345-7726

Sturgeon Bay
Door County Maritime Museum
and Lighthouse Preservation Society
920-743-5958
Fairfield Art Museum
920-746-0001
The Miller Art Museum
920-746-0865

Wausau
Leigh Yawkey Woodson Art Museum
715-845-7010

West Bend
West Bend Art Museum
262-334-9638

Whitewater
University of Wisconsin Grossman Gallery
Center for the Arts
262-472-5708

Sources

Publications

Adolph Vandertie. Ashwaubenon Historical Museum.

Alden, Sharyn. "Not your ordinary visitors center." *Madison Magazine.* April 2004.

"Alumni spotlight archive: Sr. Thomasita Fessler." The School of the Art Institute of Chicago.

"Artwork shines." *Milwaukee Journal Sentinel.* January 18, 2004.

Auer, James. "A brush with history." From the exhibition catalog Foundations of Art in Wisconsin. August 1998.

Auer, James. "Adding color to the palate." *Milwaukee Journal Sentinel.* August 7, 2003.

Auer, James. "After 50 years, couple's whimsy still connects." *Milwaukee Journal Sentinel.* December 16, 2003.

Auer, James. "Career draws to a close for indomitable teacher." *Milwaukee Journal Sentinel.* May 5, 2004.

Auer, James. "Ertz illuminated nature with brilliant technique." *Milwaukee Journal Sentinel.* January 10,2003.

Auer, James. "German-American' art contributions outlined." *Milwaukee Journal Sentinel.* April 29. 1998.

Auer, James. "Icons of state art deserve their due." *Milwaukee Journal Sentitnel.* June 30,1999.

Auer, James. "Irony of self-absorption, social analysis makes 'Dope'addictive." *Milwaukee Journal Sentinel.* August 27, 2003.

Auer, James. "Painting's history as curious as the scene it depicts." *Milwaukee Journal Sentinel.* June 28, 2003.

Auer, James. "Prophet delivers message through composition." *Milwaukee Journal Sentinel.* September 22, 1999.

Auer, James. "Self-taught Farrell outlines future without solo shows." August 5, 2003.

Auer, James. "State artists move from the fringes to the spotlight." *Milwaukee Journal Sentinel.* February 3, 2002.

Auer, James. "Terry's efforts to promote artists of color go on all year." *Milwaukee Journal Sentinel.* March 12, 2003.

Auer, James. "The artful survivor." *Milwaukee Journal Sentinel.* August 4, 1998.

Auer, James. "West Bend Museum digs up hidden treasures of state art." *Milwaukee Journal Sentinel.* May 16, 2001.

Barton, John Rector. *Rural artists of Wisconsin.* Madison: University of Wisconsin Press, 1948.

Biography Eugene Von Bruenchenhein. Dilettante Press article.

Bohrod, Aaron. *A decade of still life.* Madison: University of Wisconsin Press. 1966.

Brazill, Linda. "Fabulous Ten Chimneys." *Capital Times.* May 22, 2004.

Butts, Porter. *Art in Wisconsin.* Madison: The Democrat Printing Company, 1936.

Byrd, Joan Falconer. "Interview Harvey K. Littleton." Archives of American Art of the Smithsonian Institution. 2001.

Chicago architects oral history project. Art Institute of Chicago. Betty Blum, interviewer. August-September 1990.

Colescott, Warrington and Hove, Arthur O. *Progressive Printmakers.* Madison: The University of Wisconsin Press. 1999.

Damkoehler, David. "Norbert Kox visionary artist." Apocalypse House website.

Donohue, Gay. Society of Milwaukee Artists . Essay segment from catalog titled *Foundations of Art in Wisonsin.* Paper from the West Bend Art Museum.

"Edmund Lewandowski:Recording the beauty of man-made

objects and the energy of American industry." Paper from the West Bend Art Museum.

Ela, Janet. "Sculptor Helen Farnsworth Mears." *Wisconsin Academy Review.* Reprinted text from West Bend Art Museum. March 1986.

Elliot, Edwin E. and Wooden, Howard E. *Aaron Bohrod: Figure sketches.* 1990.

Falk, Peter Hastings (ed.). *Who was who in American art.* Madison, Connecticut: Sound View Press, 1985.

Framed! investigating the painted past. Wisconsin Historical Society exhibit 2003.

"Francesco Spicuzza an exponent of beauty and light: A family collection." *Resource Library Magazine.* October 2-November 10, 2002.

Gerdts, William H. *Art across America—two centuries of regional painting. Vol. 2: The South and Near Midwest.* Cross River Press Ltd., 1990.

Glen, Sheridan. *Behold the genius of Claude and Starck.* Downtown Living tour information.

Hambling, Marguerite Spicuzza and Newcomb, Joyce R. Francesco J. Spicuzza, *Wisconsin impressionist—clippings of a life.* 2002.

Historic Preservation Study Report. Milwaukee. Charles Allis House.

Hurt, Jeanette. "What a draw." *Milwaukee Journal Sentinel.* April 23, 2000.

"Immigration to integration: German identity in Wisconsin art." Paper from the West Bend Art Museum.

"Interview with Tom Every (Doc Evermor)." *The Bottlecap,* Vol. 1, issue 2. Summer 1998.

Jacques, Damien. "'Angel' Garton gave wings to Ten Chimneys preservation." *Milwaukee Journal Sentinel.* August 17, 2003.

John Michael Kohler Arts Center. Levi Fisher Ames menagerie. Sheboygan, Wisconsin: Leslie Umberger. 2001.

Lefevere, Patricia. "Nun teaches that we are all born artists."

National Catholic Reporter. October 22, 1999.

Lidtke, Thomas D. "A Century of Artistic Endeavor." Paper from West Bend Art Museum.

Lidtke, Thomas D. "Mid-To-Late 19th century. Essay segment from Wisconsin Art from Euro-American Settlement to 1950." Paper from West Bend Art Museum.

Lidtke, Thomas. "Carl von Marr." *Wisconsin Academy Review.* March 1986.

Lidtke, Thomas. Catalog. Carl von Marr-American German painter. West Bend Art Museum, West Bend, Wisconsin. 1986.

Lisle, Laurie. *Portrait of an artist—a biography of Georgia O'Keeffe.* New York: Seaview Books. 1980.

Lydia Ely "Hewitt." *Milwaukee Journal.* October 7, 1966.

Lynch, Kevin. "The painted past." *Capital Times.* August 15, 2003.

Lynch-German, "Lauria. Civil War veteran's beard was a clue to family's secret." *Milwaukee Journal Sentinel.* May 17, 2001.

Maller, Peter. "Sculptor wants to turn old ammo plant into work of art." *Milwaukee Journal Sentinel.* July 26, 1999.

Mary Nohl biography 1914-2001. Courtesy of the Kohler Foundation, Inc.

McCann, Dennis. "H.H. Bennett's photographs brought Dells to the world." *Milwaukee Journal Sentinel* January 7, 1998.

Mengert, Lorraine. *Door County's art history.* Door County. Lorraine Mengert. Copyright 1996.

Merrill, Peter C. "Art teachers, art schools, and art museums in early Wisconsin." Essay segment from catalog titled *Foundations of Art in Wisconsin.* Paper from the West Bend Art Museum.

Merrill, Peter C. *Elsa Ulbricht: A career in art.* Milwaukee: Milwaukee History. Vol.16, No.1. Milwaukee County Historical Society, Spring 1993.

Merrill, Peter C. "George Raab: Wisconsin artist." Section from *Prominence in 19th Century Art.* West Bend Museum.

Merrill, Peter C. *German-American Artists in Early Milwau-*

kee-a biographical dictionary. Madison: Studies of the Max Kade Institute for German-American Studies at the University of Wisconsin-Madison, 1997.

Merrill, Peter C. "Henry Vianden: Pioneer artist in Milwaukee." *Yearbook of German American Studies,* Vol. 22. pp. 137-147. Lawrence, Kansas: Society for German American Studies, Department of Germanic Languages and Literature, University of Kansas. 1987.

Merrill, Peter C. "Richard Lorenz, German immigrant artist in Milwaukee." *Wisconsin Academy Review.* March 1986.

Merrill, Peter. C. "John Ferry, artist of the Rockies." Reprint from *German American Painters in Wisconsin: fifteen biographical essays:* Stuttgart: Academic Publishing House. 1997.

Mertens, Maureen Dietzel. "Nun still nourishes the creative spirit at 83." *Milwaukee Journal Sentinel.* January 18, 1996.

Michaelson, Mike. "Catholics have the Vatican, actors have Ten Chimneys." *GlobeandMail.com.* June 2, 2004.

Miller, Ruth Morton. *Gerhard CF Miller—his life, his poetry, his philosophy and his painting.* Sturgeon Bay, Wisconsin: MAC Publishing Company. 1987.

Milwaukee's panorama painting industry. Publication of the West Bend Art Museum.

Mitchie, Mary. Essay segment from catalog titled *Foundations of Art in Wisconsin.* Paper from the West Bend Art Museum.

Moe, Doug and D'Alessio, Alice. *Uncommon sense—the life of Marshall Erdman.* Madison: Trails Media Group. Daniel Erdman Foundation, Inc. 2003.

Moe, Doug. "All aboard with Dr. Evermor." *The Capital Times.* June 20, 2003.

Nelson, Mary Carroll. "Lee Weiss:layering with a paintbrush." *American Artist.* Vol 48, Issue 503. June 1984.

"Notable black American artists." Web article. AskArt.com

Obituary of Aaron Bohrod. *New York Times.* 4-6-1992. Vol. 141, issue 48928, p.B 10.

"Old masters." *Milwaukee Journal Sentinel—On Wisconsin*

Arts. April 14, 2002.

Oxford University Press. *The Oxford dictionary of art.* Oxford: Editors Chilvers, Osborne, Farr. 1994.

Perry, Rachel. "Brown county children: Models for Ada Shulz paintings." *Our Brown County.*

Perry, Rachel. "The artists and natives of Brown County." *Our Brown County.*

Pocius, Donna Marie. "A fond farewell to Gerhard CF Miller, artist." *Door County Navigator.* August 2003.

Poser, Mary assisted by Elizabeth Groom and Helen Johnston. "Emily Groom." Essay segment from p.16-18 of the catalogue *Women's Work, Early Wisconsin Women Artists.* West Bend Art Museum. 2001.

Public works of art project: report of the assistant Secretary of the Treasury to Federal Emergency Relief Administrator. December 8, 1933-June 30,1934. U.S. Government Printing Office, Washington D.C. 1934.

Rahill, Margaret Fish. *Milwaukee paintings of the 1920s and 1930s.* Exhibit brochure.

Rath, Jay. "Backwords—building memories. Article on Arthur Peabody," *State Architect.*

Resource Library Magazine essay on the exhibit 150 years of printmaking. November 12, 1999-January 2, 2000.

Rosenthal, Debra. "Jessie Kalmbach Chase." Essay. West Bend Art Museum . 2001.

Saltpeter, Harry. "Chicago's gift to art." *Esquire Magazine.* November 6, 1939.

Sherwood, Glen V. *A labor of love—the life and art of Vinnie Ream.* Hygiene, Colorado: SunShine Press Publications, Inc. 1997.

Silvers, Amy Rabideau. "Artist Meeker was an innovator in serigraphy." *Milwaukee Journal Sentinel.* October 12, 2002.

"Sr. Thomasita Fessler, OSF, artist of the month." Passionist Research Center. December 1, 2003.

Tanzilo, Bobby. "Studio San Damiano radiates founder's commitment to art." *OnMilwaukee.com.* July 31, 2000.

Walkowski, Paul Joseph. "Michael Riddet." *The Artistic Forum Online Magazine.* September 2003.

Western Front, 1918 Artist/Lt. Claggett Wilson. Article from the Manchu Regiment. 9th Infantry. Gallery 2.

Western Pennsylvania Conservancy. Essay brochure. Frank Lloyd Wright's Fallingwater. November 2002.

"Wisconsin art from Euro-American settlement to 1950." Paper from the West Bend Art Museum.

Wisconsin art history--a chronology of Wisconsin art and history to 1950. Publication of the West Bend Art Museum. Revised January 2004.

"Women's work: early Wisconsin women artists." Exhibition at the West Bend Art Museum researched and prepared by Anne-Lee Geiger.

Organizations

Artists Rights Society (ARS) and the Georgia O'Keeffe Foundation

Captain Frederick Pabst Mansion

Charles Allis Art Museum / Villa Terrace

Fine Arts Museum of San Francisco, San Francisco, California

International Crane Foundation

John Michael Kohler Arts Center

Kohler Foundation, Inc.

Kraft Foods, Inc.

Lawrence University – Wriston Art Center Galleries

Milwaukee County Historical Society

Pentagon Renovation and Construction Program Office, Washington D.C.

Ten Chimneys Foundation

Visual Artists and Galleries Association, Inc. (VAGA)

West Bend Art Museum
Wisconsin Academy of Sciences, Arts and Letters
Wisconsin Historical Society and Museum, Madison, Wisconsin
Wisconsin Painters & Sculptors

Web Sources

AbsoluteArts.com www.absolutearts.com
Ackland Museusm at the University of North Carolina Chapel Hill www.ackland.org
  Allied Artists of America www.alliedartistsofamerica.org
All-Wright Site www.quotationring.net
Annex Galleries www.annexgalleries.com
Artcyclopedia www.artcyclopedia.com
  Artistic Forum www.artisticforum.com
Artnet www.artnet.com/magazines
Ask Art.com www.askart.com
Bergstrom-Mahler Museum www.paperweightmuseum. com
  Brandeis University http:// library.brandeis.edu/resources
Britannica Online www.eb.com
Dilettante Press www.dilettantepress.com/artists
Donald A. Heald.com www.donaldheald.com
Elvehjem Museum of Art www.lvm.wisc.edu
Fred Danziger www.freddanziger.com/mainNew.htm
Frogman's Press and Gallery www.frogmans.net
  Intuit: The Center for Intuitive and Outsider Art http:// outsiderart.org
  JSOnline Milwaukee Journal Sentinel www.jsonline.com
Kohler Art Library-UW-Madison www.library.wisc.edu
  Lawrence J. Cantor Artist Biographies www.fineoldart.com/ biographies
Lawrence University www.lawrenceuniversity.edu
Looksmart www.findarticles.com

Madison Museum of Contemporary Art www.madisonart-center.org

Marquette University www.marquette.edu/library/information/faq

Masterful Art www.masterfulart.com

Milw. Architecture/Dr. S.Reyer, Milw.School of Engineering http:// people.msoe.edu/~reyer

Milwaukee Art Museum www.mam.org

National Reigster   www.nationalregisterofhistoricplaces.com

Pabst Mansion www.pabstmansion.com

Passionist Research Center www.passionist.org/prc/artist

Patrick Farrell Studio www.patrickfarrellstudio.com

Raw Vision www.rawvision.com

Resource Library Magazine www.tfaoi.com/resource

Roadside America www.roadsideamerica.com

School of the Art Institute of Chicago for Alumni www.artic.edu/saic/alumni/news

Smithsonian Archives of American Art www.artarchieves.si.edu

Society of Architectural Historians www.sah.org

West Bend Art Museum www.wbartmuseum.com

Western Pennsylvania Conservatory: Fallingwater www.wpconline.org

Winstanely-Roark Fine Arts www.masterfulart.com

Wisconsin Academy of Sciences, Arts & Letters   www.wisconsinacademy.org

Wisconsin Federation of Museums www.wisconsinmuseums.edu

Wisconsin Historical Society www.wisconsinhistory.org

Wisconsin Painters & Sculptors, Inc. www.artinwisconsin.com

Wisconsin Stories http:// wisconsinstories.cfdev.uwex.edu

Wisconsin Union Directorate Art Committee www.union.wisc.edu/art/collection

Wisconsin Visual Arts Lifetime Achievement Award www. wvalaa.com

Wright in Wisconsin www.wrightinwisconsin.org

Film

"Frank Lloyd Wright" — A film by Ken Burns and Lynn Novick. PBS documentary. Warner Entertainment. Burbank, California. 1998.

"Statues by the Road." Bob Leff, Producer. McFarland, WI. 2003.

Acknowledgments

Many people helped me along the way with this project. Some provided valuable research. Some helped by simply answering a quick question here and there, or recommending resources, and others helped with the monumental task of procuring images for this book. In all circumstances, the people with whom I came in contact encouraged me to complete this book in the spirit of awareness for which it is intended.

My thanks to: Thomas D. Lidtke and Andrea Waala of the West Bend Art Museum, Gary John Gresl past president of the Wisconsin Painters and Sculptors, James Auer art critic of the Milwaukee Journal Sentinel, Lisa Hinzman of the Wisconsin Historical Society, Whitney Gould urban landscape writer at the Milwaukee Journal Sentinel, Evelyn Patricia Terry for input on African American artists, Madison Museum of Contemporary Art staff, Joe Kapler Wisconsin Historical Society, Russell Panczenko Elvejum Museum, VAGA Visual Artists and Galleries Association, ARS Artists Rights Society, the Georgia O'Keeffe Foundation, Terri Yoho from the Kohler Foundation, Amy Ruffo and Ruth DeYoung Kohler of the John Micahel Kohler Arts Center, James Temmer of the Charles Allis/Villa Terrace Art Museums, Lonnie Dunbier at Askart.com, Margaret Utzinger, Sean Malone at Ten Chimneys, Lady Eleanor at Land of Evermor, Ann Burke of the International Crane Foundation, Rodin International, Kelben Graf, Dawn M. Day Hourigan at the Capt. Frederick Pabst Mansion, Louise Maynard, Fred Danziger, Paula Crandall Decker, Caryn DePauw, E.N. Chan, M.C. Chan, Connie Lynch, Kraft Foods, Inc., Frank Lewis of the Wriston Art Galleries at Lawrence

University, Rick Peterson of Lawrence University, Bill Meindl of Voyageur Magazine, Jodi Wille of Dillente Press,Mary Juckem for dragging me out to walk, Robert Steeno, J.L. Adler for his astute suggestions, Marv Balousek at Badger Books, and of course, the Baroness von Bon Bon at Badger Books.

The West Bend Art Museum is located at 300 South Sixth Avenue in West Bend, Wisconsin. The extensive museum collection exists of 19th and early 20th century paintings, drawings, and other pieces. The dominant collection represents the work of Carl von Marr and contains over 300 examples of his work. A secondary continuous exhibition is the Early Wisconsin Art History Collection. Represented in this exhibit are such artists as Carl Holty, Edmund Lewandowski, Aaron Bohrod, John Stueart Curry, Frank Lloyd Wright, and many others.

The active West Bend Art Museum holds 10-14 annual exhibitions. Local and regional exhibitions are curated by the staff, and national touring exhibitions are borrowed from larger institutions.

Art Aware is a visual arts appreciation program presented to area schools each month during the school year.

Classes and Workshops in the educational program are scheduled on a trimester basis and are taught by qualified instructors.

The Art Museum staff offers free tours to most groups.

Special events at the museum include public receptions for exhibition artists, Music at the Museum, and Friends of the Art Museum Annual Gala among other events.

The Walter A. Zinn Doll House is a special attraction at the museum. The antique dollhouse was built in 1911 and completed by the family four generations later.

More About Wisconsin Art and Artists

Numerous titles on Wisconsin and all artists are available from the West Bend Art Museum. This Coupon entitles the bearer to a one-time 20% discount on the purchase price for any publications from the West Bend Art Museum. A listing of publications can be found at www.wbartmuseum.com or call 262-334-9638.

The John Michael Kohler Arts Center

The John Michael Kohler Arts Center is located in Sheboygan, Wisconsin. The Arts Center was established in 1967 for aesthetic and educational purposes. It encompasses a wide range of exhibits devoted to contemporary art, with particular interest in craft-related forms, installation works, photography, new genres, cultural traditions, and the work of self-taught artists. The Arts Center has an extensive Resource Center, and is home to excellence in the performing arts. The traditions of theater, music, and interdisciplinary forms are brought to the Arts Center by performance artists from around the world. www.jmkac.org

The International Crane Foundation

The International Crane Foundation has projects located worldwide in their efforts to conserve cranes, and their wetland and grassland habitats. The Foundation is located in Baraboo,

Wisconsin where a collection of cranes is maintained for the study of preservation and educational purposes. All fifteen species of the world's cranes can be seen at the ICF. Annual art exhibits feature fine wildlife art. Four nature trails, a chick exercise yard, a flight demonstration area, and the Ron Sauey Memorial Library are open to visitors. www.savingcranes.org

Wisconsin Historical Society

The Wisconsin Historical Society located in Madison, Wisconsin was founded in 1846, and is the oldest American Historical Society to receive public funding. The active organization holds many events and exhibits each year. A rich archive is available for research and education, along with one of the largest geneology collection in the country that encompasses genealogical histories from across the United States. Online collections and images are frequently changing and reflect a wide variety of interests. www.wisconsinhistory.org

Wisconsin Painters and Sculptors

The Wisconsin Painters and Sculptors was established in 1913, and was originally known as the Society of Milwaukee Artists which was established in 1900. Wisconsin Painters and Sculptors/Wisconsin Arts in All Media (WP&S/WAAM) is a nonprofit organization of visual artists and friends united to advance opportunities and services for artists and the public. The organization is committed to the importance and value of art and its creation in our society. Wisconsin Painters and Sculptors, along with the West Bend Art Museum and the Wisconsin Academy of Letters and Sciences, was a sponsor the for the first annual Wisconsin Visual Arts Lifetime Achievement Award. The first award ceremony was held on May 2, 2004. www.artinwisconisn.com

Index

Symbols